*The War of 1812 in Wisconsin*

# THE
# WAR OF 1812
## IN
# WISCONSIN

———————◦—————————

*The Battle for Prairie du Chien*

MARY ELISE ANTOINE

WISCONSIN HISTORICAL SOCIETY PRESS

Published by the Wisconsin Historical Society Press
*Publishers since 1855*

© 2016 by the State Historical Society of Wisconsin

For permission to reuse material from *The War of 1812 in Wisconsin*
(978-0-87020-738-9; e-book ISBN 978-0-87020-739-6), please access
www.copyright.com or contact the Copyright Clearance Center, Inc. (CCC),
222 Rosewood Drive, Danvers, MA 01923, 978-750-8400. CCC is a not-for-profit
organization that provides licenses and registration for a variety of users.

**wisconsinhistory.org**

Photographs identified with WHi or WHS are from the Society's collections; address
requests to reproduce these photos to the Visual Materials Archivist at the Wisconsin
Historical Society, 816 State Street, Madison, WI 53706.

Cover: *Showing the attack by the British, July 19, 1814, on American Fort Shelby,*
mural ca. 1940 by Cal N. Peters, courtesy of the City of Prairie du Chien.

Printed in Canada

20 19 18 17 16    1 2 3 4 5

Library of Congress Cataloging-in-Publication Data

Names: Antoine, Mary Elise, author.
Title: The War of 1812 in Wisconsin : the battle for Prairie du Chien / Mary Elise Antoine.
Other titles: Battle for Prairie du Chien
Description: 1st edition. | Madison, WI : Wisconsin Historical Society Press,
    [2016] | Includes bibliographical references and index.
Identifiers: LCCN 2016003039 (print) | LCCN 2016003550 (ebook) | ISBN
    9780870207389 (hardcover : alk. paper) | ISBN 9780870207396 (ebook) | ISBN
    9780870207396 (Ebook)
Subjects: LCSH: Prairie du Chien (Wis.) —History. | Wisconsin—History—War of 1812.
Classification: LCC F589.P8 A575 2016 (print) | LCC F589.P8 (ebook) | DDC
    973.5/2475—dc23
LC record available at http://lccn.loc.gov/2016003039

*For the many peoples who maintained their culture
and heritage in the face of Americanization.*

# Contents

# NOTE ON THE TEXT

In the twenty years prior to the War of 1812, William McKay, Thomas G. Anderson, and Pierre Grignon traded with the tribes of the western Great Lakes and upper Mississippi River. In their correspondence detailing the events of 1812 through 1815, they often referred to the tribes who allied themselves with the British. These traders and others often referred to the tribes by the names given to them by the French: Folle Avoines (Menominee), Puants (Winnebago/Ho-Chunk), Sauks (Sac), Renards or Outagamie (Fox/Meskwaki), Sauteur (Chippewa/Ojibwe), Poutewatamie (Potawatomi), Kickapous (Kickapoo), and Sioux, among others. Sometimes, the spelling had a French twist: Soque, Ouenibagoes. Robert Dickson, who became a British Indian agent and constantly met with and traveled with tribal bands, often delineated the people as the Court Orreilles (Lac Courte Oreilles Ojibwe), Sissiton (Sisseton Eastern Dakota/Sioux), or Yanctong (Yankton Western Dakota/Sioux), or named specific chiefs and their people.

After the end of the War of 1812, the British traders withdrew from United States territory and American military and Indian agents arrived to exert United States' control over the region and its people. The French tribal names were no longer used, and the United States and its agents referred to the tribes as Menominee, Winnebago (Ho-Chunk), Sac, Fox (Meskwaki), Chippewa (Ojibwe), Potawatomi, Kickapoo, and Sioux. The Sioux Nation is divided into three regionally-based groups. Zebulon Pike traveled through the lands of the Eastern Dakota, and Robert Dickson knew chiefs and warriors belonging to bands of the Eastern and Western Dakota. When referencing a specific Sioux chief or band, the individual tribal affiliation is used.

Throughout this book, the nineteenth-century American tribal names are used. Note also that original spelling is retained in quotations.

# INTRODUCTION

When asked about the events of the War of 1812 today, many Americans can recount how the British burned Washington and the White House. Patriotism swells when Americans remember that Francis Scott Key wrote the words to the national anthem while watching the British bombard Fort McHenry. And they might even hum a tune about the Battle of New Orleans. But the war is more than three events that occurred in the final months of the conflict. The War of 1812 was fought on many fronts: in the Atlantic Ocean, on the Great Lakes, in Canada, and along the upper Mississippi River. Of these, the latter has received the least attention in US history. Yet it is the battle in the Northwest Territory, where the British and Americans fought for control of the fur trade and for the alliance of Native tribes, that determined what "manifest destiny"—the push west, in terms of the land and what it promised to those who would exploit it—would mean in the decades that followed.

—‖—

On June 18, 1812, United States President James Madison signed a declaration of war against Great Britain. The conflict that ensued came to be known as the War of 1812. The issues that led to this declaration were many, but they were also regional in nature. The residents of Lower Canada and the coastal United States engaged in the fighting for reasons different from those of the people living in Upper Canada and the Northwest Territory. In the western reaches of US territory, the origins of the hostilities between Great Britain and the United States dated from before the American Revolution.

Great Britain had acquired the vast area of Quebec and the Ohio Valley from France at the end of the French and Indian War. With the land came the riches of the fur trade developed by the French. Establishing a working partnership with the American Indians of the western Great Lakes and upper Mississippi, the French had traded manufactured goods for bales of pelts beyond count. The goods the tribes received replaced their Native-made clothes, containers, personal adornments, and weapons. The greatest numbers of pelts came from the "western Indians"—west of the Appalachian Mountains and north of the Ohio River.

When Britain lost its territory south of the Great Lakes in 1783 to the newly constituted United States, it did not wish to relinquish the trade from the western Indians. By taking advantage of laws passed by the United States and the lack of United States' military power, the British from Canada continued to trade with the tribes of the western Great Lakes and the upper Mississippi.

In the vast area of the Northwest Territory, three communities with origins in the French fur trade era stood within the wilderness. The three communities were situated at important points on the fur trade routes. Michilimackinac overlooked the Straits of Mackinac through which convoys of canoes flowed each fall, bringing goods for the winter trading grounds that lay to the north and west. In the spring, canoes from the upper Mississippi and Missouri Rivers returned to the island where voyageurs sorted the pelts for which the goods had been traded before continuing on to Montreal. La Baye, on the western side of Lake Michigan, straddled the Fox River just as it entered Green Bay, and was the entrance to the Fox-Wisconsin waterway, a major trade route. Prairie du Chien, located on a prairie just north of the mouth of the Wisconsin River, was the key to the upper Mississippi. Whoever controlled the prairie commanded the immense territory inhabited by thousands of American Indians.

Michilimackinac, La Baye, and Prairie du Chien had much in common. All were French in character and culture. Economically, all were allied to Great Britain through the fur trade. And the vast majority of the residents were connected by the fur trade and marriage to the tribes of the western Great Lakes and the upper Mississippi. It was a peaceful coexistence, all participants benefitting in some way from the trade of goods for furs.

Yet on the Eastern Seaboard, war was brewing. The United States found itself in the middle of years-long conflict between Britain and France. In

## The Upper Northwest Territory

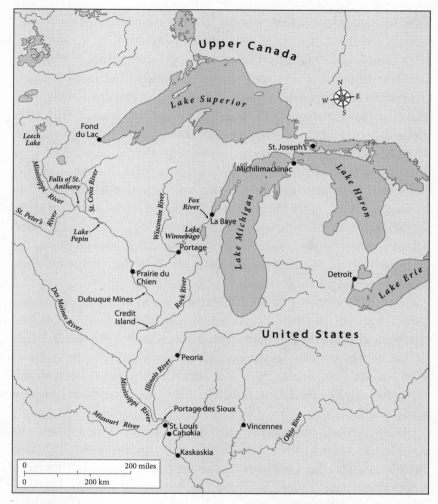

MAPPING SPECIALISTS, LTD., FITCHBURG, WI

1793, in response to the French Revolution, Great Britain and other European countries had attempted to crush the French Republic. Fighting continued after Napoleon Bonaparte seized control of the French government and as he gained power over other European countries. After a short truce, Britain had declared war on France in May 1803, sensing a loss of markets and possible threats to its colonies. The British government also felt that Napoleon was taking control of Europe, making the international economic system unstable. Great Britain and France were engaged in a fight for European supremacy, in the course of which each treated weaker powers, like the United States, with a heavy hand.

As relations between the United States and Great Britain grew more confrontational and the incidents of conflict between Indians and American settlers pushing westward increased, some government agents turned their gaze toward the upper Mississippi River. They found British flags flying at Prairie du Chien and Indian chiefs wearing British peace medals. Here, British traders operated with impunity among the tribes. There were complaints that the United States was losing a great amount of income because of the British trade. The region west of Lake Michigan began to be seen as a threat to the United States. To counteract the influence of the British among the tribes, several men, beginning with Lieutenant Zebulon M. Pike, recommended that a fort be established at Prairie du Chien, the settlement on the Mississippi just a few miles above the confluence of the Mississippi and Wisconsin Rivers.

Then in June of 1812 the United States declared war on Great Britain. Within a month, the British captured the American garrison at Michilimackinac in one of the first battles of the war. Fear of the British and their Indian allies grew and became greater when British-Indian forces captured Fort Dearborn and Fort Detroit. Rumors abounded that the British and the Indians, led by the British fur trader Robert Dickson, would descend on St. Louis.

William Clark, governor of Missouri Territory, decided he and the Americans could not sit in St. Louis anticipating an attack. Prairie du Chien must be taken "to check British influence and prevent the trade." But, as he wrote to Secretary of War Armstrong, the community needed to be under American control for it was a "very important point for the US either in peace or war."[1]

This is the story of the battle for the control of Prairie du Chien, which began many years before the three-day siege in July of 1814 for which the Battle of Prairie du Chien is named, and lasted many decades after. It is also the story of the people, Euro-American and American Indian, who lived in the western country and how the contest for control of the Northwest Territory affected their lives and livelihoods, even forcing decisions as to whether they could stay in the lands they called home.

# 1

## La Baye and Prairie du Chien: French Origins and Settlement

### 1634–1800

Throughout the sixteenth century, the major European powers sponsored explorations of coastal North and Central America. By 1600, Spain dominated the Caribbean and southern regions of North America. France was establishing missions and posts from the mouth of the St. Lawrence River into the woodlands. At that time England's endeavors in the Western Hemisphere trailed those of Spain and France. British explorers did not find a water route to the Pacific Ocean or gold and silver. But in the early seventeenth century, Englishmen began to establish colonies along the Atlantic coast. Some colonies were a financial investment, others a place to worship without the constraints of the Church of England.

The French presence in North America remained small compared to the Spanish and English. But its influence on the northern environment and Indian societies was definitive. French explorers pursued the interior of North America more deeply than others, forging trade routes and Indian relationships that survived into the 1800s.

As the western reaches of the New World beckoned, the French expanded their empire to the middle of the continent, following the watercourses of lakes and rivers. The men who ventured into the upper Great Lakes were exploring new land, but they sought to enter into trade with Native peoples and acquire the rich furs offered in exchange for

European manufactured goods. By their very presence, these French trader-explorers claimed more territory for France. Unlike the English along the Atlantic coast, the French did not desire to acquire land to farm and build villages. Rather, their travels were undertaken to expand a sphere of influence for France.[1] They sought to establish economic relations with the Native population. But the trader-explorers did assess the land through which they paddled their canoes. On each voyage, they looked for strategic locations in which to engage in trade and construct a fortified post.

The French presence in what is now Wisconsin began with Jean Nicolet, a young man who came to Canada in 1618 as a clerk for a trading company, the Compaigne des Marchands, owned by French aristocrats. He had been drawn to North America by Samuel de Champlain's plan to train young men as explorers and traders by having them live among the Indians. In 1634, Champlain sent Nicolet farther west as he hoped to establish relations with the people who lived around the western Great Lakes. In the course of Nicolet's journey, he stepped ashore at what came to be called La Baye (present-day Green Bay).

In the last quarter of the seventeenth century, the fur trade expanded as the Comte de Frontenac, governor of New France, loosened restrictions on trade. During this period, Nicolas Perrot arrived in what is now the state of Wisconsin. The tribes in the upper Great Lakes region were eager to trade their furs with the French for the goods upon which they were beginning to become dependent. At the invitation of the Potawatomi, Perrot and his partner visited La Baye. For some time they explored the area around the Fox River, establishing contact with the Menominee and Outagamie tribes.

With trade routes expanding ever westward following the rivers and lakes, the Catholic clergy wished to extend its chain of missions into the *pays d'en haut*—the upper country west of Montreal. Perrot's trade and exploration coincided with the establishment of the first Catholic outposts in the upper Great Lakes. Father Claude Allouez, superior of the mission at Trois Rivieres, had been appointed vicar general of the western region by Bishop François Laval. Allouez set out on a tour of the western missions. A mission had already been established at Sault Ste. Marie, so Father Allouez ventured westward, paddling into Chequamegon Bay. In

1669, Allouez came to minister among the tribes along the Fox River and Green Bay, and in the winter of 1671–1672, he returned and constructed the first permanent mission house on the Fox River. Located at the last set of rapids on the river before it entered Green Bay, the mission was called St. François de Pere.[2]

As they traveled the rivers and lakes of the *pays d'en haut*, traders and missionaries sought out strategic points of land that commanded a waterway and also led to other waterways. Whoever controlled such a position had access to all the land drained by the river or lake as well as the Native people who lived along the bodies of water. These locations were also desirable because, if the land was easily accessible, the sites could become places for the Native peoples to gather. Here, then, one could trade goods for the pelts the Natives had brought and also offer instruction in the Christian faith. As French explorers and missionaries traveled west, they identified such places along their routes. In the following seasons, they returned. At major gathering places favored by Native populations, the trader and the voyageurs who worked in their employ erected a fortified structure for trade, and the missionary constructed a small chapel; each event expanded contact with the indigenous people and strengthened the French sphere of influence.[3]

In 1673, French explorations reached the Mississippi River, thereby opening a vast new region for French expansion. The following year, Father Jacques Marquette returned to fulfill his desire to live among the Illinois. Louis Joliet had hoped to conduct trade along the Mississippi and make contact with the Illinois nation. He never accomplished this goal, but other Frenchmen followed the water route of Marquette and Joliet.

In 1685, Nicolas Perrot returned to trade around Green Bay. In search of expanding his fur trade connections, he paddled the Fox-Wisconsin River waterway to the Mississippi River. Breaking from the route of Marquette and Joliet, Perrot and his men turned their canoes north and paddled up the Mississippi River to trade among the Dakota. Over the next two seasons, Perrot built three trading posts on the east side of the Mississippi River: a wintering post at Trempeleau and two structures that were more substantial, one at Lake Pepin and the other on the yet unnamed prairie that lay just above the mouth of the Wisconsin River. The post on Lake Pepin he named Fort St. Antoine. The fort he built on the south end of the prairie was called Fort St. Nicolas.⁴ By the end of the seventeenth century, the French considered La Baye and the prairie, which would come to be called *la Prairie du Chien*, to be important trade locations. In time, French-speaking people would settle permanently at each location.

—||—

Green Bay and Prairie du Chien are communities that have their origins in the French fur trade. Through the military conquests of the eighteenth century that transferred the land west of Lake Michigan from nation to nation and territory to territory, La Baye and Prairie du Chien would continue to be identified with the fur trade into the 1840s. And as each nation, in turn, sought to reap the benefits of trade, the governments knew that maintaining good relations with the Native population was necessary not only to control the trade but also to maintain political dominance of the region. La Baye was the entrance to the Fox-Wisconsin River waterway. That waterway was the entrance to the Mississippi River. Numerous rivers from the Wisconsin River northward flowed into the upper Mississippi. Thus, control of Prairie du Chien, located above the confluence of the Mississippi and Wisconsin Rivers, was paramount to the control of the upper Mississippi waterway and drainage.

As the French frontier expanded westward, a small fortification was constructed near the mission Father Allouez had begun along the Fox River near Green Bay. The fort had been manned for only a few years, then abandoned. In 1717, another fort was erected. This stood closer to the mouth of the river. The fathers moved their mission into the fort, building a chapel within the walls. Though it was sometimes called Fort St. Francis because of the mission, more often the post was known as Fort de la Baye des Puants. The fortified structure and some outbuildings lay south of the marshy land where the Fox River emptied into Green Bay. This fort was planned to be a permanent outpost at the head of the Fox-Wisconsin waterway, thereby extending French military presence into the *pays d'en haut*, with the trading fort at Michilimackinac to support it if necessary. The fort at Green Bay was destroyed by the French during their first confrontation with the Fox nation and then rebuilt by the military in 1731.

To maintain the important economic alliances with the local tribes, French fur traders used the military posts as their headquarters in the wilderness to conduct trade. Green Bay was a wintering post for the Montreal-based fur traders and their employees; here they traded with the Ottawa and Menominee. Two of the men who traded at Green Bay were Augustin de Langlade and his son Charles. In 1745, they received a license from Berthelot, the governor of Montreal, to trade at Michilimackinac and Green Bay. The site of their trading post at Green Bay lay along the east bank of the Fox River, south of the fort.

At the same time the Langlades were trading at Green Bay, Pierre Paul Marin was the commander at Fort la Baye. Using the fort as his trading headquarters, Marin and his partners conducted a very lucrative trade. When his son Joseph took over the command of the post, he not only conducted trade with the Indians around Green Bay but also sought to expand it, journeying to the upper Mississippi River to trade and prospect for mineral sources. The winter of 1753–1754, he built a fort, naming it Fort Vaudreuil. This was a walled enclosure consisting of "four houses and a storehouse." Vaudreuil was on the Mississippi below the mouth of the Wisconsin River. Marin may also have refurbished Perrot's fort

Drawn by Frenchman Jacques-Nicolas Bellin, this 1775 map depicts French Canada at the outbreak of the French and Indian War. The detail shows the French fort and the Mission of St. Francis Xavier at La Baye and Fort St. Nicolas at Prairie du Chien.
WHI IMAGE ID 73182

north of the mouth of the Wisconsin in nascent Prairie du Chien at this time.[5]

During this period, France was also enlarging its posts at Detroit and Sault Ste. Marie. But French trade was not without competition. About 1750 the British began to move into French-dominated country in the Ohio Valley, engaging in fur trade among tribes that had long traded with the French. Competition for the Indian trade escalated, and in 1752, Charles de Langlade led the Ottawa and Chippewa (Ojibwe) on an attack at Pickawillany to drive British traders out of the Ohio Valley. After the defeat of General Braddock before Fort Duquesne in 1754, France and Great Britain declared war upon each other. The French and Indian War would last for nine long years, with many of the established traders taking part as commanding officers and soldiers.

Charles de Langlade had led the Chippewa and Ottawa in the 1752 attack on the Miami, who supported the British, and as a result Langlade was appointed an Indian agent for the *pays d'en haut* and in 1755, received a commission in the French colonial army. With the declaration of war, Langlade directed the western Indians in combat on Lake Champlain and above the Plains of Abraham at Quebec. Langlade and his force returned to Fort Michilimackinac to learn of the defeat of the French at Montreal. The commander at the fort departed for Louisiana, leaving Langlade in charge to surrender the post to the British. The British arrived at the Straits of Mackinac in 1761. Taking possession of the French fort, the British then sailed across Lake Michigan and also took over the fort at La Baye, which the French had abandoned in 1760. The British renamed the post Fort Edward Augustus in honor of the fourth son of King George III.[6]

As a result of the war between France and Britain, France lost its colonies of Quebec and Louisiana. Britain gained all of French Canada from Acadia to the Mississippi River. Spain acquired the vast area of Louisiana west of the Mississippi River. Britain now had control of a great stretch of North America and of the fur trade; the post at Green Bay was just one of many prizes.

Now that the French lands were part of British territory, colonists began to move in greater numbers over the Appalachian Mountains in search of land to farm. Most had no claim to the land they settled, as the local Indians had made no land cessions. This brought tension and conflict between the settlers and the Indians. British officials made the situation worse by alienating the American Indians who had fought alongside the French. The French had cultivated alliances, military and economic, among the Indians of the Ohio, Illinois, and Mississippi River valleys. Yet British general Jeffrey Amherst treated the tribes of this region as conquered people, not acknowledging their equality within the fur trade. He forbade the giving of gifts as part of the rituals of trade. In so doing, he undercut the authority of any pro-British Indians and antagonized Indian leaders.

In response to British actions and the western settlement by colonists and land speculators, Pontiac, an Ottawa chief, was able to unite several tribes, and coordinated attacks were made on British forts and settlements in 1763. When news of the uprising reached London, the British government decided to create a western Indian reserve rather than using force against the Native population. Trade was of more benefit to the British than the acquisition and sale of Indian lands to settlers. Thus, Parliament issued the Royal Proclamation of 1763, which asserted that all Indian peoples were under the protection of the king. It prohibited settlement on lands west of the Appalachian Mountains and provided for the establishment of forts to protect the land and the Indians from incursions. Only those with royal permission could inhabit or conduct business in the lands west of the Appalachians to the Mississippi River. This action stemmed the flow of western settlers and made the land west of the mountains forbidden—and intriguing—territory to many of the inhabitants of the Eastern Seaboard.

In 1764, William Johnson, British superintendent of Indian affairs, negotiated a treaty at Fort Niagara with the Indians of the upper Ohio Valley, and in 1766, Pontiac agreed to a formal treaty. The British had learned the need to ensure the safety of the Indians if they were to maintain the traditions of trade relations established by the French. These edicts would keep peace on the frontier and guarantee the continuation of profits from the fur trade. Though most of the trading licenses were given to British Canadians, these traders employed Frenchmen who had experience in the trade and knew the land and its Indian inhabitants.

One of the men who received a license to trade was Charles de Langlade, who moved his center of operations to La Baye. During Pontiac's

Rebellion, the British had abandoned the Green Bay fort; the old French post became Charles's home in 1764. Charles de Langlade is credited with being the first permanent Euro-American settler at Green Bay. With Charles and his family was Pierre Grignon, Langlade's clerk. They continued to trade with the Indians whom Langlade had led in war; Langlade and Grignon just shifted their trading contacts to the new British merchant houses in Montreal. Over the next ten years, only a very few other Canadians would settle along the Fox River.[7]

Meanwhile, trade between Indians and Europeans continued to flourish at Prairie du Chien. While Perrot and Marin had constructed fortified trading posts on the upper Mississippi River, none of these posts had been consistently manned by French military or traders. The hostility of the Sac and Fox nations and then wars in Europe between France and Great Britain had kept the Jesuits and other Catholic priests from venturing into the vast watershed of the upper Mississippi; no missions had been built along the Fox-Wisconsin waterway or the upper Mississippi. Still, the prairie continued to be an important gathering place for the Indian tribes of the upper Mississippi. After the French had reduced the power of the Fox (Meskwaki) Nation in a series of wars, the prairie became a gathering place for the fur traders who made the long journey from either Michilimackinac or the Illinois Country and New Orleans to garner the magnificent furs the Winnebago, Sac, Dakota, Sioux, and Chippewa brought to trade.

In 1766, Robert Rogers, British commander at Fort Michilimackinac, contracted with Jonathan Carver to lead an expedition westward in hopes of finding a water route to the Pacific Ocean. Leaving Michilimackinac, Carver and his men followed the fur trade route to Green Bay. He resupplied there, noting that a few Frenchmen lived along the river, and then continued on the Fox and Wisconsin Rivers to the Mississippi River. Turning north, Carver and his men stopped at the prairie. After spending the winter further north, Carver paused on his return at the prairie in the spring before continuing on to Michilimackinac. Carver came ashore at the time of the spring gathering. Though he wrote of seeing three hundred Indian houses on the prairie, one cannot be sure from Carver's account whether there was any permanent settlement there.[8]

Seven years later, the American-born British fur trader Peter Pond arrived at the prairie. He stayed there for ten days in the fall of 1773, dispatching

Jonathan Carver was one of the first white men to document his explorations of the upper Mississippi with maps and journals. In this 1769 map he recorded the names and village locations of the tribes he met and noted the rivers he traveled. WHI IMAGE ID 39773

clerks to trade on various tributaries of the Wisconsin and Mississippi Rivers, then left for the St. Peter's River (now the Minnesota River) with two other traders. Like Carver, Pond mentioned the large Native population he encountered, but he did not clarify whether there were permanent houses built upon the prairie.

Both Carver and Pond had been at the prairie at a time when the tribes of the region gathered there for trade. Both remarked upon the great number of Indians and traders that congregated on the prairie each fall and spring, either en route to wintering quarters farther up the Mississippi or returning to the trading houses. Pond found the French to be "Veray Numeres." At least 130 canoes from Mackinac were on shore alongside boats from "Orleans & Ilenoa." At the prairie, traders with connections to Montreal and Quebec drank high wine with men who would journey home to the Illinois Country and New Orleans at the end of the spring rendezvous. Carver recorded the name of the prairie: *Prairie Les Chiens.* Pond wrote the Anglicized version of the name: "Planes of the Dogs."[9]

French-speaking people from the Illinois Country, who had been to the prairie during the trading seasons, were the first to permanently settle at Prairie du Chien in the early 1770s. In 1774, Phillippe Laflamme sold "a fort, a house, a billiard table, &c" to Isaac Levy and Richard McCarty. All three were residents of Cahokia, one of the French settlements in the Illinois Country then under British control.[10] Merchants from Cahokia continued to trade at Prairie du Chien as the thirteen colonies fought for their independence from Great Britain.

Then, in the spring of 1780, the conflict between Britain and the colonies came to Prairie du Chien. For the first time, traders and Indians would have to choose with whom they were allied: Great Britain or the new United States of America. That April, Charles Gratiot, a merchant at Cahokia and an American partisan, sent a bateau loaded with furs and supplies to Prairie du Chien. Joseph Calve and Jean-Marie DuCharme, British sympathizers who traded out of La Baye, met the bateau just south of Prairie du Chien. The boat, under the direction of Jean Baptiste Cardinal, operated with an American pass. Calve and DuCharme confiscated the bateau and divided the supplies among the Canadian volunteers, traders, and 750 Indians recruited by Charles Gautier who had gathered at Prairie du Chien. Patrick Sinclair, the British lieutenant governor stationed at Michilimackinac, had planned a two-pronged attack against St. Louis and Cahokia, and the supplies were needed to support the men as they traveled toward St. Louis. According to the plan, Charles de Langlade was to leave Green Bay with his men, follow the west shore of Lake Michigan, and approach St. Louis by way of Chicago and the Illinois River. Gautier and his men and Native allies were to move down the Mississippi. Langlade, for an unknown reason, brought his contingent to Prairie du Chien, arriving after Gautier's force had left. The attack on St. Louis failed. Fearing the Americans might come to Prairie du Chien in retaliation, Gautier burned the "old French Fort" that had been used by him and his men, and the furs stored there were taken to Michilimackinac. American forces never attempted the trip to Prairie du Chien, but the influence of the American merchants from the Illinois Country began to lessen as men from Canada and Michilimackinac started to acquire property at Prairie du Chien in the 1790s.[11]

The incident of Gratiot's bateau had another effect: it caused the residents of Prairie du Chien to feel unsure as to whether they had title to the land on which they had built their houses. Some of the men who had first settled at Prairie du Chien had secured a deed for their lot of land and recorded the transfer at Cahokia or Kaskaskia, another of the French settlements in the Illinois Country. But in 1778, the American George Rogers Clark captured the British post at Kaskaskia and within a few days had secured Cahokia and the surrounding communities. The residents of the Illinois Country were forced to take an oath of allegiance to the United States. This had precipitated the failed attack on Cahokia and St. Louis. With what deeds there were now in American hands, the residents of Prairie du Chien realized the need to secure ownership of their property.

The residents decided to send representatives to Michilimackinac to meet with Sinclair, the lieutenant governor for the upper part of Canada, to ask him to help them gain title to the prairie. The fact that the residents considered the British at Michilimackinac, and not the Americans, the authority to grant ownership of land indicates that the overall sentiment at Prairie du Chien in 1781 was pro-British. Pierre Pelletier dit Antaya, Augustin Ange, and Basil Giard traveled to Michilimackinac and made the request. In response, Sinclair called a meeting of tribal representatives and concluded a treaty in which he purchased the island of Mackinac, the land along the Fox River at Green Bay, and Prairie du Chien. The treaty was signed by Sinclair and various Indians and then sent to Montreal. The three men then returned to the prairie and distributed to the Indians assembled at Prairie du Chien the goods that were payment for the land. In two years, with the signing of the Treaty of Paris, Mackinac Island, Green Bay, and Prairie du Chien would formally become part of the United States. Later, as the United States brought tribes together to sign treaties relinquishing their traditional lands, there never was a question by the Indians as to the legitimacy of Sinclair's treaty of 1781. In 1820, upon investigation, the United States would accept its validity.[12]

—╢╟—

The first permanent residents at Prairie du Chien were from the Illinois Country, and they brought with them the French method of land division. In the settlements of Kaskaskia, Cahokia, and Prairie du Rocher, people owned a village lot and a farm lot. So when the French from the Illinois Country settled at Prairie du Chien, they selected land and partitioned it in the same manner. By 1800, there were three villages at Prairie du Chien.

The Main Village was located on an island facing the east channel of the Mississippi River; the island was separated from the mainland by a *marais* or marsh. On the mainland were two more villages; one village stood directly across the *marais* from the Main Village, and a smaller village sat about three miles distant to the north. All of the village lots fronted on the waters of the Mississippi River. These village lots were measured by width in *arpents* (a unit of linear measure equivalent to about 190 feet, or 58 meters, used in New France), bounded on the north and south by the neighbor's lot. But each village lot had a defined length. In the Main Village, the back boundary of each lot was the *marais*. In the other two villages, the lots were bounded in the rear by the road that spanned the prairie north to south or by the larger farm lots. Behind the villages, the farm lots extended from the villages to the bluffs that delineated the prairie to the east. Except for the two villages, the nine-mile length of the prairie that stretched almost to the Wisconsin River had been partitioned into forty-three farm lots. Part of each lot was held in common by all the residents, and in the common grazed cattle and horses.[13]

The trading community at Prairie du Chien was far more organized than at La Baye. At Prairie du Chien, the traders lived in the Main Village, where they had their stores and homes. The men who lived in the two villages on the mainland were voyageurs and men who had retired from the trade. Almost all spoke French; they had close familial relationships and helped one another in the raising of crops on the farm lots. The trading community in the Main Village at Prairie du Chien was also far more diverse than that of the few traders, mainly French, who resided at Green Bay. Some of the traders, like Joseph Rolette, Jean Baptiste Faribault, and Michel La Bathe, had arrived in Prairie du Chien from the province of Lower Canada. Basil Giard and Louis Honore had come from the Illinois Country. But most of the major traders who operated out of Prairie du Chien were British Canadians with Scottish ancestry—John Campbell, Robert Dickson, James and George Aird, and Murdock Cameron. After the French and Indian War, British and Scottish businessmen replaced many of the French Canadian merchants in Montreal. These men learned from the French how to conduct the trade, and they invested in the western Great Lakes trade, hiring fellow Scotsmen as their agents.

The Francois Vertefeuille home was constructed using hewn logs in the French-Canadian method of *pièce sur pièce en coulisse*. This structure is typical of the houses that once stood along the Fox River at La Baye and in the villages at Prairie du Chien. Vertefeuille's home was in the Upper Village, and he was employed in the fur trade, farming during the summer. COURTESY OF ROBERT CAMARDO

As the nineteenth century began, a unique situation existed at La Baye and Prairie du Chien. Though both settlements were part of the United States, most of the men living in the communities were connected to the British fur trade. Many were of French Canadian heritage, spoke French, and lived in communities decidedly French in character. Many had familial connections to the tribes with whom they traded. At Green Bay there was not the preponderance of Scots Canadians as at Prairie du Chien. Rather, as the earlier residents of La Baye were from French-speaking Lower Canada, so too were the people who arrived in the last decade of the eighteenth century, whether French or Jewish. All were British citizens, many with business contacts in British-controlled Montreal. At La Baye and Prairie du Chien, any connection to the United States was almost nonexistent.

By 1800, the fur trade under the British had expanded. More traders resided at Prairie du Chien or used the community as a headquarters. They had pushed into the lands along the St. Peter's River, setting up wintering posts among the Dakota. Whether from love or to solidify a trading alliance, many of the Prairie du Chien traders established unions with women of the most important Dakota descent groups. Robert Dickson married

Toto-win, a sister of the Sissiton chief Red Thunder. Dickson hired as his clerk Joseph Renville, whose mother was from Red Wing's village. James Aird married the daughter of the first chief Wabasha. Archibald John Campbell married into the Mdewakanton tribe. Joseph Rolette purchased the hand of Wabasha's niece.[14]

Every resident of the western Great Lakes–upper Mississippi region was connected in some manner with the fur trade. Residents included Euro-American traders, clerks, engagés, and farmers producing crops necessary to the trade, some of whom were of mixed heritage, as well as Indian men and their families, who trapped the animals and processed the hides and pelts brought to the trade. Through the outcome of war, the fur trade had changed hands from France to Great Britain. Pontiac's Rebellion had taught Britain that if the trade was to be economically successful, the fur trade needed to continue in the manner instituted by France. Thus, traders from Canada, whether speakers of French or English, continued to go to the Indians to trade. A partnership had been formed in the seventeenth century, and the alliance continued to be maintained as the nineteenth century began. Between the tribes of the western Great Lakes and the upper Mississippi and the residents of La Baye and Prairie du Chien were economic, cultural, and familial relationships that were generations old.

This region had been called *mer de l'ouest, pays d'en haut*, and Indian country. Now under the control of the United States, it would be organized as the Northwest Territory in 1787. For the people of the thirteen colonies who had rebelled against Great Britain in part to gain access to the land west of the Appalachian Mountains, the reaches of the new territory were unknown, and the people who lived there an enigma. Even the new government of the United States was unsure how to administer the territory. Once the United States learned about the fertile lands that lay beyond the Appalachian Mountains, a movement westward began. The early-nineteenth-century movement to chart and assert United States dominance of the Northwest Territory affected all who lived on the land, including the Indian nations who for millennia had lived there; it was the origin of what came to be called Manifest Destiny.

# 2

# BRITISH TRADE IN
# UNITED STATES TERRITORY

## 1783–1802

At the end of the American Revolution, the new United States faced problems on the western frontier the magnitude of which Congress did not at first realize. The Treaty of Paris had made peace with Great Britain, but the treaty did not address the American Indians who had allied with Britain in the war. The United States was now in possession of a huge western territory, claimed and occupied by Indian nations whose friendship and allegiance had yet to be determined. Congress would have to make peace with the Indians, each nation considered sovereign and thereby requiring an individual treaty. Before any peace overture began, though, Americans pushed into the territory beyond the Appalachians. At that point, another complication became evident: the United States soon discovered the British in Canada were unwilling to give up their fur trade in the lands they had ceded to the United States north and west of the Ohio River.

Even before the Treaty of Paris was signed, the news of a peace proposal alarmed and caused discontent among the Native population from New York to the Mississippi River. To them, what had been almost a familial relationship with the British was about to be severed. The tribes feared that the Americans would attack them in revenge for their alliance with Britain during the Revolution. General Frederick Haldimand, governor of the British-held province of Quebec, felt that the preservation of the

British-Indian alliance was crucial for the defense and security of Canada.

Despite British promises to the tribes, neither the United States nor Great Britain had addressed the status of the tribes that lived west of the Appalachian Mountains. In the years between the end of the American Revolution and the signing of the 1783 Treaty of Paris, the British had maintained their long-established trade relations with the tribes and helped as they attempted to protect their land from settlement by people from the former eastern colonies. Now with the signing of the treaty, Joseph Brant, leader of the Iroquois of New York State, cried that the king had "sold the Indians to Congress." Fearing that the Indians would band together in another uprising as had occurred under Pontiac twenty years earlier, Haldimand devised a frontier and Indian policy that would form the basis of British thinking in North America into the nineteenth century. Haldimand proposed that the British military posts in the "upper country" along the western Great Lakes remain. He also proposed that the country between the United States–Canada boundary line and the Ohio River "be considered entirely as belonging to the Indians." The British Indian policy after 1783 was therefore based on the defense of Canada. For the British, there was not only fear of the united power of the tribes of the western Great Lakes but also a concern that the United States might still be considering a way to gain the western part of Quebec.[1]

Haldimand's concern may also have been economic, for in fact the British continued to dominate the fur trade in what was now United States territory. During the period between American independence and the Treaty of Paris, the British commanders at Michilimackinac had worked hard to keep the western Great Lakes tribes from warring amongst themselves and to keep them allied with Britain. After the war, the Canadian British renewed their friendship and trading relations with the Indian nations living in the Northwest Territory and provided them with supplies. Despite signing the treaty, the British army continued to hold on to its military posts located on Lake Champlain and at Oswego, Niagara, Detroit, and Michilimackinac.

The continuing British presence was counter to the expectations of the Americans. At the close of the American Revolution, the United States disbanded its army in favor of state militias. Congress believed that the British posts in the Great Lakes area would be evacuated and asked the states for seven hundred men to protect the northern frontier. As to the tribes, Congress believed that the Indians had forfeited their rights to their lands because of their support of the British. Congress felt that the tribes should sign treaties in which the United States "gave" them land.[2] In fact, that comment by Congress represented the sum of United States Indian policy in 1783.

Conversely, agents and troops of the British Indian Department continued to be present in the Northwest. As a move to reconcile differences between various American Indian tribes in the upper Mississippi and around Lake Superior and maintain their loyalty to Britain, agents of the Indian Department and traders met with tribal chiefs at Prairie du Chien, La Baye, and places in between, and convinced the various tribes to come to Michilimackinac. There the British held a peace council in July of 1787. The British promised their support for the tribes against American incursions and ended the council with presents of goods now necessary to the tribes' survival.

The United States was aware of the continuing British presence in the Northwest. But the influx of Americans into the Northwest and onto traditional Indian lands was causing greater problems on the Ohio frontier. With the lands west of the Appalachian Mountains now part of the United States, people from the first thirteen states moved westward, claiming tracts that they began to clear and farm. Several eastern states made claim to vast areas stretching from the mountains to the Mississippi River, hoping to sell land and fill their coffers depleted by the cost of war. Land companies vied over prime tracts, and competition was greatest in the area north of the Ohio River. No one had gained title to the land traditionally held by the various Indian tribes, at least not title that was recognized by the United States.

The US government knew it had to exert its authority. Congress overruled the states' claims and declared the land companies in violation. To create order, the Congress passed the Northwest Ordinance in 1787, creating the Northwest Territory. The Northwest Ordinance provided for the administration of the land south of the Great Lakes and north and west of the Ohio River and set guidelines by which a territory could be admitted as a state to the union. At the time the Northwest Ordinance was passed, about forty-nine thousand people lived in the Northwest Territory, of which approximately forty-five thousand were American Indians. From the perspective of the Indians and the French-speaking people who lived at La Baye and Prairie du Chien, the territorial policy of the United States would become a severe threat to their way of life.[3]

Though Secretary of War Henry Knox initially sent regulars and state militiamen to "extirpate utterly, if possible" the Indians who were attacking American settlers on the frontier, President George Washington and Secretary Knox rejected all-out war as a way to subjugate the tribes. Washington wanted to conciliate the Indians by negotiation, guarantees of protection, and development of trade. Through his urging, in 1790 Congress passed what would be the first Trade and Intercourse Act. Originally designed to enforce treaties that the United States was negotiating and stop white aggression, the first and subsequent acts came to embody the basic features of US Indian policy.[4]

The Trade and Intercourse Act of 1790 struck a blow to the British and French traders living in the Northwest corridor. The act stated that "no person shall be permitted to carry on any trade or intercourse with the Indians, without a license for that purpose," and established penalties for anyone trading without a license. The act also attempted to control American agressiveness, stating that any individual or group purchase of land from Indians was illegal unless made by a public treaty with the United States. Anyone committing murder or other crimes against the Indians in Indian country would be punished. Though the act was temporary, it curbed land speculators and lessened conflicts on the Ohio frontier. The act was renewed in 1793, now stronger and more inclusive. Under the renewed act, the president was authorized to give goods and money to tribes "to promote civilization" and secure "continuance of their friendship." The Trade and Intercourse Act was passed again in 1796. Using geographical features described in treaties signed with tribes in the Ohio territory, the act, when renewed in 1802, specified in detail the boundary line between settlers and Indians, calling the land west of the boundary Indian country.[5]

The acts were an attempt to lessen the influence of the British traders on the frontier, but greater tensions between the United States and Great Britain consumed President Washington and Congress. After the American Revolution, Britain had flooded American markets with goods while restrictions and high tariffs blocked American goods from being sold in Britain. British ships often stopped American merchant ships on the ocean, impressing men into the British navy if the seamen were thought to be British citizens. The border between the United States and Canada had not yet been defined, and with the tensions between the two nations, the British feared the Americans would make another attempt to invade Canada. Thus, as part of the "defense" of Canada, the British continued to occupy forts that they had agreed to vacate. Fearing a war with Great Britain, Washington sent statesman John Jay to London to negotiate with Britain.

In the resulting treaty, signed in November 1794, Britain agreed to withdraw, by 1796, from the five pre-Revolutionary forts located within the Northwest Territory, and, in turn, a commercial agreement granted the United States "most favored nation" status whereby the duties paid by ships or merchandise of one country entering the ports of the other country would be equal to duties paid by all nations. Importation duties were to be the same, and there could be no prohibitions on the importing or exporting of any articles unless it extended to all nations. The Jay Treaty, as it was called, allowed the free movement of British, Americans, and American Indians between Canada and the United States for the purpose of carrying on trade and commerce. The treaty also defined a portion of the US–Canada border; however, it failed to settle several issues, including the Maine–Canada boundary and British seizure of American goods and ships. Nevertheless, the ability of Americans to engage in trade and commerce without paying Britain's restrictive tariffs helped the US economy. For the British in Canada, the Jay Treaty specifically guaranteed the right of British traders to engage in the fur trade in US territory.[6]

Although the Trade and Intercourse acts required that anyone conducting trade among the Indians be licensed, it was almost impossible to enforce the requirement, and British traders continued to gather at Michilimackinac and Prairie du Chien and engage in trade without a license issued by the United States. When in 1796 the British turned over Fort Mackinac (now located on Mackinac Island) to the United States, the British moved their main trade depot from Michilimackinac to Fort St. Joseph on the northern shore of Lake Huron, in Upper Canada. Some of the residents of Michilimackinac relocated with the troops to St. Joseph Island. Men of the new fur-trading enterprise the North West Company, formed to compete with the Hudson's Bay Company, joined them but set up trading posts to winter in American territory in the Fond du Lac trading region so that they could engage in the upper Mississippi trade. Independent traders with connections to Montreal merchants maintained their operations in La Baye and Prairie du Chien. The goods they used for trade had been imported from Great Britain and passed into the western Great Lakes and the upper Mississippi River regions without payment of duty to the United States.

With the Great Lakes forts back in American control and treaties with the Ohio tribes opening land to settlers, the United States began to construct forts along the Ohio River and its tributaries. Americans from the eastern United States could move westward and purchase land gained through treaties in the Northwest Territory without the worry of the British or Indians stopping them. But there was a vast area of the Northwest Territory without any form of US military control. After gaining Fort Mackinac, United States troops never proceeded farther west than Mackinac Island, and no American forts existed on the upper Mississippi River. The government in Washington was barely aware of the settlements at Green Bay and Prairie du Chien, and therefore no agency of the War Department or territorial government instituted civil government in either community. In part, then, it was the inability of the United States to exert authority over the vast majority of the Northwest Territory that led the British Canadian governor to proclaim the areas west of Mackinac as Indian land, with no authority by the United States over the people who lived here.

The Jay Treaty and the Trade and Intercourse Acts had little effect on the daily life and commerce at La Baye and Prairie du Chien. The traders at La Baye and Prairie du Chien continued to purchase their trade goods from British merchants and in return sold their pelts through the commercial houses in Montreal. Trading activities at Prairie du Chien increased as more British traders made the community a center for their operations. The Mississippi River was an economic highway giving access to the St. Peter's River to the north and the Missouri River to the south. Both rivers flowed into the vast lands of the Sioux nation.

—⊣⊢—

In an attempt to further counteract the presence and economic power of the British traders and maintain the friendship of the Indians, in 1796 Congress passed "An Act for establishing Trading Houses with the Indian Tribes." The trading houses, or fur factories as they were sometimes called, would be operated by the United States. The houses would be located at military posts and places on the western and southern frontiers, or in Indian country. The president of the United States was given the power to appoint an agent, the clerk, and any other employees necessary to conduct business. All trade was to occur only at the factory. President Washington felt if the United States carried on the trade, the Indians would receive goods at a fair price and "engross their Trade, and fix them strongly in our Interest." Thus, prices of the goods supplied to the Indians in exchange for furs were to be regulated so that the United States would not make a profit. Agents, clerks, and other employees would be paid by the United States. The act emphatically stated that no one employed at the trading houses was to benefit personally from the trade.[7]

Yet the Americans had another motive in mind. Unlike the French and British, who sought only to trade with the Indians for the furs and pelts, the United States sought the lands on which the tribes lived and hunted—an initiative that would be pursued in earnest by Washington's successor, Thomas Jefferson.[8] When Jefferson was elected president of the United States in 1800, he had already left his imprint on the Northwest Territory. His suggestions on the method by which western territories could become part of the United States had been written into the Northwest Ordinance of 1787. As president he pursued an Indian policy that greatly expanded US Indian policy and furthered the creation of territories. Jefferson's Indian treaties had two goals: to acquire land and direct the fur trade to the United States, and to "civilize" the Native population. By signing a treaty, a tribe agreed to give the United States its traditional lands, agreed to trade with government traders at fur factories, and were removed onto lands where they would become sedentary and turn to agricultural pursuits. In return, the tribes received annual annuity payments. This agreement would open lands to settlement, bring income to the United States by trade and land sales, and make the tribes dependent on the government.[9]

In his instructions to the government representatives dealing with tribes, Jefferson told them never to coerce the Indian nations to sell their lands. But he hoped to accelerate the process. Jefferson wrote to William Henry Harrison, governor of Indiana Territory, suggesting that if the Indian nations could be encouraged to purchase goods on credit, they would likely fall into debt, which they could relieve by the sale of their lands to the government. "In this way," he wrote, "our settlement will gradually circumscribe and approach the Indians, and they will in time either incorporate with us as citizens of the United States, or remove beyond the Mississippi. . . . [W]e presume that our strength and their weakness is now so visible that they must see we have only to shut our hand to crush them." Jefferson also supported the concept of fur factories. These he saw could be of use among the tribes who had not yet accepted the "protection" of the United States. He felt that if factories could be established near the western Great Lakes and on the Mississippi, "[t]hose this side of the Missipi [sic] will soon be entirely with us."[10]

The method of conducting the trade at a factory or any set location was counter to all trading traditions established by the French and continued by the British. For close to one hundred and fifty years, traders had gone to the Indians, taking their goods with them and establishing wintering posts close to Indian villages. Where competing traders had posts close to one another, the Indians could play one trader against another, having a say in the value received for furs. If the United States took control of the fur trade in Indian country under the factory system, the Indians would be forced to journey, sometimes hundreds of miles, to a factory to trade their pelts for goods, accepting what goods and prices the United States offered.

Not surprisingly, the idea was met with disregard and disapproval by those who lived in the upper Northwest. Americans such as John Kinzie, Thomas Forsyth, and John Jacob Astor operated independent trading houses. Governor Harrison issued trading licenses to individuals even though a US factory existed at Fort Wayne. Ninian Edwards, governor of Illinois Territory, criticized the system. William Clark, though an Indian agent, carried on a private trade. Even so, the factory system expanded; but with a lack of United States military presence in the upper Mississippi at the end of the eighteenth century, it was impossible to even consider establishing a government trading house at La Baye or Prairie du Chien. As such, British traders carried on with no governmental competition.[11]

—||—

At La Baye, Pierre Grignon continued de Langlade's trading contacts in the country around Green Bay and sent goods to Pierre Antaya at Prairie du Chien. In 1796, the same year Congress ordered the establishment of fur factories, Jacques Vieau established a trading post along the Menomonee River for the North West Company, where he wintered, and several posts along the eastern shore of Lake Michigan.

At the same time, the Main Village at Prairie du Chien was expanding. Most of the men who had come from the Illinois Country remained at Prairie du Chien.[12] In the 1790s, there was an influx of British Canadian traders to the upper Mississippi, and many began purchasing lots in the Main Village. They strengthened the British economic hold on tribes into the farthest reaches of the Northwest Territory. Many of these men would be key players in the rising conflict between US and British interests in the region, including during the War of 1812.

Andrew Todd was a junior partner in the Montreal trading firm of Isaac Todd and James McGill. Sent west as his uncle's representative, in 1792 Andrew bought a village lot just north of Louis Honore's. Admitted to the Beaver Club for his years spent in the wilderness, Todd must have ingratiated himself with the Spanish governor of Louisiana. Since 1762, Spain had controlled the vast lands west of the Mississippi River from New Orleans to Canada, which contained great riches in furs. In 1794, Baron de Carondelet granted Todd an exclusive right to the trade on the Mississippi River above St. Louis and the Missouri River. This area of trade was highly sought after by the Canadian British, and for two years Todd sent considerable trade goods into the region.[13]

The trading opportunities west of the Mississippi River drew others as well. Julian Dubuque, trading with the Fox, learned that the tribe mined for lead on their lands. Meeting with the Fox chiefs at Prairie du Chien, Dubuque received a grant to work their lead mines. He moved to Catfish Creek on the west side of the Mississippi and soon had a monopoly on the mining and trade of lead between Catfish Creek and St. Louis. Concern over encroachment by Americans caused Dubuque to petition de Carondelet for title to the land. The governor granted Dubuque title on the condition that Dubuque made no attempt to take over the trade granted to "Don Andrew Todd."[14]

With this foothold, British traders expanded into Spanish territory. In 1790, Jean Baptiste Faribault came from Michilimackinac and settled in the Main Village of Prairie du Chien, using it as his base for trading. Nine years later, Faribault settled two hundred miles up the Des Moines River, trading there for four seasons. Each spring he paddled down the Des Moines to the Mississippi River where he transferred the pelts to Lewis Crawford, also of Prairie du Chien, who then ensured that the pelts reached Montreal. About the same time, Thomas G. Anderson of Michilimackinac traded for Jacob Franks with the Ioway as far west as the Missouri River.[15]

In 1799, Louis Honore of Prairie du Chien, who often traded in St. Louis, received a concession of land from Carondolet of three miles square about ten miles above the mouth of the Des Moines River. With the grant, Honore obtained a monopoly on the fur trade of that region. He was "to watch the savages and to keep them in fealty which they owe His Majesty."[16]

About the same time, Basil Giard received a grant of land of more than five thousand acres from the Spanish lieutenant governor. The land was situated on the west side of the Mississippi River across from Prairie du Chien. Giard, like Honore, traded with the Indians west of the Mississippi River, and Giard's instructions may have been similar to those given to Honore. Whether Honore and Giard kept their Indian trading partners loyal to Spain or not, they freely traveled from Spanish territory through American territory to British territory.[17]

While people could pass freely from Canada to the United States for the purpose of commerce and trade, the United States expected British merchants to pay custom taxes on merchandise brought into the country. In 1799, a US customs house was opened on Mackinac Island, and all traders traveling with goods into the upper portion of the Northwest Territory were expected to stop and pay taxes on their merchandise. Custom taxes, trade restrictions by Spain, and the increased competition from American traders caused the British traders, many of whom operated independently, serious economic problems. Perceiving the need for a united front, British traders began to form trading agreements or companies.

The North West Company had formed twenty years earlier, in 1779, in an attempt to break the Hudson's Bay Company's monopoly of the fur trade in the northern reaches of Canada. Two of the men associated with the company were Peter Pond and Isaac Todd, both of whom had connections to Prairie du Chien. The North West Company also extended its operations to the western Great Lakes and as far south as the junction of the Illinois and Mississippi Rivers. These traders soon had competition from former compatriots. In 1797, several traders formed the XY Company. Disenchanted with Simon McTavish's leadership of the North West Company, they called themselves the New North West Company. Since the North West Company labeled its packs *NW*, the new company labeled its packs with the two letters that follow *W*, and the company came to be known as the XY Company.[18]

Jacob Franks had traded in the region, and in 1794 he obtained a 999-year lease from the Menominee for twelve hundred acres of land located on both sides of the Fox River at Green Bay. Three years later, Franks came to Green Bay with his nephew John Lawe. Franks had purchased the Ogilvy, Gillespie, store at La Baye and now operated it as the XY post. It was Franks, as agent of the XY Company, who had sent Jean Baptiste Faribault to trade along the Des Moines River. North of Prairie du Chien, the North West Company and the XY Company were in close competition for the same trade with the Chippewa and Dakota. The companies manned trading posts directly across from each other on the Yellow River, in what is now northern Wisconsin, and at Grand Portage and Rainy Lake in present-day Minnesota.[19]

By 1800, there were many traders residing at La Baye and Prairie du Chien. Some lived permanently in the communities at each location; others operated seasonal trading posts or stores and lived at Michilimackinac during the summer. Most operated with British trading licenses, and they did not pay the United States duty on the British goods they used for trade. Their trading contacts and influence stretched from Lake Michigan to the Missouri River and from the Des Moines River northward into the lands of the Chippewa and Dakota. It was stated that because of the inability of the United States to enforce its laws on the fur trade, the government lost twenty-six thousand dollars annually in the upper Mississippi region alone.[20]

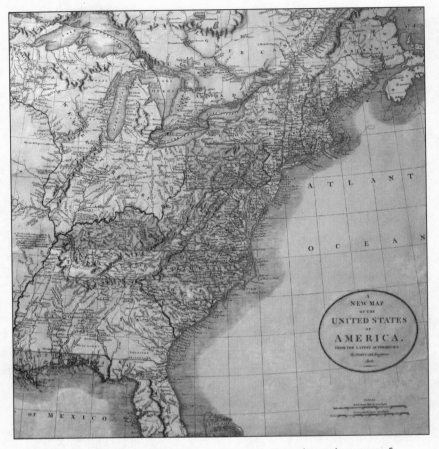

John Cary's New Map of the United States of America, 1806, shows the extent of
the United States after the formation of the Northwest Territory in 1787. COURTESY OF
MAPSOFPA.COM

In 1802, the first semblance of US jurisdiction in Prairie du Chien came
in the form of political appointments by the governor of the new Indiana
Territory, created by an act of Congress made effective on July 4, 1800.
Indiana Territory included all of the Northwest Territory except Ohio
and was divided into three counties, Knox, Randolph, and St. Clair. The
northernmost part of the territory, which included present-day northern Illinois, Wisconsin, eastern Minnesota, and northern Michigan, was
unorganized. La Baye and Prairie du Chien were within the unorganized
area. The local justices and a regional militia were tasked with enforcing

and interpreting the laws of the nation within each county.[21] The newly appointed territorial governor, William Harrison, quickly appointed officials for the three counties. Having never visited Prairie du Chien, he must have relied on the recommendations of people who were familiar with the community's residents to decide whom to appoint. Of the five men appointed to positions, four had trading connections in St. Louis. It is not clear whether Harrison was aware that each also had agreements with British trading houses.

Governor Harrison appointed John Campbell and Robert Dickson justices of the peace for St. Clair County, of which Prairie du Chien was made a part. Henry Munro Fisher was commissioned captain of the Prairie du Chien militia, with Basil Giard the lieutenant and Michel La Bathe an ensign.[22] Although each of these men resided at Prairie du Chien, each was engaged in the fur trade and operated in association with a British Montreal-based trading company. Given that background, one could question each man's compunction to enforce the laws of the United States, especially in regards to licenses, payment of import duties, and trade and commerce with the Indians.

A year after these appointments, Ohio was admitted to the Union as a state, so Harrison redefined the boundaries of some of the counties within the Indiana Territory to include La Baye and the lands along and west of Lake Michigan. He then appointed Charles Reaume from La Baye another justice of the peace for St. Clair County. With these appointments, Governor Harrison must have felt he had established American authority in the farthest corners of US territory. Of all the men appointed by Harrison, only Reaume had demonstrated at least a modicum of allegiance to the United States. During the American Revolution Reaume had supported the British. Captured by the Americans at Detroit, he took an oath of neutrality. About 1792, he moved to La Baye from Detroit, and after some attempt at trading he turned to farming.[23]

John Campbell was also engaged in the fur trade, with his regular trading place a post on the St. Peter's River. Campbell was part of the influx of Irish and Scots who came from the British Isles to Canada to work in the fur trade. He arrived at Prairie du Chien in the 1780s. Making Prairie du Chien his headquarters, he traveled seasonally from St. Peter's River to Lake Huron.[24]

Like Giard, Michel La Bathe traded among the Indians of the upper
Mississippi. Working under an agreement with the North West Company,
for several seasons La Bathe had been trading with the Sioux who resided
along the west bank of the Mississippi above Prairie du Chien.

Henry Munro Fisher, although born in the province of New York, had
been raised in Montreal. His parents were Loyalists who had fled to Canada
during the American Revolution. At the age of sixteen, his mother appren-
ticed Henry to Isaac Todd, who instructed Fisher in the trade, sending him
as his representative to Michilimackinac. After Fisher's marriage to Mad-
elaine deVierville in 1796, he moved to Prairie du Chien. With the death
of his nephew Andrew, Isaac Todd may have assumed that Fisher would
continue Andrew's St. Louis connection and also secure a large share of
the trade in the Mississippi valley.[25]

Robert Dickson was the most prominent of the traders in the upper
Mississippi. Working for his cousin, Robert Hamilton, Dickson was sent to
Michilimackinac in 1786 "to learn the art and mystery of commerce." For
a couple of years he was the clerk and storekeeper for the British Indian
Department. Having mastered this side of the trade, Dickson ventured into
the country of the Sioux, operating posts on Lake Traverse, Sauk Rapids,
Leech Lake, the Rum River, and other sites. Like Campbell, Fisher, Giard,
and La Bathe, Dickson owned a lot in the Main Village of Prairie du Chien.
Each, except for Fisher, had married a woman from the tribal band with
which he traded.[26]

Of these Prairie du Chien men who held offices of the United States
government, only Fisher could possibly be considered a citizen of the
United States. Campbell, Dickson, Giard, and La Bathe had all been born
within the British Commonwealth. And all held trading agreements with
British trading houses headquartered at Montreal.

In the decade after the end of conflict between the United States and
Great Britain, American governmental leaders faced issues and crises that
threatened the future of the new country. During that time, with the passage of the Northwest Ordinance, the young confederation set in place the
mechanisms to regulate and control future expansion of the American
nation. The Constitution replaced the Articles of Confederation, thereby
creating a central government with the powers needed to administer a
country more vast than the thirteen colonies. The Jay Treaty was an at-

tempt to settle outstanding issues between the United States and Great Britain that had been left unresolved since American independence. The Trade and Intercourse acts were an attempt to settle another unresolved issue: the continued British trade with the Indians. The Jay Treaty did accomplish the goal of maintaining peace between the two nations. But in the northern reaches of the Northwest Territory, the British remained in control. Trade with the Indians endured in spite of American laws, and British traders held American governmental posts. If the United States wished to control the region, it needed more than unenforceable laws and uninformed political appointments. The acquisition of Louisiana in 1803 would initiate the first American presence in the upper Mississippi.

# 3

## ZEBULON PIKE EXPLORES
## THE UPPER MISSISSIPPI RIVER

### 1803–1806

As the United States spread westward and new states and territories were organized, the Mississippi River became increasingly more important as a means to transport agricultural and other trade products. Control of river trade would determine, in large part, which western power controlled the surrounding land. Though as yet unexplored by agents of the United States, the upper Mississippi was no exception. It is no surprise, then, that in addition to commissioning Meriwether Lewis and William Clark to investigate and report on the newly acquired Louisiana Purchase, the far reaches of the Northwest Territory would receive similar study.

A young lieutenant whose father had fought under George Washington became the first American to act as an agent for the United States, traveling up the Mississippi to its source to determine the scope of trade, establish friendship with the Indian tribes, choose sites for US forts, and help set the scene for American control of the fur trade. Though Lieutenant Zebulon M. Pike accomplished some of these goals, his assumptions—often misguided when it came to his treatment of the Native population and his overblown sense of authority as an American agent—also set the tone for the unstable Indian alliances that would influence the War of 1812.

The acquisition of Louisiana from France in 1803 doubled the territorial size of the United States. With the western and northern boundaries yet undetermined, Louisiana was unknown to the new owners residing in Washington. President Thomas Jefferson determined to change this situation, and during his administration five expeditions explored the vast regions of the Louisiana Purchase, the most famous of which was the expedition of Lewis and Clark.

The first expedition was to travel the northern portion of the Louisiana territory all the way to the Pacific Ocean. The men involved were to gather geographical facts about the land and acquire information about prospects for the Indian trade. Jefferson commissioned his private secretary and neighbor, Captain Meriwether Lewis, to lead the expedition to map the northern and western parts of the Purchase by following the Missouri River. He was to determine if the river connected to the Columbia River and thereby to the Pacific Ocean. Lewis chose his close friend, Second Lieutenant William Clark, as second in command. In May 1804, Lewis and Clark and the "Corps of Discovery" left St. Louis.

The year after its acquisition, the Louisiana Purchase was divided into two parts; this was further refined in 1805 to be the New Orleans Territory and the Louisiana Territory. President Jefferson reassigned General Wilkinson to be the governor of the northern portion, the Louisiana Territory, and Wilkinson established his headquarters in St. Louis. Perhaps Wilkinson desired to know the range of the land that he governed. Or perhaps learning what lay to the north of St. Louis would be of benefit to him as he corresponded with Aaron Burr to set up an independent nation in the west. For whatever reason, unknown to President Jefferson, Wilkinson decided to organize an expedition up the Mississippi River. He selected Lieutenant Zebulon Montgomery Pike, one of the many young officers with whom Wilkinson surrounded himself, to lead the expedition.

Pike's father, also named Zebulon Pike, had served in General George Washington's army and remained in the military at the end of the Revolution. Like his father, Pike decided to make the army his career and began serving at western forts. Pike received a commission as a first lieutenant in the First Infantry in November 1799. General Wilkinson, who had commanded Pike's father, had come in contact with the young officer at Fort Massac and Fort Kaskaskia and had taken an interest in Lieutenant Pike.

On July 30, 1805, Wilkinson instructed Pike to travel the Mississippi River to its source. Pike was to plot the course of the river, describing the land and its resources from St. Louis to its source. He was also to report the number and residences of the Indians and the extent of their trade; select sites for and acquire land from the appropriate tribes for two military posts; treat with the American Indians; and arrange for delegations from the various tribes to visit "the Great Father" in Washington. As the fur trade was an important consideration, Pike was to note the current state of the fur trade on the upper Mississippi, finding out what he could about the British traders.[1]

Lieutenant Zebulon Montgomery Pike, ca. 1807, by Charles Willson Peale. COURTESY OF INDEPENDENCE NATIONAL HISTORIC PARK

So, while Meriwether Lewis and William Clark continued their trek to the Columbia River, a young lieutenant of the First Regiment of United States Infantry prepared to lead a party of soldiers in an expedition up the Mississippi River. Some of the goals of Zebulon Pike's expedition would be the same as Lewis and Clark's, while others were specifically military in nature.

Pike left St. Louis on the ninth of August with twenty men on a seventy-foot keelboat, carrying provisions to last them four months. Unlike Lewis and Clark, Pike did not travel with an aide, a slave, or an interpreter. Nor did he have the benefits of preparation, training, or funding. His only scientific instruments were a thermometer, a theodolite for determining latitude, and a watch. The expedition had been hastily assembled as Wilkinson wanted Pike to observe the British traders during the fall gathering and winter trapping seasons.

Pike and his men sailed up the river, only slightly deterred by sunken logs, strong head winds, sandbars, and rapids. As they proceeded northward, the only people they met on the river were various parties of Sac and Fox, including Black Hawk, bateaux coming from Michilimackinac, and some traders. Pike found James Aird of Michilimackinac encamped below the Rock Island rapids to repair his canoe. Pike stopped and had breakfast with him to learn about navigating the rapids. Aird was on his way to trade on the Missouri River. On September 1, Pike and his men arrived at the lead mines, where Pike met with Julien Dubuque. Wilkinson had ordered Pike to learn what he could about Dubuque's mining operation. There were no horses available to take Pike to the mines, so he had to content himself with proposing "10 queries" to Dubuque. Pike reported to Wilkinson, "[T]he answers seem to carry with them the semblance of equivocation." Continuing onward, Maurice Blondeau overtook the party. Pike offered to take Blondeau to Prairie du Chien. With Blondeau as translator, Pike was able to communicate with several bands of Indians who paddled from shore to his boat. He was surprised to learn that the Sac and Fox he met had a "dread" of Americans. He blamed their fear on the British traders and surmised, "When they find that our conduct toward them is guided by magnanimity and justice . . . it will have the effect to make them reverence at the same time they fear us."[2]

On the morning of September 4, Pike's company arrived at Prairie du Chien. Pike's description of the settlement, written after he returned, would mark its first depiction in the historical record. He found the remains of the early French fortification on the southern end of the prairie now deserted. "The present [Main] village lay to the north of the old fort and contained 18 houses on two streets. Behind the village on the mainland were eight dwellings. Beyond the two villages were scattered other houses, some on the prairie but also three across the Mississippi on Giard's river."

Pike speculated that the population numbered 370. The number greatly increased in the spring and fall trading seasons when traders and engagés from Michilimackinac gathered at Prairie du Chien, accompanied by three hundred to four hundred Indians. In Pike's opinion there were a few gentlemen who resided at Prairie du Chien "and many others claiming that appellation." He commented on the connections that had been formed between the men and Indian women so that "almost one-half of the inhabitants under 20 years have the blood of the aborigines in their veins."[3]

At Prairie du Chien, arrangements had been made for Pike to be quartered with Henry Munro Fisher. At Fisher's home, Pike was introduced to James Fraser. The following day, Fisher and Fraser guided Pike on a tour of the Wisconsin–Mississippi confluence. There Pike examined the bluffs as a site for an American fort. He chose a spot atop a bluff overlooking both rivers, which Pike thought "most eligible" as "being level at the top, having a spring in the rear, and commanding a view of the country around."[4]

Pike stated that James Fraser, who clerked for a Montreal trading house, was preparing to travel north and winter among the Dakota of the Sioux nation. Fraser helped Pike procure supplies for the rest of their journey and accompanied Pike as far as the St. Croix River. While at Prairie du Chien, Pike engaged Pierre Rousseau and Joseph Renville as interpreters, as no man in his company knew the languages of the Native tribes who lived above Prairie du Chien. Fraser paid the men to accompany Pike as far as the Falls of St. Anthony. This was Pike's first meeting with the men at Prairie du Chien who were engaged in the fur trade. As he continued northward, he would meet others.[5]

That evening, as he would throughout his journey, Pike wrote to General Wilkinson. He reported that besides the site to the south of Prairie du Chien, he had selected two other sites for American forts. One was on the west bank of the Mississippi River north of the Des Moines River rapids; the other was three miles up the Wisconsin River at the Petit Gris. Pike stated he found Robert Dickson's clerks not very accommodating but wrote of Fisher's hospitality and recommended James Aird for his "humanity." He asked Wilkinson to send two medals to Fisher, who would give them to the band of Dakota Sioux led by La Feuille (Wabasha). Pike met with La Feuille at Prairie du Chien to secure his friendship with the United States and would stop at La Feuille's village, where the Dakota chief would profess his loyalty to the Americans. Knowing the significance of medals to the Indians, the gift of which they saw as the sealing of an alliance and agreement, Pike wanted the medals for La Feuille to underscore the importance of their talk. In preparation for their trip, Lewis and Clark had been given medals cast with the impression of Thomas Jefferson. Pike's expedition had been so hastily organized that there had not been the luxury of time to wait for medals to arrive from the East.[6]

### Pike's Journey, 1805–1806

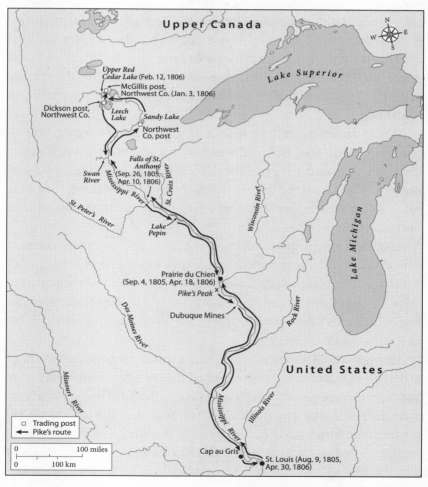

MAPPING SPECIALISTS, LTD., FITCHBURG, WI

Pike found all the residents of Prairie du Chien to be very polite, though he noted a distinction between the Americans and the French Canadians. In the comments made in his journal, Pike exhibited the American attitude toward the French-speaking people of the upper Mississippi that would be very evident in the treatment of the residents of Prairie du Chien after the War of 1812. Pike found the kindness of Fisher, Fraser, and a Mr. Woods, "all Americans," to be "spontaneous effusions of good will," while the French Canadians "appeared attentive rather from their natural good manners than sincere friendship." Pike wished to recommend Fraser to Wilkinson because of the help he gave Pike in organizing the next leg of his journey and the loan of his interpreters so Pike could communicate with the Sioux and Chippewa. Fraser exuded "candor, bravery, and that *amor patria* which distinguishes the good of every nation." Fraser rose even greater in Pike's opinion when Fraser, after Pike prohibited the practice of giving the Indians rum, removed the alcohol from the merchandise in his canoes.[7]

Pike and his men left the prairie the next day. As explained to Wilkinson, the keelboat they had used was too large and unwieldy to navigate the Mississippi north of Prairie du Chien. So Pike borrowed two Schenectady barges from the traders. Smaller and flat-bottomed, they were better suited to the upper Mississippi. Pike would find them crowded and uncomfortable.

Pike's less than favorable opinion of people who were not American extended to those who spoke English. At Lake Pepin, Pike found Murdock Cameron, who had unpacked his goods on the shore in anticipation of trade. To Pike, Cameron lived in "all the ease of an Indian trader . . . indolent in his habits"; Pike described Cameron "as a Scotchman by birth, but an Englishman by prejudice."[8]

Pike exhibited a naiveté, thinking that because a person had been born in the United States, that person espoused and lived the same beliefs as Pike and his contemporaries. Though James Fraser had been born in Vermont, and was therefore an American, as Pike recounted, Fraser was engaged in the fur trade with Blakely of Montreal. This "Blakely" was in fact Josiah Bleakley, a British trader. Bleakley had accompanied two canoe loads of goods to Michilimackinac in 1782 and soon secured British governmen-

tal positions as clerk and Indian storekeeper. Headquartered at Michilimackinac, for several seasons Bleakley came to Prairie du Chien and the
upper Mississippi to trade. In 1806, Bleakley and Fraser would be two of
the founding partners in the Michilimackinac Company, organized to
compete with Americans in the fur trade.[9]

Two days' travel from Prairie du Chien, Pike engaged in his first meeting with Natives on their land. As promised, on September 10 Pike stopped
at the village of La Feuille. La Feuille had sent a pipe by Fraser acknowledging the United States, graciously stating that Pike "was a chief of their new
father, and that he wished me to be treated with friendship and respect."
Pike sat with La Feuille, who expressed his desire not to be at war with
"their new father," and then watched a dance. Returning to his boat, Pike
felt he had conveyed the position of the United States clearly. Pike sent La
Feuille presents of tobacco, salt, vermillion, and, at Fraser's request, rum.

Pike had had no experience in the complex protocol and rituals of
Indian diplomacy, and he spoke no Native language. Yet Pike had been
ordered to represent the United States in country claimed by the United
States where the British were allowed to trade by the Jay Treaty and inhabited by Indians who were not impressed with the acumen and power of the
United States. His letters to Wilkinson indicate he felt he had the ability
to change Indian allegiance to the United States. He had met with small
groups of Indians along the way but Pike's ability as a diplomat would be
determined by a meeting he would have with the Native people towards
the end of September.

September 21, Pike arrived at the St. Peter's River with Red Wing, whom
Pike had met on the way. Progressing up the river, Pike's force passed the
encampment of Jean Baptiste Faribault. Two days later, gathered on an
island at the confluence of the St. Peter's and Mississippi Rivers, Pike met
in council with Petit Corbeau and representatives of various bands of the
Dakota. As this was to be a very important meeting, Pike ordered the fabrication of a formal bower or shade made from the boat's sails "into which
only my gentlemen and the chiefs entered." Pike addressed the chiefs in
a "long and touching" speech that addressed many topics, the object of
which was to acquire land for a military installation. They settled on a tract
at the mouth of the St. Croix River. The majority of the land, however,

stretched from the confluence of the Mississippi and St. Peter's Rivers up the Mississippi nine miles along both banks and included the Falls of St. Anthony, the present-day site of St. Paul.[10]

With this aim accomplished, Pike shifted to an issue not covered by his instructions. Pike attempted to negotiate a peace between the Sioux and their Chippewa neighbors. Listing the advantages of peace, Pike ended with a threat. If the chiefs did not listen "to the voice of their father," Pike warned, "they will call down the vengeance of the Americans." After discussions, Pike drew up a treaty draft in which the Sioux agreed to give the United States land for "the purpose of establishment of military posts." Some of the chiefs did not wish to sign the treaty as they felt their word of honor should be accepted, but Pike insisted. In the treaty, the Sioux also agreed to end hostilities with the Chippewa. Pike commented to Wilkinson, "We have obtained about 100,000 acres for a song." He then reported he had had to present the Dakota with about two hundred and fifty dollars' worth of goods. Since Wilkinson had sent no trade goods with the expedition, Pike had purchased the items from the traders with his own money; he hoped that he would be reimbursed.[11]

At this gathering were several chiefs who had traveled to St. Louis the previous spring. At the insistence of Pierre Chouteau, a US Indian agent, they had surrendered their British medals. Chouteau had promised them American medals in return. As he had none at the time, he said he would send some medals to their village "by some officer." The chiefs asked Pike for the medals, saying the medals "were their commissions—their only distinguishing mark from other warriors." Pike promised he would write to Wilkinson, which he did, asking Wilkinson to "remedy this evil." It is not clear, however, that Pike understood the significance of the medals to the Native tribesmen.[12]

As early as the mid-seventeenth century, the French, Spanish, and British had distributed medals bearing the image of their monarch, as well as flags and certificates of friendship, to the Indians in North America. By distributing the medals and flags, the colonial governments sought to secure political, economic, and military alliances between their nations and the tribes, who held the true balance of power in the interior of North America. For the Indians, a medal was a visual symbol of the honor given by the bearer to the wearer; it also represented a pledge of trade goods. For the Europeans, a peace medal was a visual symbol of an alliance that secured for their country a source of military strength against competing countries. The medal was also a pledge that the country would receive a secure supply of furs into their trading system. The giver of the medal always sought a person with power to receive the medal. By the mid-eighteenth century, the British had raised the medal to an established diplomatic symbol of friendship, a symbol that the United States adopted after the American Revolution as it began political relations with the Indian nations. For Pike, new to this system, his promises to tribes to replace their British medals with American medals was a gesture aimed at swaying the Indians to the American side. Yet it wasn't until he reached St. Louis, when his promises to the tribes went unfulfilled, that he fully comprehended their value.[13]

After his meeting with the Santee and Mdewakanton Sioux, Pike outlined his plans to reach Sandy Lake and Leech Lake. Part of the impetus to keep going, even though the weather was getting cold, was Pike's knowledge that the North West Company had posts at both lakes. Pike was not sure "in what manner I shall conduct myself towards them." He had heard that Hugh McGillis, who had charge of the two posts, was "a sworn enemy of the United States." McGillis and his employees were "the very instigators of the war between the Chipeways and Sioux, in order that they may monopolize the trade of the Upper Mississippi."[14]

Returning to the Mississippi, Pike pressed onward. The journey from the falls northward was hard, as winter had arrived. They transferred supplies to sleds they had to make, food often was scarce, and many suffered from frostbite. Finally, on February 1, 1806, Pike and his men reached Leech Lake, which Pike recorded "is the main source of the Mississippi." Pike's legs were so swollen he was forced to lodge at the North West Company post with Hugh McGillis, the very man he had called an instigator and enemy. McGillis gave Pike some of his own clothing, as Pike could no longer wear his. Soon after his arrival, Pike and McGillis had an exchange about the presence of British flags. McGillis politely asked if the British flag could be raised "by way of complement" to the American flag. Pike remained silent, but several days later after hoisting the American flag in the fort, Pike "directed the Indians and my riflemen to shoot at [the British flag] still flying at the top of the flagstaff."[15]

Seeing the British flag flying at the North West post and other posts Pike had visited greatly incensed Pike. On February 7, he addressed his displeasure in a letter to McGillis. Acting on his own authority, Pike informed McGillis that he and other company traders were in US territory and had to obey import laws and custom regulations set by the federal government. Pike then issued an extensive list of demands. In tersely written, adversarial language, Pike ordered McGillis to tell the agents of the North West Company to declare all goods that had been brought into the United States at the customs house at Mackinac and also to secure licenses to trade within the boundaries of the United States. While admitting the Jay Treaty gave the British the right to trade with the Indians, Pike expected the traders to conform to United States law. Additionally, as he traveled the Mississippi, there were two actions that Pike came to consider "more particularly injurious to the honor and dignity of our government." He therefore directed McGillis to command all North West Company posts not to hoist "or suffer to be hoisted, the English flag." Pike also ordered McGillis not to present a British flag or medal to any Indian or hold council with them on any political subject.[16]

Eight days later McGillis wrote a gentlemanly reply, demonstrating that McGillis was more adept at diplomacy than Pike. McGillis agreed to present Pike's requests in regards to duties and licenses to his superiors. He attempted to explain the difficulty that declaring all goods at Mackinac would involve, since most of the North West Company supplies were located at Kamanitiguia on Lake Superior. McGillis also tried to explain to Pike that the North West Company posts were enclosed by pickets to protect the stores and the inhabitants and not for the reasons Pike had surmised. McGillis was appalled that Pike would think that the stockading of posts might be considered "useful in the juncture of a rupture between the two powers." He went on in an attempt to clarify that the gift of flags and medals to the chiefs with which they traded was a time-honored custom that his agents had continued. He assured Pike that political subjects would not be discussed with the Indians, and reference would be made to American agents, "should any application be made worthy such reference." McGillis felt "honored" that Pike had accepted "accommodations as my humble roof could afford." He closed by expressing "my esteem and regard for yourself."[17]

When Pike indicated his leave-taking, McGillis provided Pike with a sled and dogs, and the Americans departed to return to St. Louis. On February 19, recording that "Mr. M'Gillis' hospitality deserves to be particularly noticed," Pike retraced his route and gathered up the men and the supplies he had left behind at various temporary forts, and then waited at the stockade encampment on the Swan River until the Mississippi River opened. As Pike and his men continued southward, they met traders returning to Prairie du Chien from their wintering posts. At Red Wing's village, gifts of brandy, sugar, and coffee awaited Pike. Murdoch Cameron and his partner, Joseph Rolette, had sent them up the river. Though he considered the gifts "trifling" in value, Pike did not know whether he should accept the gifts, as he was going to prosecute both men for selling liquor to the Dakota. Pike did accept them and justified his decision assuring the person who had brought the items that "the prosecution arose from a sense of duty, and not from any personal prejudice."[18]

At two o'clock on April 18, 1806, Pike and his flotilla arrived at Prairie du Chien. Pike again quartered in Henry Munro Fisher's house while Pike's men were thoughtfully cared for by John Campbell, who gave them a barrel of pork, and by Fisher, who provided biscuits, bread, and meat. The following day, Pike dined at John Campbell's house. Among the guests was Nicolas Jarrot of Cahokia. Jarrot was to leave for St. Louis the following day, so Pike wrote a long letter to Wilkinson recapping all he had accomplished during the winter. With self-adulatory humility, Pike felt that his voyage and exploration would provide "new, useful, and interesting information for our government, although detailed in the unpolished diction of a soldier of fortune."[19]

After two days of meetings with the Winnebago and then representatives of several Sioux nations, Pike left Prairie du Chien to return to St. Louis. As he had with the Dakota and Chippewa, Pike convinced the Winnebago to relinquish their British medals. He added them to the British flags and medals he had already collected. Pike promised the Winnebago that the British medals and flags would be replaced with American flags and medals as soon as possible.[20]

Now at St. Louis, Pike finished his reports, explaining what he had accomplished. He had selected two sites for forts, one overlooking the confluence of the Wisconsin River with the Mississippi and the other where the St. Peter's River flowed into the Mississippi. He had elicited a promise of peace between the Sioux and Chippewa and brought back a very detailed description of the region through which he had traveled and all the tribes with whom he had conversed. Having met with traders and tribal representatives all along his journey, Pike had gained promises from traders to comply with the US customs laws on trade goods and convinced the Indians to give up their British medals and flags. Besides requesting medals, Pike warned Wilkinson that unless military troops and an agent "to watch the rising discontent" were sent among the Sioux and Chippewa, "the weapons of death will again be raised, and the echoes of savage barbarity will resound through the wilderness."[21]

Pike had worked hard to gain the friendship of the tribes for the United States and curb the influence of the British trade. But a single expedition up the Mississippi by a United States lieutenant with twenty men—a lieutenant who could only offer promises—would not be sufficient to diminish the power and influence of the British traders and a way of life for the residents of the upper Mississippi that had been in existence for more than one hundred years.

—ıⱶ—

When General Wilkinson had ordered Lieutenant Pike to ascend the Mississippi River, Wilkinson had been very specific as to what he expected Pike to accomplish. Pike assiduously followed the general's directives, arriving back in St. Louis after an absence of "eight months and 22 days." Pike proudly reported to Wilkinson that he and twenty men had traveled seven hundred miles and found the source of the Mississippi River, negotiated a peace between the Sioux and Chippewa, and introduced an American presence in the trading region of the upper Mississippi without the loss of one man. Upon one topic, though, Pike found little satisfaction. He had often brought the subject to Wilkinson's attention and ended his final report on the journey with the comment, "I hope the subject may not be forgotten."[22]

General Wilkinson had told Pike that on the expedition, Pike was "to spare no pains to conciliate the Indians and to attach them to the United States." For Pike, this included collecting British medals and flags from the Indians and promising to replace them with American ones. As part of his report to Wilkinson, Pike once again asked that American medals be sent upriver to Prairie du Chien in care of Henry Munro Fisher.

This medal of George III, found at Prairie du Chien, may have been one of the British medals surrendered to Lt. Zebulon Pike while on his expedition. COURTESY OF BLAIR E. DILLMAN

Pike's letters from that time indicate negotiating without medals was somewhat stressful for him. After dealing with the subject again at Prairie du Chien, he wrote to Wilkinson just a few days before his journey's end.

> My faith was pledged to the Savage Chiefs for the replacement of the medals and flags of the British government, which they surrendered me, by others of the same magnitude of the United States. . . . This has left a number of Sioux and Sauteur [Chippewa] chiefs without their distinguishing marks of dignity, and had induced them to look on my conduct toward them as premeditated fraud.[23]

Pike warned Wilkinson that if medals were not given to the Sioux and Chippewa, should he return to negotiate with either tribe, his life would be in danger. Any other American officer who should attempt a council and treaty with either nation would be in an "extremely delicate" position. Pike tried to impress upon Wilkinson that the medals were declarations of the good faith of the United States government. Therefore, the promise of medals "should be held inviolate."[24] Pike made sure to say that he understood that the lack of medals was not Wilkinson's fault but was caused by "the change of agents, and a variety of circumstances."[25]

By the change of agents, Pike may have been referring to the change in US Indian policy. In April 1806, Congress had passed an act creating the position of superintendent of Indian trade. This law continued the system of government trading houses begun in 1796 and authorized a superintendent to direct the business. The superintendent would be appointed by the president with the authority "to purchase and take charge of all goods intended for trade with the Indian nations." This would include the minting and distribution of medals. Prior to the enactment of this legislation, the secretary of war designated what goods would be acquired for the Indian trade. The keeper of military stores at Philadelphia purchased goods, and the military distributed the goods to the US trading houses. The president of the United States had established trading houses on the frontier and appointed an agent for each trading house. The goods would be distributed to the American Indians through the agent. The frontier was far removed from the nation's capital, so soon the territorial governors became *ex officio* superintendents of Indian affairs within their territory.[26] The territorial governors then appointed agents for specific tribes or regions. Wilkinson would have this power, but he had not been given authority to order trade goods, including medals.

By the time the "change of agents and other circumstances" had been settled and John Mason appointed superintendent of Indian trade, a change in the administration of the upper Louisiana Territory had occurred. President Jefferson had turned to two old friends to direct the future of that region.

Meriwether Lewis and William Clark had completed their Voyage of Discovery in September 1806. By January 1807, both Lewis and Clark were in the nation's capital, where President Thomas Jefferson honored them. In the first week of March, Lewis was appointed governor of the Louisiana Territory, and Clark was named brigadier general of the territorial militia and a principal US Indian agent. That April, William Clark returned to St. Louis. He was to oversee the Indian trade and relations within an enormous region that stretched from New Madrid and the Arkansas River in the south, to Illinois and the western Great Lakes in the north, to the entire Missouri River watershed in the west.

# 4

## United States Indian Agents at Prairie du Chien

*1807–1811*

Unlike his requests for medals, Zebulon Pike's recommendation to Wilkinson that a US Indian agent be sent among the Sioux and Chippewa did not go unheeded. Wilkinson may have forwarded Pike's correspondence to Henry Dearborn, the secretary of war, or Dearborn himself may have seen the necessity of appointing an agent to the upper Mississippi to bring the influence of the United States to the region and secure the allegiance of the tribes. In either case, William Clark, newly appointed as principal US Indian agent, would make the recommendation as to whom should be appointed agent for the vast region of the upper Mississippi and western Great Lakes. Unfamiliar with the area and its residents, Clark relied on the opinion of Josiah Dunham, commander of the American forces at Fort Mackinac.

In August 1807, Dunham wrote a long letter to Clark in which he informed Clark of the formation of the "Macana Company," the object of which he perceived "to be a complete Monopoly of the Fur trade." He found the members of the company to be in "Opposition to the American Interest; & who would but not wish to Annihilate the Arm of American power, so far as it extends over the Indian Country!" Dunham warned Clark that some of the members of the company would be visiting Clark soon. Though they were "certainly gentlemen of eloquence, talents

& address ... [t]here is not among them a friend to the American Government."[1]

After making dire predictions as to how the Michilimackinac Company would bring "Misery, oppression & wretchedness to the Aborigines," Dunham stated he had "one thing which I wish to suggest." He felt that it would be of great advantage to the United States to have an Indian agent at Prairie du Chien who could explain to the tribes, in their own language, the "real views & disposition towards them" of the United States.

William Clark, ca. 1807, by Charles Willson Peale. COURTESY OF INDEPENDENCE NATIONAL HISTORIC PARK

The most suitable man for this position, in Dunham's opinion, was John Campbell of Prairie du Chien, who was still serving as justice of the peace for St. Clair County and was one of the men who had offered hospitality during Zebulon Pike's journey. Dunham had known Campbell for five years and recommended him because he was

Friendly to our Country & government—he has extensive property there—Speaks the language of the different nations around him—is considered by them all as their Father—and has, perhaps, a more extensive influence over them than any other man in the Union. ....

[T]his man alone, in such a Capacity, would render the Government
more essential service, than a regiment of soldiers along the banks of
the Upper Mississippi.

But of more importance than all of these capabilities to Dunham was
the fact that Campbell "has refused several shares in the [Macana] company."[2]

After this sterling recommendation, Dunham informed Clark that
Campbell would be in Washington that coming winter. He ended his letter
by stating, "Any service you could render him by letters to Head Quarters
would be gratefully acknowledged by him & us." Dunham apologized to
Clark for his frankness, but as the two men were personally acquainted, he
felt that Clark would accept his thoughts and understand he had written
them from a sense of duty.[3]

The recommendation was well received. By the ninth of December,
Campbell was in Washington meeting with Secretary Dearborn. A com-
bination of Dunham's recommendation and Campbell's knowledge of the
upper Mississippi were sufficient for Dearborn to determine that Campbell
would be a good US Indian agent. On that day, Secretary Dearborn presented Campbell with his appointment as

agent of Indian affairs to the several nations of Indians within that
part of the Louisiana Territory, which lies on the waters of the Mississippi, above the river Iowa, and that part of Indiana Territory which
lies to the Northward of the river Illinois, except such part as lieth to
the Eastward of a line drawn from a point on said River, twenty miles
above the village called Piorias, to the mouth of the Sakies river on
Lake Michigan.

A month later, Secretary Dearborn informed both Governor Harrison and
Governor Meriwether Lewis of Campbell's appointment, for Campbell's
duties as Indian agent would involve the tribes living in the Indiana and
upper Louisiana territories.[4]

As stated by Dunham, John Campbell had extensive property in the region. Within a few years of his arrival at Prairie du Chien, he had acquired
two lots in the Main Village, one of which he purchased from Andrew

Todd, and a large farm lot that stretched into a coulee east of the village. In 1805, he purchased two lots on Mackinac Island within the village set along the lakeshore below Fort Mackinac. On one lot was a house, and the other lot contained Campbell's store.[5]

Dunham may have embellished Campbell's position among the tribes of the upper Mississippi and ability to communicate, but Campbell did have personal and business relations with many tribes. He had a permanent trading site on the St. Peter's River located between the mouth of the river and Little Rapids where he wintered. By 1790, he had established a personal relationship with Ninse, a Dakota Sioux. They had five children born between 1790 and about 1800. It can be presumed, then, that Campbell knew the Sioux language. In the course of conducting the fur trade at Mackinac and St. Joseph Island, he probably had acquired a proficiency in other Indian languages as well.[6] William Clark, from all he had been told from men who knew Campbell, later relayed to Secretary Dearborn that Campbell "has more influence with the upper Mississippi Indians than any other man in the quarter," but Governor Lewis was more circumspect. Because of their proximity to St. Louis, Meriwether Lewis wanted an agent who had great influence with the Sac and Fox. Lewis believed that Campbell's influence was only with the Sioux along the St. Peter's River, the lower bands of Chippewa above Prairie du Chien, and the tribes at Green Bay and along the west side of Lake Michigan.[7]

In promoting a candidate, Dunham could have made the same arguments for appointing Robert Dickson the Indian agent for the region. Dickson owned a lot in the Main Village of Prairie du Chien and another one in the village on Mackinac Island. In both communities, Dickson and Campbell were next-door neighbors. Like Campbell, Dickson was a justice of the peace for St. Clair County, and Dickson's connections with the tribes were just as extensive as Campbell's. While Campbell traded from Mackinac to Prairie du Chien, Dickson had trading posts along the St. Peter's River and between the Mississippi and Red Rivers. But outweighing all of Dickson's abilities and connections was Dickson's association with the "Macana Company."

Although Campbell was not a member of this consortium of traders, he had constant contact with the men Dunham had castigated. The western Great Lakes–upper Mississippi region was a vast area inhabited by an

Indian population numbered in the thousands, but only a handful of men engaged directly with the Native people in the course of trade. All the traders and their employees knew one another, and most operated out of and had a house or store at Prairie du Chien. Periodically, Campbell traveled to St. Joseph Island where he was acquainted with several Michilimackinac Company traders. The island had become the center for the British fur trade after the British forces relinquished Fort Michilimackinac in 1796.[8]

These concerns, however, did not impede Campbell's appointment, and John Campbell returned to Prairie du Chien commissioned as the Indian agent for the upper Mississippi. In February 1808, Governor Harrison sent Campbell a few trading licenses. Harrison told Campbell that only a few licenses were enclosed, and he would send more if needed. In the meantime, Campbell could issue a certificate that would be acceptable until a regular license arrived at Prairie du Chien. Campbell was to make sure to obtain a bond, charging the trader what he felt was necessary for the work involved in preparing the bond. Then, Campbell was to "furnish them with a copy of my Proclamation relative to selling liquor to Indians which is still in favor."[9]

Campbell spent the spring and early summer fulfilling his duties as US Indian agent for the upper Mississippi. He engaged Pierre Fournier as his interpreter and ordered goods for distribution to the tribes. He met with chiefs of the tribes and issued licenses for the trade. He must have been persuasive, for James Aird and Robert Dickson applied for American licenses to trade.[10]

—||—

Though Governor Lewis and William Clark acknowledged the influence Campbell had with the tribes of the upper Mississippi, neither believed his range included the Sac and Fox. Lewis wrote to the Secretary of War:

> [W]ith the Saucs he has none, and with the Foxes his influence is confined to a few stragling bands who usually trade at Prairie du Chien and with these even he dose not possess as much influence as Mr Julian Dubuke.[11]

Lewis had been struggling with the need to neutralize the Sac warriors who had attacked homes on the Missouri frontier and waged war against the Ioway and Sioux. He decided, therefore, to engage someone who had influence among the Sac; in 1806 he commissioned Nicolas Boilvin, a personal acquaintance, as assistant Indian agent. Boilvin was to make the Sac village along the rapids of the Des Moines River his "principal place of residence."[12]

Nicolas Boilvin had been born in Quebec in 1761, the son of a French soldier. As a young man he traveled to Spanish-controlled St. Louis. By the summer of 1783 he was in Detroit, which was then under British control. He was employed by Patrick Sinclair to manage Sinclair's farm near Detroit. In 1779, Sinclair was a captain in the British army and had been appointed lieutenant governor and superintendent of Michilimackinac. Within a short time, Boilvin decided to return west and left Detroit for St. Louis. He was living in the St. Genevieve District by 1805.[13] Boilvin married Marie-Helene St. Cyr, the daughter of a prominent St. Louis resident. Hyacinthe, Marie-Helene's brother, had been in Prairie du Chien since at least 1800. Hyacinthe seems to have had a union with a Winnebago woman, and these family connections may have been the means by which Boilvin became familiar with the region of the Mississippi above St. Louis and received the appointment.

Boilvin took his responsibilities as assistant Indian agent very seriously. In April 1808, Robert Dickson wrote to Frederick Bates, secretary of the Louisiana Territory, praising Boilvin's work among the Sac. In Dickson's opinion, "Mr. Boilvin has done everything in his power to accommodate matters and has hitherto prevented them shedding blood"—a gentlemanly compliment from Dickson whom, in less than two years, US officials would consider an enemy.[14]

That summer, as tensions grew between the Sac and settlers, Boilvin was to travel to the Des Moines River and induce the Sac to end their disputes with the Ioway and Sioux. He was also to distribute gifts to the tribe. Lewis enclosed with his orders a speech that he had written; Boilvin was to read the speech to the Sac. The real reason for the directive, however, was to keep the Sac from descending on St. Louis.[15]

The negotiations proved to be successful, but Lewis felt that the success lay in a maneuver he had directed. Through Boilvin, Lewis had made an offer to Maurice Blondeau to assist in maintaining peace with the Sac.

Part Sac-Fox, Blondeau was a clerk in the employ of the Michilimackinac Company who traded on the Des Moines River. Lewis convinced Blondeau to end his service with the company with a promise that Blondeau would be appointed a US subagent. Blondeau agreed to the offer and then assisted Boilvin at all the meetings with the Sac. Showing little regard for Boilvin, Lewis told Dearborn that Blondeau "has more personal influence with the Saucs & Foxes, . . . than any man in this country." Lewis then boasted, "Through Blondeau I paved the way in a great measure to the final success of Mr. Boilvin."[16]

With Campbell at Prairie du Chien working with the Sioux, Chippewa, and tribes that lived around Green Bay and western Lake Michigan and Boilvin and Blondeau at the mouth of the Des Moines River to control the Sac and Fox, Lewis informed the secretary of war, "We shall be enabled to keep the Indians on the Mississippi . . . in good order."[17]

—11—

Even before Lewis wrote to Dearborn on August 20 confident with what he had accomplished, the "good order" had been disrupted. In August, Campbell had traveled from Prairie du Chien to Mackinac. He probably had business to attend to but also met with acquaintances on the island. At one gathering, Robert Dickson and Redford Crawford, a trader on the upper Mississippi, were among the men present. They were drinking and a discussion arose. Jean Baptiste Faribault later recalled that they were talking about the North West Company. Whatever the topic, the discussion became heated, and Crawford felt that a comment made by Campbell was a personal insult. Crawford challenged Campbell to a duel. Campbell accepted and seconds were chosen; Dickson stood as second to Crawford. Hearing the challenge, the justice of the peace at Mackinac forbade the duel. Crawford and Campbell, therefore, agreed to meet at a place along Lake Huron in British territory. The duel occurred, and Campbell was mortally wounded. Others were present, for American soldiers placed Campbell in a canoe and took him to St. Joseph Island. Campbell died August 13, having survived two days. In accordance with a request he had made, his body was taken to Mackinac Island for burial.[18]

Campbell had been well regarded by the US officials and military officers at Mackinac. Feeling deeply the loss of Campbell and as a testimony to their regard and respect, on August 26 they resolved that all Americans at Mackinac wear black crepe on their left arm for forty days. A copy of the resolution was sent to Secretary of War Dearborn, Superintendent John Mason, and the editor of the *National Intelligencer.*[19]

About three weeks later, the same men gathered and wrote a letter to Dearborn in which they protested the rumored appointment of Robert Dickson as US Indian agent to replace John Campbell. They had heard that Dickson had started for Washington City "for the express purpose of applying for the Office of Indian Agent for the Upper Mississippi." Dickson, they conceded, was "a man of very handsome education—and his manners are not disagreeable." He had also performed services for the United States conducting "Indian offenders and their friends from the river Moin" to St. Louis "into the hands of justice." However, they warned, although Dickson may have been carrying with him letters of recommendation written by "persons of great respectability & in high office," these had only been obtained by Dickson's "insinuating & imposing manners."[20]

The gentlemen informed Dearborn that Dickson "is better known at this place [Mackinac] than anywhere else." Dire consequences would occur if Dickson were appointed the agent, they argued, because he was connected "with a very formidable company of British fur traders." They even intimated that Dickson was responsible for Campbell's death. They acknowledged there had been a dispute between Campbell and Crawford, but according to the writers, Dickson had interfered and "exerted himself so as to carry the dispute to extremity."[21]

The angst of the Americans at Mackinac over Robert Dickson was for naught. Campbell, as he lay wounded, expressed his wish regarding whom should be appointed US Indian agent for the upper Mississippi, and he had recommended Julien Dubuque. This request proved satisfactory to Governor Lewis, as he had met Dubuque many years before and had held the opinion that Dubuque had more influence with the Fox than Campbell.[22]

Julien Dubuque had been born in the Three Rivers District of Quebec. Having received an education, about 1780 he arrived at Michilimackinac to work as a clerk in the fur trade. Soon after, Dubuque and his brother came to Prairie du Chien where they established trade. According to Nicolas Boilvin, in the course of only a few years Dubuque "gained the esteem and affection of the Sac and Fox." This was done through his acts of generosity; Dubuque often presented the Indians with gifts and "refus[ed] in many instances to take their furs in exchange, contrary to the custom of the traders among them."[23] Dubuque may have married a Fox woman, as Zebulon Pike and others referred to Madame Dubuque. Whether he had or not, Dubuque obviously had the respect of the Sac and Fox.

Through his friendship with the Sac and Fox, Dubuque obtained the sole rights to mine for lead on Fox land south of Prairie du Chien. By an agreement made at Prairie du Chien on September 22, 1788, "the Fox permit Julien Dubuque called by them Little Night, to work at the mine as long as he shall please." Dubuque moved to the mine located on the west bank of the Mississippi River at Catfish Creek. He brought with him ten or eleven men from Prairie du Chien to assist in the mining operations. In 1796, he petitioned the Spanish governor of Louisiana to grant him legal possession of the mines and the surrounding land. As it was easier to ship lead downriver, St. Louis became the principal market and Dubuque made semiannual visits to the city, conducting business mainly with Auguste Chouteau and participating in society and attending dances and social dinners. At one function, Dubuque met Meriwether Lewis.[24]

Though Governor Lewis approved of Dubuque and Campbell had expressed his wish for Dubuque's appointment, George Hoffman and Samuel Abbott, the American customs agent and the notary at Mackinac, did not write to Dubuque to inform him of Campbell's or Lewis's request that Dubuque be appointed Indian agent until February 17, 1809. In the meantime, William Clark sent Boilvin to Prairie du Chien for the winter. Though Boilvin was subagent to the Sac on the Des Moines River, Clark found Boilvin to be "a man on whom we can depend." Upon receiving the letter informing him of his new position, Dubuque began to perform his responsibilities as agent. He journeyed to Prairie du Chien and met with the tribes who gathered on the prairie. He informed them of Campbell's death, which caused a great upset within the tribes. At his own expense, Dubuque distributed presents to reassure the Indians gathered of the friendship of the United States.[25]

Despite a promising start, Dubuque's tenure as agent was short-lived. He was not in good health. After "one month and twenty-eight days" of holding office, his "languorous disease" overwhelmed him. Feeling he could no longer carry out the responsibilities of an agent, Dubuque wrote to Governor Lewis requesting that he be replaced. Lewis respected Dubuque's request and gave the responsibilities—but not his position—to Nicolas Boilvin. On the twenty-eighth of November, 1809, Dubuque "ceded all the papers in [his] hands" to Boilvin. He died in March 1810. Following Dubuque's death, the Fox burned the buildings at the mines on Catfish Creek and refused to permit any other person to work the lead deposits.[26]

As Dubuque had prepared to take on the responsibilities of Indian agent that Campbell had bequeathed, changes were also occurring in Washington City. James Madison had been elected the fourth president of the United States and was sworn in on March 4, 1809. As the head of a new administration, Madison selected a cabinet to fulfill his policies and purpose. He appointed William Eustis the new secretary of war. Eustis came to the office lacking military experience and administrative abilities, unlike his predecessor Henry Dearborn. Mason continued as superintendent of Indians, but he exerted little authority.

The political governance of the upper Mississippi River valley was also changing. Three days before James Madison was inaugurated, the US Congress divided Indiana Territory into two separate governments. Indiana Territory was now the land east of the Wabash River, slightly smaller than the present-day state of Indiana. The territory west of the Wabash River to the Mississippi River became a separate territory called Illinois. Ninian Edwards was appointed governor and Nathaniel Pope secretary of the new Illinois Territory. It encompassed what is now Illinois, Wisconsin, part of the Upper Peninsula of Michigan, and northeastern Minnesota. Prairie du Chien and La Baye became part of Illinois Territory.

The creation of Illinois Territory caused uncertainty as to who would direct the duties of the Indian agents in the upper Mississippi valley. Would it be the superintendent for the west, William Clark, or Ninian Edwards, who in his capacity as governor was considered Indian agent for his territory? As agent for the upper Mississippi, Boilvin was headquartered at Prairie du Chien, in Illinois Territory. He met with many tribes that lived east of the Mississippi River in Illinois Territory. He also was in charge of regulating trade and convening councils with the Sac, Fox, and Sioux who lived west of the Mississippi River in upper Louisiana Territory. Boilvin now had the responsibility as agent for the Sac who lived on both sides of the Mississippi, the Winnebago, the Fox, and the Dakota, and he was expected to deal with the Menominee who came to trade at Prairie du Chien, all without the promise of being promoted to Dubuque's position. The lack of defined authority threatened to hamper Boilvin's effectiveness at a time when he had been directed to secure the friendship and loyalty of tribes. But Boilvin had a plan. He would solve the problem of who was his superior by corresponding directly with President Madison and Secretary of War Eustis.

—‖—

In the spring of 1809, as Dubuque's illness worsened, Nicolas Boilvin was in Prairie du Chien reporting to William Clark that at present he was "in the fire." A Winnebago, appointed chief by General Wilkinson, was attempting to gather and lead "all the Nation of Indians" to Detroit to meet with the British. The Winnebago had asked Boilvin three times to council with them at Henry Munro Fisher's house, wishing to tell Boilvin that they had but one father, the British monarch. They wished to join the British and keep their lands, which they protested the Americans were taking. Through an interpreter, Boilvin told them he refused to "answer them in a British house"—Fisher was decidedly on the side of the British. If they would come instead to his home, Boilvin would answer them.

The Winnebago arrived the next day. Boilvin counseled them to "become good," saying he had no confidence in them as they "vary like the wind and the leaf of trees." His words were the same as he had spoken to the Fox and Sioux the day before. Boilvin felt he made some impression upon the Winnebago, but the Sioux repeated what they had said to Zebulon Pike several years before:

> The Sioux say that they have given Major Pike their British Medals
> and flags, but that they have received none in return, [and] that puts a
> bad impression on the minds of the Nations of Indians.

As Pike had warned, the issue of the medals was indeed proving to hinder the prospects for the Sioux to ally with the Americans. Boilvin concluded his report with a caution that the British were encouraging the Indians to attack the fort at Belle View. Boilvin then made a pointed request. "If

I had a few goods, ammunition Tobacco &c I could do a great deal more, with the Indians."[27]

In July, Boilvin pressed the issue further, writing directly to President Madison, not doubting that Madison would "understand French perfectly." Boilvin informed the president of all that he had done on the frontier to keep the tribes friendly to the United States. Boilvin described Prairie du Chien as the center of five tribes: six nations of Sioux, Menominee, Winnebago, Fox, and Sac. Having visited the villages of each tribe, Boilvin told Madison that three things were necessary so that "all harmony will reign among the different tribes and between the tribes and our government":

> To know that there are small presents for them every year; or a company of brave soldiers to control the Company [Michilimackinac] mentioned above, as well as the Indians; or to prohibit the Company from trading with them.

Boilvin proudly asserted he had recently stopped a party of forty Menominee men who had been on their way to Detroit to ask the British to give them clothes for their women and children "who were in a pitiable state." Boilvin instead gave them something to drink—"to the health of their Good American Father"—as well as tobacco and something to eat. He sent them home telling them that their Father "watched them always and looked upon them as his children and maintained towards them at all times a fond affection."[28]

If Boilvin's requests seem forceful and his desire to prove his worth overeager, it is likely due to his growing concern about Dubuque's position, not yet officially filled. Indeed, he had some justification to feel insecure in his position as an Indian agent at Prairie du Chien. Clark had ordered him to the community as an agent, but instead Julien Dubuque had received the appointment to direct the agency. Then Dubuque had requested that he be replaced and in November had ceded all his papers to Boilvin, implying that Boilvin would receive the position as agent for the upper Mississippi. This made Boilvin anxious, for he had already committed himself and his family to the prairie.

In May 1809, Nicolas Jarrot from Cahokia, Illinois Territory, had conducted an auction of the estate of John Campbell, which included personal furnishings, livestock, and real estate at Prairie du Chien. At the sale, Boilvin purchased a substantial amount of Campbell's personal property. He had also bid in the lot and improvements "where there [were] two houses & other bildings in the village of prairie du chien joining Mr. R. Dickson."[29] Boilvin may have wondered whether he had committed himself and his family to a position that might be taken from him.

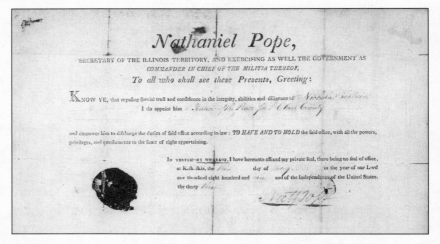

Nicolas Boilvin's appointment as justice of the peace was signed by Nathaniel Pope, then commander in chief of the Illinois militia. COURTESY OF VILLA LOUIS HISTORIC SITE

When he went to Washington in the fall of 1809, Boilvin hoped to see the secretary of war and press his arguments. Not able to do so, Boilvin wrote the secretary in October:

> I have done all the Business of Mr. Campbell since the time of his Appointment, and after his Death for the whole Mississippi, and also my own, including the greatest Part of the Missouri, for which I was promised a compensation by General Dearborn as also to be placed on the same footing as other Agents in the Indian Department employed by Government.[30]

In January 1810, Boilvin wrote to the secretary of war again in greater aggravation and uncertainty. Boilvin explained he had placed his hopes for the appointment and thereby an increase in salary in Governor Lewis. When Clark had informed Boilvin that Governor Lewis was planning a trip to Washington, Boilvin wrote to Lewis, asking him to petition the secretary to appoint him as agent for the upper Mississippi. But Lewis never arrived in Washington. Instead, he took his own life along the Natchez Trace. Learning of Lewis's suicide, Boilvin vented his frustration. Now that "the unhappy Fate which has brought this Gentleman to an untimely death, has frustrated my Hopes, to hear of a Result in the Spring," Boilvin questioned whether it was the "Will of Government that I shall stay here, or be relieved." He became even more frustrated when Frederick Bates, who had been appointed acting governor of upper Louisiana Territory, told Boilvin to follow the directives of the governor of Illinois Territory.[31]

For all his complaining, Boilvin was assiduously performing the duties of the US Indian agent for the upper Mississippi. He had met with various tribes within their villages, talking with them to convince them to be loyal to the United States. He had kept tribes who were displeased with traders from pillaging the stores. He had countered tales of the influence of the British at Detroit with assurances that the United States cared for the Indians along the Mississippi. He had maintained peace. But now the concern of others about political jurisdiction had become an issue.

Acting as governor before Edwards arrived, Nathaniel Pope had learned of the councils Boilvin had conducted at Prairie du Chien and other locations within Illinois Territory. He had also been informed that Boilvin had been issuing licenses to people to trade. Pope wrote about what he'd learned to Frederick Bates, complaining that Boilvin had been proceeding without Pope's knowledge and approval. Bates wrote Boilvin relaying Pope's complaint and expressed surprise at Boilvin's actions. Bates then enlightened Boilvin:

> The Orders of the Superintendent of Indian Affairs for Louisiana can have no operation East of the Mississippi—And no Licenses in Gov Lewis' name aught to have been issued at Prairie du Chien or for any other part of the Illinois.

Bates recommended that Boilvin correspond with Pope.[32] Feeling that his letter had been harsh, Bates wrote two days later cautioning, "There are many expectations of change in the Indian Department." Boilvin was to "be extremely circumspect in everything you do." He was to especially grant no trading licenses or enter into any arrangements within Illinois Territory unless under the direction of Acting Governor Pope.[33]

For the next year various difficulties, beyond politics and the uncertainty of his position, beset Boilvin. He purchased goods and met with representatives of the tribes that visited Prairie du Chien to ensure their friendship to the United States. In these gatherings, the tribes complained to Boilvin that their American Father did not take care of them, as no American traders visited them. Rather, the British traders came to their lands with goods. As the British traders spread out the gifts and goods, they told the tribes "that if it were not for their old English father, they would not have a Single blanket to cover themselves with." The British traders also told the tribes that soon the English would declare war against the Americans. If that happened, their English father "will again take under his protection his beloved red children, that if they will Side with him they will have everything in abundance." To Boilvin, such pronouncements only "diminish the confidence they have in this government." Boilvin knew he would constantly have to argue against British rhetoric, but supposed he would have the support of his own government in countering verbal attacks. But US policy and lack of chain of command hindered Boilvin.[34]

The United States had opened a fur factory at Fort Michilimackinac in 1808. Fort Belle View, which would be renamed Fort Madison in 1809, had been built the same year close to the mouth of the Des Moines River. Poorly sited to be a defensive fort, the garrison was seen as protection for the government trading house that was established at the same time. With the factory in place and John W. Johnson factor, the Department of War felt the influence of the British traders would be diminished and the Sac and Fox would trade with the United States. The picture at Prairie du Chien was very different. There, Boilvin continued in difficult negotiations with the Sioux.

In council with Boilvin in early 1811, the Sioux questioned statements made by Boilvin and the US policy of annuities. They asked why gifts were given every year to the Sac and Fox for lands that did not belong to them. The Sioux had been told that their land also belonged to the United States, yet they did not receive gifts. Boilvin, therefore, gave the tribes "small presents" when they came to hold councils with him at Prairie du Chien. He found that "Spirits, Tobacco, Salt—Ammunition, paints, and Such like articles" made good gifts, as the chiefs could share the articles among their people. In the year previous, he had given these items to about eight thousand seven hundred men who had come to the prairie. Boilvin insisted this practice of gift giving must continue. He admitted, "[T]he expenses must be great, but they are absolutely necessary, if the government wish to preserve the good will of those people."[35] At William Clark's request, Boilvin had submitted vouchers for the cost of the goods to Clark. Thereupon, Clark had refused to reimburse Boilvin unless the secretary of war approved. General Benjamin Howard had concurred.

Greatly in debt for the goods he had acquired to help assure the Indians' loyalty to the United States and still without a clear commission as Indian agent for the upper northwest, Boilvin traveled to Washington to present in person his account for disbursement on behalf of the United States from August 1, 1809, to the first of January, 1811. Boilvin must have met with Secretary of War Eustis, or at least his representative, for per the secretary's request, he wrote a series of reports in February and March 1811 and submitted them to Eustis.[36]

In his first report, Boilvin enumerated the villages of the tribes that inhabited the Mississippi valley from St. Louis to the St. Peter's River. He recounted conversations he had at Prairie du Chien with the representatives of the tribes. He believed that the discontent that the tribes had directed toward the United States for two years would cease if a fur factory was opened at Prairie du Chien as it had been at Fort Madison. The factory would also lessen the influence of the British traders. Boilvin reiterated his recommendation that a fort be built on the prairie and manned by a permanent garrison. This would "keep those different nations at all times, in awe." He enclosed sketches so that a map could be drawn of the Mississippi, from the source to St. Louis, locating all of the Indian villages.[37]

Secretary Eustis must have responded with a request for more information about Prairie du Chien. On March 5, Boilvin responded. His letter described the geographic setting of the prairie and a bit of its history as a seasonal gathering place of the Canadian fur traders and tribes. Boilvin estimated the population of Prairie du Chien at one hundred families with the men "generally French Canadians who have most married Indian wives: Perhaps not more than 12 white females are to be found in the

Settlement." The residents farmed the prairie, providing annually eighty thousand pounds of flour for the traders and Indians. The prairie was surrounded by "numerous Indian tribes." He then repeated his continual arguments that Canadians posed "Great dangers." However, the United States could "turn the current of Indian trade on the upper Mississippi" if it would open a factory and establish a garrison on the prairie. Then the Indians would turn their attention to other pursuits such as mining lead. The Canadian traders would then, in his estimation, "wholly abandon the country."[38]

## Tribes of the Upper Northwest Territory, ca. 1810

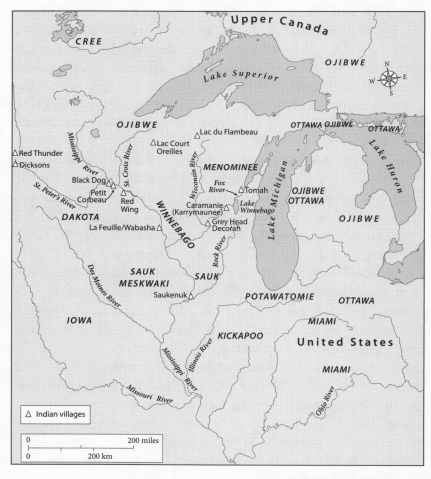

MAPPING SPECIALISTS, LTD., FITCHBURG, WI

With this report, Boilvin demonstrated that he knew more about the country and the people of the upper Mississippi than any other American official. Yet Boilvin's recommendations, which he based on his personal knowledge and experience, fell on deaf ears. Speculations were later made that as Boilvin wrote all his reports in French, the reports often lay unread.[39]

Instead of reimbursing Boilvin, Eustis responded that in the coming year, the government of the United States could not make as large an appropriation for the Indian Department as it had in the past. He therefore asked Boilvin to make a list of expenses for only "absolutely necessary" articles. Boilvin responded with the caution that he expected more Indians at the prairie than had come in the past. He included an observation that it would be in the government's interest to have a blacksmith stationed at Prairie du Chien to mend guns and tools for the Indians. Boilvin attached a list of goods he felt necessary to retain Indian friendship to the United States. The list included tobacco, whisky, salt, gunpowder, vermillion, knives, ribbon, flints, looking glasses, thread, wampum, and provisions for the Indians for one year. His final item was "6 Medals to return to the Indians for those Major Pike took from them." The Sioux were still patiently waiting for their medals from "their American father."[40]

Even though his budget for gifts had been reduced, with these reports, Boilvin must have finally proved to the secretary that he was worthy to be appointed US Indian agent for the upper Mississippi. After two years, on March 14, 1811, Secretary Eustis wrote to Nicolas Boilvin:

> As you have for some time past performed the duties of Indian Agent at Prairie du Chien, in the room of John Campbell deceased, you will herewith receive a Commission appointing you his successor.

Though Eustis did not afford Boilvin the respect of giving him a title, he did clarify to whom Boilvin would be responsible: General Clark. However, Boilvin would have to continue to correspond with the governor of Illinois. Eustis informed Boilvin his principal place of residence was to be Prairie du Chien, but he was expected to visit other places "within the limits of your commission." Eustis detailed Boilvin's duties for which he would be compensated "twelve hundred dollars per annum." [41]

Having been in Washington when he received his commission, Boilvin returned to the Mississippi valley soon afterward, stopping at St. Louis. Though Boilvin had recommended that the Sac, Fox, and other tribes be encouraged to mine lead as a way to lessen their economic dependency on the British traders, his line of reasoning had been ignored. Dubuque had been in debt to Pierre Chouteau when he died. So even though the mines did not belong to Chouteau, Chouteau had given two men a contract to work Julien Dubuque's mines.

Arriving at the Rock River, the Sac and Fox met Boilvin. Learning that sixty men were en route to Dubuque's mines, the Sac and Fox voiced their opposition. They explained to Boilvin that they had given the mine only to Dubuque with the understanding that at his death the mines returned to the Fox nation. Boilvin was embarrassed by the situation in which he had been placed. When he arrived at the mines, the Fox assembled. They accused the American men of depriving them and their families of bread. Boilvin used all his power of persuasion to prevent an attack on the men. He convinced the chiefs to meet with Clark as a means to settle the problem. He then proceeded to Prairie du Chien.[42]

The Sac and Fox were upset because of the presence of Americans on their land, but all the tribes of the upper Mississippi were in great distress. Rumors of impending war between the United States and Great Britain heightened the unease of the residents of Prairie du Chien and all the tribes and led to questions about the supply of trade goods now desperately needed. All looked to see which country would provide what was required.

# 5

## TECUMSEH'S REBELLION
## AND THE DECLARATION OF WAR

### *1811–1812*

France and Great Britain had renewed warfare soon after President Jefferson acquired the Louisiana Purchase. The two countries sought to damage each other's commerce by seizing the ships of neutral nations carrying their adversary's trade. As the largest neutral nation, the United States suffered greatly. Many ships were seized and valuable cargo taken. Britain also impressed sailors from American ships into the British navy. To prevent the destruction of the US merchant ships and preserve its seamen, the United States instituted an embargo that made it unlawful for American ships to leave port. This embargo caused economic distress to American shippers and all producers of goods and crops. With threats of rebellion coming from all parts of the country, Congress ended the embargo and passed the Non-Intercourse Act in March 1809. This prevented trade with Britain and France. Soon after James Madison was inaugurated president, he reopened trade with Britain. Relations did not improve, however, and Madison once again declared non-intercourse, which resumed on March 1, 1811.

Under the Non-Intercourse Act, it was unlawful to import goods from either Britain or France or their dependencies, either directly or through third parties. English traders could no longer legally bring goods into

United States territory. That August, John Askin Jr., storekeeper for the British Indian Department at St. Joseph Island in Upper Canada, wrote his father that the traders associated with the South West Company remained on the island in the "hopes that the Act will be repealed."[1] As British agents, Lewis Crawford and Robert Dickson were two such traders who had goods they planned to transport into Indian country. The Non-Intercourse Act would affect American traders and Indian agents more severely. Without goods to trade, they would have nothing to offer the Indians, who had become dependent on the goods, to help retain their loyalty to the United States.

With goods of the South West Company, a subsidiary of the American Fur Company, unable to leave St. Joseph Island, concern grew among the Indians as to whether any of the goods needed for the winter would be coming into the country. Boilvin spent the summer of 1811 meeting in council with the chiefs and warriors of the upper Mississippi. To him, they were "terrified at the prospect of war between Great Britain and the United States." Since Boilvin's return to the prairie in mid-July, "there has not been a single day but what there has been a council on their situation to anticipate what would happen if war began." He often told them what would be the consequences if they were to "take up arms against their new American father." He worked tirelessly, sometimes cajoling and resorting to frightful predictions of US retaliation, to keep the tribes from joining the British. As the weeks progressed, the tribes began to prepare to depart for their wintering locations along the rivers, expecting traders to join them as they had in previous seasons.[2]

Robert Dickson had been acquiring trade goods and supplies from the Montreal merchants who operated stores by the fort on St. Joseph Island in preparation for the trading season on the Mississippi and St. Peter's Rivers. Under the Non-Intercourse Act, all these goods and his attempt to bring them to the upper Mississippi were unlawful. At the end of August Dickson left, taking a circuitous route from Queenston to Fort Pitt down the Ohio River to the Mississippi then northward to be "amongst the Siouxs." Where Dickson acquired the goods and the "manner he escaped the Yanky Collectors," Askin was not "authorized to say."[3] Dickson arrived at the prairie in early September with the much-needed merchandise. As he unloaded the goods, Boilvin found all that Dickson had brought to be contraband goods and challenged him. Dickson replied that he came "in no unfriendly way, only to carry on the same trade as was his custom." Boilvin reported Dickson's actions to the Illinois governor and William Clark, but neither responded. Boilvin therefore wrote in frustration to Secretary Eustis almost begging him to respond with some small "benevolence, that you cast your fatherly eyes from time to time on the Indians." Evidently, he expected the United States to supply the goods needed for trade.[4]

While Boilvin worried about the goods Dickson had brought into the country, Dickson was distressed to find the tribes to be in a "Calamitous state." For two years, lack of rain had affected the crops of the Winnebago, Sac, and Fox. The tribes that existed by hunting were also suffering because the hot, dry weather had driven the game farther north in search of food.[5]

Indeed, as Boilvin reported to the secretary, many parties of Menominee, Fox, and Sac had passed through the prairie on their way to see their "English father." They knew he would give them the clothes their women and children needed. They were probably on their way to the British trading center on St. Joseph Island where the goods imported by Americans languished; only Dickson and Crawford had chosen to ignore the nonimportation act. Crawford also bypassed the Americans at Michilimackinac by taking a route through Lake Superior to Lac du Flambeau.[6]

From mid-July through the fall, Boilvin conducted meeting after meeting with the Indians. By the end, he felt he had changed their minds with "a drop to drink, something to smoke, a little ammunition, and the wherewithal to clothe several of the unfortunate ones."[7] Yet his gifts to the tribes and invitations to the chiefs to visit Washington did little to address the real needs of the Native population. Realizing the requirements of the tribes for food, Dickson decided to remain in Prairie du Chien instead of continuing to the St. Peter's River. From his home in the Main Village, Dickson distributed his entire stock of trade goods amounting to 20,975 Quebec livres, which he had purchased on credit. This benevolence, more persuasive than the promises of Boilvin, more firmly attached the tribes of the upper Mississippi to Dickson and the British.[8]

The winter of 1811–1812 added to the distress of the Indians of the upper Mississippi and western Great Lakes in many ways. The bands that had come to Prairie du Chien were in great need of not only food but also ammunition to try to gain something from the winter hunting season, but the season would be disrupted by events to the south.

For several years, the Shawnee leader Tecumseh had traveled into the Rock River valley recruiting tribes to be part of a Native confederacy that he had begun to form in the early nineteenth century. Following the 1795 Treaty of Greenville, tribes in what is now the eastern and southern parts of Ohio moved off lands ceded to the United States. They traveled northwestward and settled on the traditional lands of other tribes. Here, they lived in harmony, creating a village rather than a tribal form of government. Seeing this, Tecumseh began a movement to attempt to unite the tribes west of the Appalachian Mountains into a confederation. Tecumseh believed that the land did not belong to a single tribe. Rather, no one owned the land except for the Master of Life, the Shawnees' principal god. Tecumseh believed that the only way that American Indians could transfer land to the United States was if every tribe agreed to it. Tecumseh wanted to force the Americans to deal with all of the tribes in unison. Separately, the individual tribes did not have much power. Together, Tecumseh hoped, they would be a major deterrent to white expansion. Tecumseh's vision was to establish an independent nation, where all could live secure in the possession of land held in common.[9]

In 1804, William Henry Harrison, representing the United States, had negotiated a treaty with the Sac and Fox. Many members of the two tribes, including Black Hawk, refused to acknowledge the legitimacy of the treaty, as the Sac who signed the treaty were not chiefs and did not represent the tribe. As a result of the treaty, the Sac lost their largest settlement. The treaty also affected the Winnebago, Kickapoo, and Potawatomi, who lived between the Mississippi and Fox Rivers. Tecumseh met with the Winnebago and Sac in 1809, and approximately fifty Winnebago had then moved to Tippecanoe on the Tippecanoe River in present-day Indiana. More Winnebago, Potawatomi, Sac, and Fox joined their brothers the following year.[10]

In the fall of 1811, William Henry Harrison prepared to attack Tippecanoe, called Prophetstown by the whites, as it had been founded by The Prophet, Tecumseh's brother. Not only was Tippecanoe the largest Native community in the Great Lakes region but it also served as a major center of Indian culture and the final rampart of defense against whites. It was an intertribal, religious stronghold along the Wabash River in Indiana for three thousand American Indians. Gathering about one thousand men, Harrison marched his men to the Tippecanoe River and encamped on a hill close to Prophetstown. On November 7, the Indian confederacy attacked the camp. In the battle of Tippecanoe, Harrison's men held their ground, and the Indians withdrew from their village after the battle. Harrison ordered the town burned, and then he returned to Vincennes. The Indians who had supported the confederacy disbursed after the defeat. The defeat convinced many Indians in the Northwest Territory that they needed British support to prevent American settlers from pushing them further out of their lands. Boilvin informed Benjamin Howard, who had been appointed governor of Louisiana Territory, that the "news of Gov' Harrisons Victory does not appear to please the Indians here." He worried about the safety of those who lived on the frontier if Harrison did not "follow up his conquest."[11]

At the end of December, about forty Winnebago from the Rock River arrived at Prairie du Chien and sought out Boilvin. Boilvin wrote of his encounter with these men in two reports submitted to Secretary Eustis and a letter to Governor Howard. The occurrence made such an impression upon Boilvin that he wrote to Eustis again in June providing more details. The band of Winnebago, with Pokor an Fleche leading them, were brought to Boilvin's house. "Armed to the teeth," he wrote, they stood at his door, "shrieking out the most barbaric terror." They said, "We have been killed; your comrade Harrison has killed us; look at us who have escaped; look at the way our blankets are pierced with bullets."

With them were two Winnebago chiefs, Decora and Caramani. Decora relayed the results of the battle at Tippecanoe as bad news, saying, "We have been killed by the Americans at the Shawanies." At first "too surprised for suitable language," Boilvin reminded them that the previous fall he had counseled the Winnebago not to follow The Prophet. Then, with no apparent sympathy, Boilvin added, "You probably have deserved it." He told them to rest and return the next day, and then he would listen to them.[12]

Boilvin had made Decora a chief, so Decora spoke somewhat contritely, explaining that the Winnebago with him were from three bands. These men had been foolish and were now in affliction. Decora suggested that Boilvin "inform them below that they may take care of those bad men."

Boilvin may have assumed that Decora found the men "bad" because they had fought with The Prophet. But after the Winnebago left, Boilvin learned that thirty Winnebago had attacked the American traders who lived by the mines about eighty miles below Prairie du Chien. Two men had been killed and cut into pieces, and all the houses and buildings had been set on fire. According to Maurice Blondeau, these acts were in retaliation "for what Governor Harrison had done to their nation, at the time they went to see the Prophet."[13] The arrival of the Winnebago and news of the attack upon the American traders threw all the residents of Prairie du Chien "into great consternation."[14]

Howard forwarded copies of Boilvin's and Blondeau's reports to Ninian Edwards, governor of Illinois Territory. Edwards forwarded the copies to Secretary Eustis, with the comment that Howard had received more information to corroborate the "opinions" expressed by Boilvin and Blondeau. Their reports finally reached the secretary's desk on March 10, more than two months after they had been written.

William Clark submitted his own report on the killing of the two men and the destruction of the trading houses at the mines to Eustis. Most of the report detailed a proposal that he believed "necessary for the protection of . . . the Frontiora [sic] of this quarter." He suggested that companies of US Rangers be sent to the western territories. They would be "kept in Continuel motion" patrolling the unsettled lands of the Illinois and Louisiana Territories, with detached "Spys" to warn of the "approach of the Enemy." A line should be drawn, he said, between the friendly bands of Indians and the "Indian Bands towards the Lakes." The friendly Indians would be given signals known only to the Rangers or written permits issued by the Indian agents. No Indian could cross the line without a permit or knowledge of the signals. Additionally, Clark said that all communication between the tribes and the British traders needed to be cut. This could be accomplished

> [i]f possession was taken of a point about the Fox river where it enters into Green Bay[.] Communication would be Cut off between the Traders and Indians on the Mississippi below Prariedechien [sic], and the British Trading houses on the Lakes[.]

If the United States controlled La Baye, then "smuggling might be prevented thro' that Channel" by Robert Dickson and other British traders who "grasp at every means in their power to wave the affections of the Indians from anything that is American." For the next two years, Clark would put forth various proposals to curb the influence of the British traders. Like the American commandant at Fort Mackinac and Nicolas Boilvin, William Clark in his reports and comments had acknowledged the preeminence of Robert Dickson in the region, dismissing others engaged as "other British traders."[15]

The weather that winter also affected all residents of the upper Mississippi. On December 16, the first of three earthquakes that came to be known as the New Madrid earthquakes occurred. For five weeks after the first quake, a series of aftershocks shook the region. Extremely cold weather set in and froze the Ohio River. By the third week of January, 1812, there were few, if any, travelers on the Mississippi River from the Ohio southward.[16] If the Ohio River was frozen, it can be assumed that the Mississippi River above St. Louis was also closed to water travel. As no goods could get through to St. Louis, any trade goods or supplies that Boilvin needed either remained in St. Louis or never arrived.

As the Winnebago had been engaged in the fighting against General Harrison, they had not participated in the fall hunt for food for the winter. And though Dickson had arrived in Prairie du Chien with trade goods and distributed all he had, other British traders had not been able to bring enough goods and ammunition to the western Great Lakes. Reports had come to Boilvin that among the Sioux who lived along the St. Peter's River, more than one hundred lodges had died of starvation. The fierce winter and lack of ammunition had forced "3705" Sioux, Menominee, Winnebago, Fox, Sac, and Ioway men and women to come to Prairie du Chien in search of powder and supplies. Three wagons filled with provisions reached the prairie by some means, and Boilvin shared them the best he could. But Boilvin believed that the English traders had "brought more than I to provide for quite a number of Indians of different nations." Boilvin reported that these Indians, led by their chiefs, were now on their way to Michilimackinac to meet with the British.[17]

When Boilvin wrote this letter, he was en route to Washington City. During Boilvin's previous visit, Secretary Eustis had requested that Boilvin bring chiefs from the upper Mississippi to visit the president. Boilvin had questioned whether he should fulfill this request because of the unrest among the tribes brought about by the battle at Prophetstown. He felt his presence was required at Prairie du Chien to keep the tribes friendly and at peace. Governor Howard considered it very necessary for the chiefs to meet the president of the United States, as this would be a means to influence the chiefs against the power of Tecumseh and the British. Boilvin, therefore, called a council of Sioux, Menominee, Chippewa, Winnebago, Fox, and Sac. For twenty days, Boilvin met with the chiefs; he would talk, they would leave and return with their responses or questions, and Boilvin would talk again. During this time, the Indians met with Boilvin in his house up to five times a day. They discussed what the tribes should do in case of war between the United States and Great Britain. Should they take the side of the British, who encouraged them to do so, or should they take the side of the Americans, "whose wrath they might some day have to fear"? Boilvin told them:

> Their American father asked nothing [in way of concessions] from his red children; that he was able to defend his cause without using unfortunate people like them; he gives a living to your wives and children; you will one day be happy and your American father will relieve you.

But privately, Boilvin had his doubts. Bluntly, he wrote Eustis that he had had

> [p]lenty of trouble and talking all winter and this spring but I cleared up this bad reputation the Americans have had among all the nations who were being deceived and made promises which were never fulfilled.

Boilvin listed some of these deceptions, and all he laid at the feet of the United States. The United States had a bad reputation because the Indians had been chased from their lands; American agents and officers took their English medals and promised that they would receive medals and flags from their American father but had never delivered them; and the Indians had been promised other things by American officials who deceived them.

Boilvin told Eustis that he had promised that the American father would fulfill all that had been promised and would do so without deceit. Boilvin seemed to be implying that the United States needed to live up to its word and carry out all that had been pledged to the tribes under his care.[18]

Dickson and Boilvin were both distributing as much as they could to the tribes. As Boilvin reported, he also had sat in counsel with the Winnebago, Sac and Fox, Menominee, and Ioway and given them presents. From his house next door, Dickson watched the comings and goings of the chiefs. To him the agents of the American government "were using every means in their power to influence Indians in their behalf," not only distributing presents but also "inciting them in the most pressing manner to visit the President of the United States at Washington, where it was held out to them, they would hear something of the utmost importance." Dickson presumed Boilvin, through his interpreters, was suggesting the Indians do "something hostile" against the British. In response, since Dickson found himself to be "the only individual in that Country possess'd of means of frustrating their intentions," he also met with the chiefs, encouraging them to remain loyal to the English. Each man achieved some results. Some of the chiefs agreed to journey to Washington City with Boilvin. The rest of the Indians, Dickson believed, returned to their homes in a peaceful and satisfied state of mind.[19]

Both Boilvin and Dickson left Prairie du Chien early in the summer of 1812. Boilvin left in June, accompanied by five Sioux, three Ioway, and two Winnebago chiefs and interpreters, one of which probably included Joseph Roc, an interpreter for the Sioux who had originally been engaged by John Campbell. Boilvin and his party stopped in St. Louis, and there they learned that William Clark was also on his way to Washington. In May, Clark had left St. Louis with an entourage that included nine chiefs and warriors from the Great and Little Osage, Shawnee, and Delaware, three Indian women, several interpreters, and Maurice Blondeau. Arriving at Cincinnati, Boilvin learned that what he and all living in the vicinity of the prairie had feared: the United States had declared war on Great Britain. On June 1, 1812, President James Madison had sent a message to Congress asking for a declaration of war. The House of Representatives passed the declaration on June 4; on June 17, it passed the Senate. Madison signed the declaration on June 18. The War of 1812 had officially begun.

The reasons for President Madison's declaration had their origins in Europe. First and foremost were the vitriolic trade relations with Britain over the past several years. According to the Non-Intercourse Act renewed by Madison in March 1811, the United States prohibited trade with Britain, which continued to seize American ships and merchandise and to impress American sailors into the British navy. Madison felt that impressment of American seamen was the greatest injustice, and he saw it as a first step in the possible reconquest of the new nation by Britain. He was also aware of British attempts to gain the loyalty of the western Indians in US territory. That spring, a group of influential Americans began agitating for war. New members of Congress elected in 1812 and led by Henry Clay and John C. Calhoun were at the forefront of the movement. They encouraged war as a means of retaliation for the blockade and what they perceived as British activities encouraging the Indian resistance to American expansion into the West. To preserve the territory and sovereignty of the United States, Madison asked for the declaration of war.

Learning that a state of war existed, Boilvin's immediate concern was the trip to Washington. He wrote the secretary of war questioning whether he should continue on to Washington, explaining that the chiefs with him, especially the Winnebago, were from bands friendly to the United States. He was apprehensive and informed Eustis that he could not catch up with Clark. He would appreciate instructions. The next stop was Pittsburgh, where a letter awaited Boilvin telling him to continue his trip to the nation's capital.[20]

The journey for Clark's and Boilvin's parties was long. At Pittsburgh, they left the ease of river travel and rode and trekked overland. Clark arrived in Washington on August 1; Boilvin and his party reached the capital in mid-August. President Madison had planned a visit to impress all. The chiefs, interpreters, Clark and Boilvin, and department heads attended a dinner at the White House hosted by Dolley Madison on August 16. Three days later, the chiefs led a day of feasting and dancing on Greenleaf Point overlooking the Potomac and Anacostia Rivers. The culmination of the visit was an address to the Indian nations by President Madison on August 22.

Madison was concerned about Indian alliances to the British in the American West. He knew that these tribes could potentially be Britain's allies. Thus, Madison now needed to make any attempt to gain Indian loyalty, or at least neutrality. As Madison stood before the assembled chiefs and warriors in Washington, the speech he was about to give had extremely great importance, for, unbeknownst to him, the American fort on Mackinac Island had already surrendered to a combined force of British and Indians.

Madison began by complimenting the nations who lived on and west of the Mississippi River who "shut their ears to the bad birds hovering about them for some time past." He continued, saying the "red people" live on the same "great Island" as the "white people of the 18 fires" (fires meaning number of US states) and all were made the same by the same spirit. But he was concerned by the hostility between the Osage and the Sac, and the "Winibagoes and some other tribes, between the Mississippi & Lake Michigan & the Wabash" who had shut their ears to his councils. As their father, he was going to give them advice, and as his children it was their duty to hearken to what he was to say. First, Madison declared the British to be weak, calling their agents "bad birds" who try to decoy the Indians into war on the British side. Conversely, he said, he does not ask them to join the Americans but to "[s]it still on your seats; and be witnesses." The Americans had beaten the British before, when they were only "13 fires," and would do so again. Then Madison asked the chiefs to look closely at the men, women, and children of the eighteen fires. None ever perished of hunger, he said, in contrast with the red people. Why?

> The white people breed cattle and sheep. They plow the earth and make it give them every thing they want. They spin and weave. Their heads, and the hands make all the elements & productions of nature useful to them. Above all; the people of the 18 fires live in constant peace & friendship.

Madison concluded that it was in the power of the Indians to be like the people of the eighteen fires. As the Great Spirit "is the friend of men of all colours," all should be friends. Madison asked that they take his message home and share it. In the future, his words would be spoken by Clark and others "who may be near you."[21]

Many of the chiefs responded to Madison. Afterward, presents were distributed, including medals. But in a note sent to Clark, Madison indicated that the United States was still having difficulties procuring medals with the image of the American father. Once the proper medals could be had, Clark was to exchange the medals given that day for one "of a Proper description." After six hours of speeches, Madison closed the day, and Clark and Boilvin left with their parties to prepare for the trip home.[22]

The return trip to St. Louis in September proved to be difficult. There were threats against Boilvin and his party by white people committing acts of vengeance against any Indian who traveled on the river. Boilvin had to wait at Pittsburgh for an armed escort, fearing for the Indians who were with him. He arrived in St. Louis, where he received orders to remain there, for to return to Prairie du Chien would put his life in danger. The War of 1812 had begun in earnest. Boilvin would not return to Prairie du Chien until the summer of 1814. The Indians returned without him.[23]

# 6

## ROBERT DICKSON AND "HIS MAJESTY'S FAITHFUL INDIAN ALLIES"

### *1812–1813*

Robert Dickson departed Prairie du Chien for St. Joseph's Island about the same time Boilvin started down the Mississippi bound for Washington City early in the summer of 1812. Having supplied the Indians and their families with ammunition and provisions, Dickson's stock was depleted. He left promising he would return with more supplies. As occurred with Boilvin, Dickson received a message while on his journey eastward. Arriving at the portage of the Fox and Wisconsin Rivers, Dickson was met by two runners from Amherstburg, bearing a message from Major General Isaac Brock. The runners had left the British fort at the mouth of the Detroit River, traveling cross-country to Lake Michigan. American soldiers at Chicago had apprehended them. Sensing their capture, they had been astute enough to hide the letters in their moccasins and bury them. When nothing had been found after a search, they were allowed to proceed. Retrieving their moccasins, they continued to the portage. There they found Dickson, James Fraser, and a large contingent of Sioux, Winnebago, and Menominee.[1]

Brock had been made responsible for the protection of Upper Canada. Believing that the United States and Great Britain would soon be at war, he had prepared the army and militias under his command for military engagement. For some time Brock had corresponded with Dickson, respecting his knowledge of the western Great Lakes region and the esteem in which the Indians held him. Therefore, as the tension between the two countries increased, Brock turned to Dickson to learn more about the possibility that the Indians would ally themselves with Great Britain.

The two runners carried a "Confidential communication" written in February 1812 and sent from British headquarters in York. Brock had dictated to Captain Glegg, his aide-de-camp, the message: "War may result from the present situation: I wish to know—" There followed nine questions about Dickson's "friends." Brock inquired as to the number of friends upon which the British might depend, their disposition, whether they would "assemble and march" under Dickson's orders, what succor Dickson may require and the best means to convey it, what equipment Dickson could procure, the necessity to establish direct communication, and whether Dickson might select from his friends "a few *faithful* and very *confidential* agents" (original emphasis) and send them to York. Brock asked when and where they could meet. He warned that Dickson was to avoid the use of names in his written communication.[2]

Dickson penned an immediate response enumerating the friends, all of whom were "ready to march under proper persons commissioned for the purpose." He requested provisions of all sorts and especially asked for "flags, one dozen large medals with gorgets and a few small ones." If his request was met, the tribes would finally receive flags and medals to replace those they had relinquished to Pike and Boilvin, but this time with a new allegiance, to Britain.[3]

At the same time he sent his reply, Dickson also dispatched seventy-nine "friends." These friends carried speeches for the British commander. In them, La Feuille, Little Crow, and another chief stated that they had been amused for some time by "bad birds." They had for a long time lived near the English traders and would stand by the English. They would join the British forces at Fort George at Niagara-on-the-Lake. Dickson then chose a band of thirty Menominee under Weenusate, a chief, to travel to Fort Amherstburg, which stood at the mouth of the Detroit River across from the American fort at Detroit.[4] Dickson and about 130 warriors, commanded by their chiefs, continued on to St. Joseph Island. The troupe included Sioux, Winnebago, and Menominee. They arrived at the fort by July 3.

Captain Charles Roberts of the Tenth Royal Veteran Battalion commanded the garrison at Fort St. Joseph on St. Mary's River above Lake Huron. Stationed at the post were about forty-five other men of the Tenth Veterans with only a small supply of arms and ammunition. On July 9, an express arrived from General Brock announcing that on June 18, the United States had declared war against Great Britain. Roberts immediately understood the gravity of the situation. His was the lone British post at the juncture of three of the Great Lakes through which supplies, furs, and men flowed to and from Montreal. To the south, the American force at Fort Mackinac was now the enemy and was in position to attack and block necessary supply lines. Roberts determined to take immediate action against the American garrison.

Anticipating orders from General Brock, the following day, Roberts requisitioned all the boats, arms, and ammunition that were located in the store of the South West Company. Roberts sent requests to the North West

Little Crow (left), called La Petit Corbeau by the French and British, was a hereditary chief of the Kaposia band of Dakota. Petit Corbeau supported the British during the War of 1812, serving in the attack on Fort Sandusky. A strong ally, Petit Corbeau vowed to attack any American force that attempted to retake Prairie du Chien. WHI IMAGE ID 26790.

Wabasha (right), called La Feuille by the French and British, was a hereditary chief of the Mdewakanton and was highly respected by the Dakota. Alongside other First Nation warriors, Wabasha participated in key battles during the War of 1812, including the Battle of Fort Mackinac and throughout the western frontier. After the Treaty of Ghent, Wabasha continued to be an important spokesperson for the Dakota and his people's rights against growing American expansionism. WHI IMAGE ID 26926

Company headquarters at Fort William for more munitions and men to assist, and he commandeered the *Caledonia*, the North West Company's seventy-ton armed schooner. He called on the traders at Sault Ste. Marie and St. Joseph and their employees to be part of the expedition against the American fort. Roberts gathered the Indians who had arrived with Dickson and the Chippewa and Ottawa who lived around St. Joseph Island, asking them to be part of the attack.

Dickson volunteered his services and that of the Indians who had traveled with him to assist in the attack on Mackinac Island, placing all under the command of Captain Roberts. With the exception of the Ottawa, the Indians' support was unanimous, championed by "the Western Indians whose animated example had great influence upon the concurrence of the others."[5] Within two days, Roberts had accumulated a force of 140 Canadian volunteers led by Lewis Crawford and about one hundred warriors led by Robert Dickson. Roberts held a council with most of the principal chiefs of the Ottawa, and after a long consultation, they consented to gather their warriors to join the British. Besides these, Roberts learned that more men and supplies were on their way from the North West Company post.[6]

Familiar with Mackinac Island, Dickson offered Roberts advice as to the position of the American fort, the best place for a landing, and the nature of the buildings and residents along the shore. Roberts appreciated Dickson's assistance and felt "much may be looked for from him and his party in the event of an Attack upon the American fort." Dickson was pleased with the attention Roberts had given him and the Indians in his party. In response, he noted, "the Indians are much gratified with his comportment towards them, and in him they repose the highest Confidence." They would be led by John Askin Jr., the interpreter at Fort St. Joseph, whose mother was Ottawa.[7]

On July 15, Roberts received orders from Brock to do whatever was necessary to secure Mackinac Island. A force of about 230 Canadian traders and voyageurs, 320 Indians composed of Sioux, Winnebago, Menominee, Ottawa, and Chippewa, and the soldiers of the garrison left St. Joseph Island on July 16 at 11:00 a.m., sailing aboard the *Caledonia* and paddling canoes down the St. Mary's River and into Lake Huron. Not far from the island, the flotilla met Michael Dousman paddling toward St. Joseph. Dousman, commissioned an officer in the militia, had been sent by Lieutenant

Porter Hanks, in command of Fort Mackinac, to the British settlement in an attempt to learn what Roberts proposed now that war had been declared. A fur trader operating out of Michilimackinac, Dousman was well acquainted with Dickson and the other traders. He was soon captured and taken aboard the *Caledonia*, where he quickly changed sides and told Roberts all he knew about the strength and weaknesses of the American fort. Landing in a cove on Dousman's farm about three o'clock in the morning, Robert's force quietly crept through the woods to the high ground that rose behind the fort. The height secured, Roberts ordered one of the six-pound cannon from the ship to be brought ashore and dragged to the top of the hill. The sight of the cannon and the Indians ranged along the rise and into the woods was enough to make the commander of the American fort realize that surrender was the best option. Toussaint Pothier succinctly reported, "[We] summoned the garrison to surrender at 9:00 and walked in at 11:00 am."[8]

Captain Roberts presented to Lieutenant Porter Hanks the terms of capitulation by which the fort at Mackinac was to be immediately surrendered to the British force. The garrison would march from the fort with honors of war, lay down their arms, and, since they were to be returned to the United States as prisoners of war, could not take up arms against Britain until exchanged. In the terms, Roberts ensured that all private vessels at harbor and their cargoes would remain in the possession of their owners and all private property would "be held sacred." The citizens of the island who would not take the oath of allegiance to the crown were given one month to leave the island with their property. Roberts was very happy to report to General Brock that "not one drop of either mans or animals Blood was spilt."[9] Thus ended the first major victory for the British in the War of 1812.

At the end of July, General Brock was headquartered at Fort George at Niagara-on-the-Lake. With Roberts's reports in hand and aware that Dickson had sent a band of Menominee to Amherstburg, Brock wrote to Sir George Prevost, governor general and commander in chief of British forces in North America, that Dickson was "a gentleman every way capable of forming a correct judgment of the actual state of the Indians." Soon after he had written to Prevost, Brock received a communiqué from Colonel Proctor, who was commanding the British forces at Amherstburg. Proctor recommended that reinforcements be sent to the post, as this would ensure "a powerful Aid from the Indians of whom the Enemy are much in dread."[10]

The Menominee Dickson had sent to Amherstburg were part of a force of Indians placed under the command of Tecumseh. In mid-August, about two hundred Indians who had journeyed from Mackinac Island joined them. General Brock arrived about the same time and decided to attack Fort Detroit. Crossing the river above the fort, the Indians under Tecumseh executed maneuvers, making the American general, William Hull, think that the force was far greater. Fearing a slaughter by the Indians, Hull surrendered the fort—another early victory for the British.

With Mackinac Island and Detroit in the control of the British, Dickson took an optimistic view of the future. He wrote to Louis Grignon saying, "My opinion is that peace will come very soon, and I hope that all things will be well." With this outlook, Dickson turned to business. He sent a letter to Jacob Franks, a trading partner of Dickson's at La Baye. Franks had been the second largest provider of equipment for the Indian forces that had served under Dickson at Mackinac. Franks himself had commanded a detachment of "Canadians or Boatmen" during the attack and a week later he provided the barge to move the British headquarters from St. Joseph Island back to Mackinac. Dickson reported on the taking of Detroit, praising the service of Weenusate and the Menominee, and then focused on the trade. It had been a long campaign, and Dickson needed to organize his business affairs, for he had committed much to ensure the Indians had gone to Michilimackinac and Amherstburg. So, unlike the Winnebago and Sioux who had fought at Michilimackinac and returned to their homes to prepare for the winter, Dickson remained on the island.[11]

Dickson fully believed in the British cause and worked to ensure the western Indians maintained their loyalty to Great Britain. Over the years, he had garnered their respect. He talked to them, and when he asked the tribes to support Britain and go with him to defend their lands, Dickson made sure they had supplies for the journey and the days they stayed away from home. Dickson had already provisioned the Sioux, Menominee, and Winnebago from his own stores. He had purchased additional goods at Prairie du Chien and La Baye, where the British were still supplying trade goods, and purchased two oxen to supplement the dry provisions. After the capture of Fort Mackinac, Dickson once more withdrew goods from his own stores for the Indians, and Captain Roberts ordered that a number of bullocks be purchased from the island residents. By his account, Dickson had spent £1875.5.9.[12]

The taking of Detroit had guaranteed the security of the Great Lakes for the British. Supplies for the winter were soon to arrive at Michilimack-inac from Montreal by the *Nancy.* Dickson returned to his house on Mackinac Island. From there, he would send a boat to La Baye with all that was necessary for Franks and others to winter over and be prepared for the spring trade. John Lawe, Franks's nephew, would leave with goods to the Mississippi River where he would meet James Aird and arrange for his wintering. Thomas G. Anderson, a fellow trader, needed to be well supplied "as the best peltries come from that quarter." All the goods plus high wine, spirits, and two hundred pounds of tobacco Dickson expected to be at La Baye by the twenty-sixth of September. When the supplies arrived, five additional canoes filled with presents for the Indians arrived with them. Dickson did "everything in his power" to make sure the presents left the island to arrive "among the Indians," as he knew the importance of the gifts as symbols of friendship and as a necessity for the winter months.[13]

Though the goods had successfully arrived at his store, and he had organized men to leave with the provisions for La Baye, Prairie du Chien, and the St. Peter's River, Dickson's optimism of the previous month for a quick peace had left him. A longer war seemed inevitable and that would affect the trade. He told Franks,

> We have no chance of doing any thing in the Country in the way we have been, this some time past. We are as yet in the dark respecting Politics, nor can any one form an opinion respecting the duration of the war.[14]

Dickson himself would not return immediately to Prairie du Chien or the St. Peter's River and his family. Since hostilities would continue, he felt that he needed to travel to Montreal and place recommendations before the British commander in chief as to how to retain the friendship and cooperation of the Indians. He also wished to be reimbursed for his expenses in bringing the Indians to Michilimackinac. By mid-October, Dickson left the island for Montreal. As Dickson traveled eastward, Proctor sent a letter to Major General Sheaffe in which he stated that Dickson could give him any information on the defenses at Detroit and British interests in Indian country. He then commented, assuming that the general would understand this inference, "The great defect in the Indian Department, is the want of a leader of influence in the field."[15] On the way east, Dickson stopped at York, the provincial capital of Upper Canada. When he left, he carried with him a letter of introduction written by Captain Glegg to Colonel Baynes, the principal staff officer to Sir George Prevost, governor general of Canada.

Glegg's letter demonstrates the esteem in which the British administration for Upper Canada held Robert Dickson. Introduced as closely connected to families known as friends to His Majesty's government, Dickson was praised for his influence and assistance with the "Tribes of Indians" who had performed services for the British cause. His services of preventing starvation among the tribes and leading the warriors in the capture of Mackinac Island were explained in detail. Glegg did not know if Dickson planned to request an interview with Prevost, but he reinforced the staff's opinion that

> there is no Gentleman in the Province more capable of giving accurate information respecting the Western Indians than himself, and I am authorized in saying, that had General Brock survived the last contest, he intended pointing out Mr Dickson to the notice of His Majesty's Government, as a Gentleman who by his zealous and faithful services had proved himself deserving of their special protection.[16]

Arriving in Montreal early in December, Dickson presented a statement of his activities on behalf of the British government with an itemized account of the expenses incurred. He also put forward a series of actions that the British government should take "if the active cooperation of the Indian Tribes is required." He suggested that a "large Wampum Belt with proper designations & an appropriate speech" be sent among the tribes, that the tribes should rendezvous in the spring at Chicago and La Baye, and provisions should be sent to the two places prior to the gathering. To demonstrate the sincerity of the British, "One silk Standard & one large medal" should be produced for each tribe. In addition, a person needed to be authorized to draw from the Indian stores all that would be needed by the tribes and receive a commission from the commander in chief to command the western Indians. That person would need twenty interpreters and officers. Dickson then offered his services to set out for the Mississippi, stopping along the route at Kingston, York, Niagara, Amherstburg, Detroit, St. Joseph, Chicago, and the Rock River to gather the Indians in support of Britain.[17]

With Dickson's statement of expenses in hand, Sir George Prevost convened a confidential board of inquiry to assess the circumstances and authority under which Dickson had acted by giving supplies to the Indians, determine if Dickson received any personal gain, and judge whether the prices he paid were fair. The board also had at its disposal the letter of recommendation written by General Brock's aide-de-camp and the written proposal Dickson had submitted to the commander in chief for conciliating and acquiring the services of the western Indians.[18]

The board met on January 8, 1813, and unanimously recommended Dickson to the position of agent for the Indians for the western nations retroactive to January 1, 1813.[19] On January 14, 1813, Robert Dickson received written notification from Prevost of his appointment. Prevost informed Dickson that the members of the board had "especial trust in your Zeal, loyalty and ability." Prevost set Dickson's salary at two hundred pounds per year, payable through the accounts of the Indian Department, and allocated an additional three hundred pounds for travel and expenses, to be paid out of the secret service fund. Prevost authorized that Dickson be reimbursed for the trade goods and supplies he had distributed to the Indians

> as compensation for the eminent services which he had rendered to His Majesty's government by his loyalty, zeal and exertions in bringing forward the Indians to aid in the capture of the post of Michilimackinac and that of Brigadier General Hull and his army at Detroit.[20]

The powers that came with the appointments of superintendent and agent were extensive. Dickson was given the authority to employ five officers and fifteen interpreters and to make requisitions for goods and provisions from the Indian Department storekeepers or other officers that he would consider "necessary to successfully carry out the Object." In all policies that he should invoke, Dickson was to

> endeavour to consolidate them [the tribes] to act together harmoni-ously, that you should restrain them by all the means in your power from acts of cruelty and inhumanity.

Finally, Dickson was to encourage the preservation of the British–Indian alliance against the common enemy. The extent of his authority was so great that it caused some jealousy within the Indian Department. There-fore, to make certain that Dickson would not have to contend with ob-structions caused by envy, he was given greater autonomy and instructed to report only to senior officers of the British army.[21]

In his letter of December 23 to the commander in chief, Dickson had made suggestions on the rituals that should be observed to retain the sup-port of the tribes. These suggestions had come from the many years of experience Dickson had accumulated in trading with the tribes of the west-ern Great Lakes and upper Mississippi. His own recommendations were now given back to him as orders. La Baye and Chicago were designated as the places of rendezvous for the Indians. Sir John Johnson, superintendent general of Indian affairs, approved the fabrication of a wampum belt and ordered six silk flags and five large medals as presents for the tribes Dick-son would gather in conference. As the means to put forward the belt as a symbol of unity and distribute the flags and medals, Dickson was provided with a policy speech and instructions to deliver it to tribes living west of Lake Huron.[22]

The speech provided to Dickson had been written by General Rotten-berg and Sir John Johnson. It exuded warmth and affection and traced the strong bonds of trust and friendship between the Indian people and the British crown since the promise made by Sir William Johnson at Niagara in 1764. At the Niagara Conference, Sir William had created a new covenant chain between Britain and the Indian nations of the western Great Lakes. Johnson promised the nations support and gifts "as long as the sun shone and the grass grew, and the British wore red coats." British Indian agents had recited these promises every year since 1764 during the annual gift-giving ceremonies.

In his speech, Dickson would address each tribe and harken back to this promise that the British "would never forsake or abandon" the western Indians. Since the promise had first been made, the king had kept his word by sending traders "amongst you with Cloathing, and with Arms and Ammunition" so that the young men could provide sustenance for all. They were then asked to compare the situation in their country now with what it had been fifteen winters ago, when "you then wanted for nothing—Your Country was full of Traders and Goods—You were happy." Now they were reduced to making use of bows and arrows to hunt deer because of "the wicked policy" of the Americans forcibly taking the land of the Indians and depriving them of goods and ammunition. The speech warned that the Americans wanted "to possess themselves of all the Indian land and to destroy one Nation after another until they got the whole country within the Rocky Mountains."[23]

As he began the speech, Dickson was to lay a belt of wampum before the chiefs and reference the belt given to them by Sir William Johnson, saying that the British king had never lost his hold on the belt. Addressing the chiefs, the call would then be made:

> My Children, with this Belt I call upon you to rouse up your young Warriors, and to Join my Troops with the red Coats, and your ancient Bretherin the Canadians, who are also my Children, in order to defend your and our Country, Your and our wives and Children from becoming Carriers of Water to these faithless people . . . our common enemy.

The speech concluded with the gifts of a flag and medal to demonstrate the renewal of the alliance between the tribes and the king's white children. The gifts were to be preserved by the Indian nation forever:

> By looking at this Flag you will remember it came from your English Father, and when any of my Chiefs shall see it, they will be happy to take you by the hand and do you all the good they can.

As final proof of the regard in which the king held the Indians, Dickson would then read what Sir John Johnson had written:

> I have made your old friend the Red Head [Dickson] a Chief in order to carry to you my Speech, and have also given him a Flag as a pledge that I consider him as your Brother.[24]

In this ca. 1920 photograph, Chief Mike Flatte is wearing two British medals and holding a British "red ensign" that had been passed down for generations within the Grand Portage band of Ojibwe. The medals have been identified by scholar Carolyn Gilman as a 1778 medal used until the War of 1812; another dated 1814 given to allies of Great Britain in the War of 1812; and an 1853 Franklin Pierce medal. The flag was made after 1801 as the Union Jack includes the red cross of St. Patrick. Chief Flatte also wears a silver gorget and silver armbands.[25] PHOTOGRAPH BY GEORGE MILES RYAN, MINNESOTA HISTORICAL SOCIETY E97.1F 19234

The ritualized speech and gift giving followed a long-established diplomatic protocol that even the United States had begun to adopt when in council with a tribe. But unlike any US agent, Dickson could recite the long history of alliance between the British and the western tribes and the care the British had provided without requesting land in return. Most important, Dickson would bring to each council a symbol far greater than the medals and flags. On the wampum belt were symbols signifying the agreement between Great Britain and the western tribes. Beads of

In this undated photograph taken by Charles Van Schaick, a British flag flies from a Winnebago (Ho-Chunk) feast lodge. The flag was given to the tribe when they allied themselves with the British during the War of 1812. WHI IMAGE ID 63782

wampum made from white and purple mollusk shells are sacred to the Haudenosaunee (Iroquois). When their chief, Hiawatha, unified the nations into the Iroquois Confederacy, a belt of wampum was woven in a pattern to represent the agreement. In 1677, when the Iroquois formed an alliance with Great Britain, the British adopted the ceremony of presenting a belt of wampum to signify the importance of the agreement. At the Niagara Agreement of 1764, William Johnson had presented a belt to the western Indians, and in 1811, Tecumseh had produced a wampum belt to rejuvenate the alliance between the British and the Indians.

With the speech, the wampum belt, and the flags and medals in hand, Dickson left Montreal for the west. He stopped at Niagara and by mid-February was at Sandwich. He had not yet delivered the speech to any nation, as messengers had to be sent to all the bands of a tribe asking them to travel and assemble at a designated place. But the individual bands that Dickson had spoken with were greatly buoyed by learning of Britain's support. Also, the Indians were coming to Sandwich to join Colonel Proctor and the British troops in response to the victory at Frenchtown.[26] American forces had secured Frenchtown on the River Raisin after the loss of

Detroit. On January 23, 1813, British and Indians surprised the Americans. The result was one of the bloodiest battles of the war, and General Harrison was forced to cancel a winter campaign to retake Detroit.

Arriving at St. Joseph, Dickson found a letter waiting for him. Concerned with the actions of some of the Indians who had massacred wounded American prisoners after the battle at Frenchtown in which the Americans suffered great losses, the command at Montreal instructed Dickson to take measures to forestall such happenings in the future. Dickson responded that he would "use my utmost endeavours to restrain the Indians, from committing any insults on their Enemies who may fall into their hands." Dickson then spoke to the Potawatomi, who were then planning on joining the Shawnee, Kickapoo, and Delaware and would leave shortly for Detroit. Dickson reported that he would leave St. Joseph the following day to travel to Chicago and Milwaukee. He hoped to reach the Mississippi by the beginning of April.[27]

—||—

As Dickson journeyed the frozen waterway from Montreal to Niagara, some unsettling letters arrived at Prairie du Chien. Though Nicolas Boilvin had been forced to remain in St. Louis, he was still attempting to maintain the United States' hold on Prairie du Chien and the Indian residents of the upper Mississippi valley. Joseph Roc, an interpreter in the employ of the US Indian Department, had remained at the prairie as an American subagent, and he kept Boilvin informed of happenings on the upper Mississippi the best he could. In early 1813, Boilvin accompanied some Sioux and Fox who were returning home from their trip to Washington. Boilvin went as far as Fort Madison where he met with other Fox and Sac warriors. The Sioux planned to continue northward, but before they left, Boilvin gave Red Wing letters that he had written to Michel Brisbois, one of the most influential residents on the prairie, Francois Bouthellier, a fur trader who operated the South West Fur Company store, and Henry Munro Fisher. Red Wing was to give the letters to Jean Baptiste Faribault, and Faribault would distribute them to the recipients. From his experience while living at Prairie du Chien, Boilvin must have assumed that these men were loyal to the United States. In the letters, Boilvin invited the residents of the prairie to join with the Americans in the fight against Great Britain. Included with the letters was the text of a talk that Boilvin had written, which was to be presented to the various Indian nations.[28]

Boilvin's attempt to rally Prairie du Chien to the American side backfired spectacularly. Either Faribault or one of the recipients of the letters shared Boilvin's correspondence with several British-leaning residents of Prairie du Chien. The letters caused a great "unease" among the traders and inhabitants of the prairie, and they showed them to Lieutenant Duncan Graham of the Indian Department, the ranking British authority at Prairie du Chien when the letters arrived. At their request, Graham brought the letters to Joseph Rolette, who was at his place of trade fifty leagues north on the upper Mississippi. Rolette immediately left his place of trade, even though it was "when the Indians were coming out of the lands with their credits at the critical time that Traders depend for their returns." He arrived at Prairie du Chien. Outraged at the contents of the letters and the tenor of the talk to be read before representatives of the Indian nations, copies were made of each communication. One set of copies was sent by an express runner to the St. Peter's River "to raise all the nations to go to war" against the Americans in the Illinois district and Boilvin in particular. Another set of copies was given to Lieutenant Graham, who volunteered to take the letters to Mackinac Island, Rolette advancing the expenses for the trip and giving Graham letters of credit. With the copies, Graham was given a letter from the traders and other residents of Prairie du Chien, asking that Roberts send a military force and supplies to the prairie. Graham then left for Michilimackinac. The Menominee were so upset about the contents of the talk that they destroyed the personal property that Boilvin had left in his home and killed his cattle.[29]

During the absence of Robert Dickson, Captain Roberts at Michilimackinac had asked to be informed of any occurrence at Prairie du Chien that would be of importance to the British government. The traders at Prairie du Chien considered the letters and talk to be of such importance. In their correspondence with Roberts, the traders told Roberts that Boilvin's letters pointed out the intentions of the Americans, and that the chiefs returning from Washington reinforced what Boilvin had written. The chiefs and warriors held a conference at Prairie du Chien with the traders. With

La Feuille as their spokesman, they stated that although they had received many presents while in Washington, they had not faltered in their allegiance to the British.

To those who read them, Boilvin's letters may have suggested that the Americans were planning to come up the Mississippi and attack Prairie du Chien in the near future. Now, directly counter to Boilvin's intentions, all the Indians agreed to join together and prevent the US forces from coming to the prairie. The traders' letter informed Roberts that there were about five thousand Indian men in the region and about two hundred residents on the prairie. These, they assumed, the British did not want "to perish." Therefore, the traders asked Roberts for assistance. In the meantime, they questioned whether they might have the authority to take the powder held by the merchants in order to defend themselves. If he did not grant their request, they argued, "the Indians will be obliged to throw themselves at the feet of those people they detest so much." If the Indians were forced to subject themselves to the Americans for want of powder and other necessities, "[t]hen the *English influence* adieu! among the nations of the Mississippi" (original emphasis). The fourteen men who signed the letter concluded by assuring Roberts of their devotion to the British cause. Among the signees were the men to whom Boilvin had written his letters—Michel Brisbois, Henry Munro Fisher, Francois Bouthellier—and Jean Baptiste Faribault.[30]

Included with the traders' letter was a short statement from La Feuille, in which he informed Roberts that the Sac, Outagamie, and Winnebago were all of one heart. But they needed assurances of aid.

> As a cloud is approaching over the heads of thy Children whom thou hast put under my care, and that the Americans mean to take possession of this piece of land. I would wish it clear, but I want help—Come and assist me as soon as possible.[31]

La Feuille's words demonstrate what the Indian nations most feared: loss of their lands. That fear was what drove La Feuille and the tribes to ally themselves with the British. La Feuille had surrendered his British medal and flag to Pike, but now he realized where the threat to his people and land lay.

On his way to Michilimackinac, Lieutenant Graham stopped at La Baye. He informed the residents of his mission and what had occurred at Prairie du Chien. He must have shared the request for British aid, for the main traders at La Baye wrote a letter joining their "friends at La Prairie" in a request for assistance. The men at La Baye chastised their "Government" for asking the Indian nations to help in the war and then refusing to furnish them with the necessary quantity of powder. In a similar argument to the one made by the Prairie du Chien traders, they wrote, "May this want of Energy not put them under the necessity of turning those arms that are disposed to serve us, against us." The men estimated that thirty barrels, or fifteen hundred pounds, of powder would be sufficient, as five hundred pounds of powder were already at Prairie du Chien and two hundred pounds were at La Baye. With this total amount "the Indians will be in a situation to oppose the Americans," until the spring when the rivers opened and more supplies could reach the prairie.[32]

Joseph Roc, the person Boilvin had asked to remain at Prairie du Chien as his representative, wrote to Boilvin in March telling him of the adverse reaction to his letters. He concluded his report with dire words:

> In short, Sir, I must tell you every thing is against you Americans[.] [A]ll nations in general have given their word to the English. The traders together are setting them on against you all.

Roc had assessed the situation on the upper Mississippi and now determined where his own loyalty lay. On the tenth of February Roc had taken the oath of abjuration against the American government. He then accepted employment in the British Indian Department.[33]

As Lieutenant Graham began the trek to Michilimackinac, Boilvin attempted once more to counteract the influence of the British among the tribes. He had become aware of Dickson calling the Indian nations to a council at Chicago. Maurice Blondeau, subagent to the Sac, had seen the runners Dickson had sent to the upper Mississippi. Carrying a wampum belt and a pipe with a red handle for each nation, the runners had announced the war against the Americans and invited all to gather at Chicago where they would be given arms, ammunition, and presents. According to Blondeau, Dickson then planned to use Prairie du Chien and a point on the Illinois River as gathering places for an attack on St. Louis. To verify what Blondeau had reported, Boilvin sent spies, including Augustin Ange, an interpreter with the Indian agency, "in all directions as far as Chicago." He sent Blondeau to Prairie du Chien and on to La Baye. If he found the threat of attack to be true, Boilvin planned to post guards along the frontier "against the fury of the barbarians who trouble us." Boilvin cautioned Secretary of War Eustis that the recent murder and scalping of a young Sac by a US Ranger could "change the disposition of the Indians," especially since the commandant at Fort Mason had not shown respect and given the Sac chief presents to take back to the relatives of the dead man. Boilvin, therefore, had sent presents with Blondeau that he would give to the Sac when he met in council with them. While many of the Sac refused to join the British, Boilvin communicated that "Eight Sac Lodges had abandoned their nation for the council of the English." Trying to maintain the loyalty of the Sac to the Americans was a problem with which Boilvin constantly dealt.[34]

Boilvin kept Secretary Eustis and William Clark informed of his actions. But apparently what he was doing was doing too much, for Frederick Bates, secretary of Louisiana Territory, wrote to General Howard on February 27 expressing displeasure. "Mr. Boilvin does not conduct himself as I could wish. So far in acting in concert he adventures into the most delicate and important matters without my knowledge."[35] But nothing, least of all political considerations and advancement, would deter Boilvin. He felt he had a duty to the Sac and Fox and bluntly wrote Secretary Eustis,

> For me, I hope for no better appointment; my duty is to the Mississippi where I would sacrifice all I hold most dear to put the Indians on the right path or I would sacrifice my life for all to be destroyed if the government gives me power, sir. The commercial interests of this country are bringing about our ruin and destroying the government.[36]

# 7

## DICKSON UNITES THE TRIBES

### 1813–1814

As Nicolas Boilvin was sending spies into the country, Robert Dickson left St. Joseph Island in a sloop for Chicago. He sailed as far as Milwaukee, but the frozen waters of Lake Michigan prevented him from going farther. He finally reached Chicago in mid-March. In the meantime, men from La Baye and Prairie du Chien were rallying the Indians for what the Americans in Illinois and St. Louis feared would be an attack on their settlements.

Maurice Blondeau reported that a party of Englishmen had traveled on the ice from La Baye, one of whom was John Lawe. They had arrived at Prairie du Chien, and Lawe had successfully gathered "a great number of Indians of various nations" to join the British forces in defense of Detroit. Major Nicolas Jarrot had learned that several Prairie du Chien residents, namely James Aird, Joseph Rolette, John Anderson, Jean Baptiste Bertholet, and Joseph Renville, were also actively recruiting among the tribes and named them British agents.[1]

The runners Dickson had sent out among the tribes of the Mississippi, carrying a belt of wampum and a pipe with a red handle for each nation, had reached Chicago, bringing with them a good number of chiefs and warriors. Dickson met with them in a long-anticipated council and reported that the tribes on the Wabash River were all "on their march for Detroit." Soon, Dickson promised, he would be sending others. Upon completing his report, he continued to the Mississippi. Dickson left Chicago on the twenty-second of March heading westward along the Rock River. As he journeyed, Dickson met Potawatomi, Kickapoo, Ottawa, and Winnebago. To each group Dickson gave guns, ammunition, and supplies.[2]

Black Sparrow Hawk, the leader of the eight Sac lodges that Blondeau had reported had "abandoned their nation for the council of the English," came upon Dickson's encampment as he journeyed to the Mississippi River. In hopes of bringing the great chief to his side, Dickson explained to Black Hawk, "Your English father has found out that the Americans want to take your country from you." Dickson and the other Indians had been sent to drive the Americans back "to their own country," and, to that end, Dickson had great quantities of arms and ammunition. Speaking for himself and Britain, he said, "[W]e want all your warriors to join us." In his memoirs, Black Hawk remembered:

> He then placed a medal around my neck, and gave me a piece of paper, (which I lost in the late war,) and a silk flag, saying—"You are to command all the braves that will leave here the day after to-morrow, to join our braves in Detroit.

Black Hawk explained that he preferred to descend the Mississippi and attack the settlements that now existed on Sac lands. Keeping in mind the promise he had made to keep Britain's Indian allies from engaging in wanton killing, Dickson explained that he had been a trader for many years on the Mississippi. He had always been treated kindly and would not consent to send men to kill women and children. There were soldiers where he was sending Black Hawk and the others. These were the people to defeat, because if they did so, "the Mississippi country should be ours!" Black Hawk understood the message. The next day guns, ammunition, other arms, and clothing were given to Black Hawk's band. After a night of feasting, Black Hawk left with about five hundred warriors to join British forces at Fort Wayne. Beginning with this association with the British in the spring of 1813, Black Hawk and his followers, who would continue to reject the treaty the Sac had signed with William Henry Harrison, would eventually be known as "the British Band."[3]

From this meeting, Dickson continued to the Rock River. There, in early April, he met with the Fox bands that lived around Prairie du Chien.

Black Hawk was the leader of a band of Sac (Sauk) that opposed American expansion.
He refused to acknowledge the legitimacy of the 1804 treaty in which the Sac lost their
land east of the Mississippi River, and allied with the British during the War of 1812.
Black Hawk refused to participate in the 1815 treaty of Portage des Sioux from which he
and his followers came to be called the "British band." WHI IMAGE ID 25690

They had broken with the Fox who lived along the Des Moines River. The
Fox from Prairie du Chien met in council with Dickson. He once again presented the wampum belt and told them not to listen to the rumors about
the Americans coming up the Mississippi River. He explained that the US
forces were too busy attempting to retake Detroit to consider Prairie du
Chien. For that reason, Dickson wished the Fox to send fifty warriors to
join the British at Detroit.

Three agents of the British Indian Department, Michel Brisbois Jr.,
Dominique Perrin, and James Fraser, had arrived at the gathering with
powder, strouds, and liquor. These were given to the Fox and the band of
Sac led by Black Hawk, with some of the powder reserved for the Sioux.
La Feuille had sent a representative from the Sioux to the gathering. La
Feuille had given the man two belts of wampum, two silver breastplates,

and one medal. In a message delivered by the young man, La Feuille said the presents had been sent by their English father, "who invites you to join him at Detroit, & the rest of your Nation to go and join the Northern Indians at Prairie du Chien." Heeding the request, La Feuille had sent warriors to join Dickson and the other tribes.[4]

From the Rock River, Dickson turned northward to Prairie du Chien. Having heeded the insistence of the residents of Prairie du Chien and La Baye and fearing the possibility that the Americans were launching a force of two thousand to "impede the progress of Dickson," Sir George Prevost had authorized reinforcements to be sent to Michilimackinac and provisions to La Baye for the supply of the Indians. Organized by William McKay, large North West canoes carrying armed men from the Corps of Voyageurs transported the goods and served as reinforcements for the island. Once the stores and provisions had arrived at Michilimackinac, Roberts had sent several boats manned by Canadians to La Baye. Within the supplies had been the powder, strouds, and goods Dickson and his agents distributed to the Fox, Sac, and other tribes who had met with Dickson. The remainder of the powder and provisions awaited Dickson at Prairie du Chien.[5]

Dickson arrived at the prairie on April 17. Along the way, Captain Hamilton of the Upper Canada Militia had joined him. Together, they held councils with the Indians at Prairie du Chien. Dickson also gathered with his friends living at the prairie. In the course of their conversations, Michel Brisbois cautioned Dickson several times "to be on his guard." Francis Michael Dease, a fur trader who often assisted Dickson, warned Dickson that the "Country is in a state of confusion." After the incident of the letters from Boilvin and rumors of possible movement by American troops up the Mississippi, Dickson realized Prairie du Chien needed some form of defense and appointed Dease captain of militia. Feeling he also needed a representative in the community when he was absent, Dickson ordered Dease to act as his agent among the Indians.[6]

Despite their success in allying Indian tribes, the uncertainty of the war and the loyalty of residents and Indians caused tensions among the men at the prairie, especially those charged with responsibilities by the British government. One evening while sharing a drink in Michel Brisbois's home, Captain Hamilton and Joseph Rolette began to discuss the history of the conflict between the United States and Great Britain. Rolette made a flippant analogy comparing the United States to a youth who had matured. Hamilton took the remark to be "seditious" and lodged a charge against Rolette. As the senior British official, Dickson instituted a court of inquiry and appointed officers of the British Indian Department, including Lieutenant James Fraser and Lieutenant John Lawe, to hear the testimony. The court assembled in the house of one St. John. After hearing testimony from Hamilton and Rolette, they determined Rolette's words were not well chosen but not "seditious." Rolette promised to "be more cautious in the future." The written complaint was then burned.[7]

The Indians on the prairie also were uneasy. Preparing to leave, Dickson was standing on the shore between his home and Nicolas Boilvin's when he learned that a Sioux warrior had killed a calf belonging to Rolette. When Rolette heard this, he ran past Dickson to his backyard threatening to kill the man. Dickson yelled to Rolette to stop, saying he would pay for the calf "sooner that any disturbance should take place amongst the Indians." Ignoring Dickson, Rolette ran on. Only quick action on the part of Duncan Graham stopped him from attacking the Sioux warrior. Rolette later said that his "passion had prevented him" from hearing Dickson. This would not be the last time Rolette's temper got him in trouble.[8]

Hoping he had established some order and authority at Prairie du Chien, Dickson canoed up the Mississippi to La Feuille's village. There, he addressed the principal chiefs of the Dakota, asking for a reaffirmation of the long-standing ties between the Dakota and the British. As spokesman for all the branches of the Dakota, La Feuille responded. He began by stating that there was no reason for his people to renounce the British as the British had kept all the promises they had made to the Dakota. The matter of the present conflict between the British and the Americans had been discussed by the assembled chiefs and warriors, and, the chiefs concurred,

> from the last band of our nation to the west, we hold each others hands. . . . [W]e rejoice again in hearing the voice of our English Father who has never deceived us, and we are certain never will.[9]

According to Dakota tradition, the people called the War of 1812 *Pahin-shashawacikiya*. This translates to "When the Redhead Begged for Our

Help."[10] The "redhead" was none other than Robert Dickson, whose flaming hair was well known among the Sioux.

—⊩—

For months, General Proctor, stationed at Sandwich, had been inquiring as to where Dickson might be. The general greatly needed the Indians Dickson had promised. Pierre de Boucherville, aide-de-camp to Sir George Prevost, wondered whether the people in whom Dickson placed his confidence had betrayed him and whether the supplies Roberts had sent from Michilimackinac had ever reached Dickson. Finally, on June 10 Dickson arrived at Michilimackinac. With him were upwards of six hundred warriors from the western Indians. He listed them as

|     |     |
| ---:| --- |
| 116 | Chippeways |
| 220 | Menominies |
| 42 | Ottawas |
| 97 | Sioux |
| 18 | Foxes or Renards |
| 130 | Winnebagoes or Puants |
| Total 623 | |

He reported that he had sent eight hundred more warriors by land to Detroit. By June 23, Dickson and his "Indian Warriors" had embarked for Detroit.[11]

Dickson had been forced to delay his departure for want of supplies to feed the Indians on their journey. Once again, Dickson had had to requisition stores from the Indian Department store and the traders at Michilimackinac. Madeline Askin, wife of the storekeeper John Askin Jr., was glad to see Dickson and his Indian force leave. Her husband had been "plagued with Indians, the house never empty of them from morning to night." They had killed six or seven cattle and several sheep, which was a great loss as cattle could be sold for forty dollars on the island. In a letter to her mother, she explained the enormous expense and logistics in supplying the Indians who fought for the British. In three to four days, the six hundred warriors had eaten three hundred bags of flour. They additionally consumed five hundred *minots*, or bushels, of corn a day, plus pork grease, beef, fish, and sugar. Her husband's store was now empty and much of the merchandise had been sold. All the guns in the village, old and new, had been requisitioned.[12]

Much to Proctor's relief, Dickson and the warriors arrived at Sandwich in mid-July. The eight hundred Indians whom Dickson had sent directly from the Mississippi and Rock Rivers and were already at Sandwich had proved to be a challenge to Proctor; there were more in camp than he could feed, as many had brought their families with them. Lacking the supplies to adequately provide for such a great number, Proctor reported that if they had not been "very warm in the cause," they would have deserted him. Writing to Prevost, Proctor admitted that the "Indian Force should not remain unemployed." He therefore decided that though the size of his army was smaller than desired, the force that he had under his command could no longer wait for the Canadian militia. He needed the militia for the success of any maneuver, but the men, per the agreement at their enlistment, had returned home to harvest their crops. By early August, Proctor decided the force, including the Indians under his and Dickson's commands, must advance "where we might be fed at the expense of the Enemy." But the number of Indians in camp was not easily organized to begin movement. Proctor commended Dickson's ability to control his contingent of Indians, who "were restrainable, and tractable." But even Dickson's influence couldn't keep them in check. Proctor reported that they were soon "contaminated" by the Indians already in camp.[13]

In mid-July, Dickson and the western Indians moved with Proctor's troops in a second effort to capture Fort Meigs, built above the rapids of the Maumee River. The British force attempted to draw the Americans out of the fort by staging a mock battle. The subterfuge did not work and a strong thunderstorm compelled the British and Indians to withdraw. Proctor then ordered his troops to move on to capture an American supply base on the Sandusky River guarded by Fort Stephenson. Disgusted with the lack of victory and spoils of war, when the Sioux with Dickson heard Proctor's order, they turned to Itassipah, whom La Feuille had designated his representative. Itassipah refused to go. Dickson sent Lieutenant Fraser and Lieutenant Colin Campbell after him, and Itassipah again refused to enter the canoe. As a result, most Sioux left to return home. Of the Sioux, only the Dakota chief Petit Corbeau and sixteen of his young men remained with Dickson.[14]

Black Hawk and his band continued toward the Sandusky with Dickson. Black Hawk recalled how Proctor gave Dickson a flag to carry as the British and their allies gathered before Fort Stephenson. Dickson told Black Hawk, "You will see, to-morrow, how easily we will take the fort." Black Hawk believed Dickson, but when the British began making preparations to retreat in the face of the strong defense by the Americans, Black Hawk became "disappointed." Black Hawk "was now tired of being with them— our success being bad, and having got no plunder." He decided to leave the British and return to the Rock River to see his wife and children. In the evening, Black Hawk and about twenty of his warriors quietly walked away and began their journey home.[15]

Soon after losing the faith of the Indians, Dickson also left Proctor. At the end of August, orders were written in Montreal that Dickson "should be sent forthwith to Michilimackinac," as he needed to fulfill other responsibilities as agent to the western Indians. The canoes containing the supplies the Indians required for the upcoming winter were about to leave Montreal. Dickson needed to be on hand to sort the goods "in order to avoid collision and partialities." The goods, together with the presents from the British government, needed to be delivered to Dickson at Michilimackinac where they would be distributed to the tribes. Keeping promises made to the Indians was of utmost importance in retaining their alliances, which became all the more pressing as the war continued. Indeed, the British government acknowledged that all had not gone as they had hoped at Detroit. As a result, some of the tribes had become disgruntled and others were starting to contemplate changing their allegiance to the United States. Therefore, it was essential that Dickson be the person to distribute the presents and supplies. Dickson had been "the ostensible organ of Government, in any promises made to them" and "must necessarily be the fittest agent for fulfilling those promises." The British command at Montreal realized "a much stronger impression should be made upon these Nations, than if the same articles were distributed by other hands."[16]

On the last day of August 1813, the same day these orders were being penned in Montreal, Dickson wrote from Sandwich to John Lawe in La Baye. He requested that once Louis Grignon arrived with powder for the Indians, Lawe was to proceed to Prairie du Chien to "get intelligence of what is doing in the Mississippi." If the Americans were advancing up the river, Lawe was to do all he could to encourage the Indians to drive them back down the river. Dickson then departed to intercept the supplies, as they were to leave Montreal on September 11. Sheaffe strongly hoped that Dickson would be at Michilimackinac when the goods arrived. If he could not be there, Sheaffe recommended that Captain William McKay be sent in his stead.[17]

—||—

Anticipating the arrival of the presents and supplies, the Sioux and Menominee came to Michilimackinac in early September. Lieutenant Louis Grignon had been at Michilimackinac and there received Dickson's orders, which, he replied, he would "execute to the best of my ability." The Indian supplies had not arrived, however, and the Sioux had become demanding. Grignon was keeping the Sioux quiet with help from others at Michilimackinac. The most discontented was the son of Red Wing, who was advocating attacking the Chippewa. A talk by Petit Corbeau calmed the Sioux for a while, but Captain Richard Bullock, who had just arrived as the new commandant at Fort Mackinac, decided to take action. The Sioux had complained that the winter season was coming and they had to return home in order to hunt. They had the farthest to travel, so they issued an ultimatum. The Sioux "fixed a date for their departure" if the presents and supplies did not arrive at Michilimackinac.[18]

Bullock knew that to retain the service and friendship of the Sioux, he had to give them supplies. To that end, he borrowed from the merchants "a sufficiency of goods" for the Sioux. The merchants would be reimbursed once the Indian goods arrived from Montreal. Grignon was to be given arms and gunpowder for the Mississippi, but Bullock could give him only the powder, as there were no arms in the Indian store or with the merchants. Satisfied, the Sioux and Menominee left for their homes on September 19, and Grignon departed for the Mississippi on October 5 with just gunpowder. He had left the gunpowder intended for the Chippewa and Ottawa with Mr. Cass. He believed the powder would suffice for the time being as Bullock had ascertained that there was no immediate threat of the Americans ascending the Mississippi.[19]

But that was the only good news at Michilimackinac, for there was only a month of provisions left at the post, and no public money either. Bullock requested that both be sent immediately before the close of navigation on the lakes. Finally, the company of Michigan Fencibles—units composed of civilian volunteers—was "in a deplorable state for want of clothing." These were Canadians who had been in the employment of the traders. Bullock found them to be good men and well disposed, but to be of any service to the British, they too required supplies.[20]

At the end of September, Dickson intercepted the Indian presents and supplies at York. Since he had left Sandwich, the American squadron on Lake Erie, commanded by Oliver Hazard Perry, had engaged a British squadron commanded by Robert Barclay off the shore of Put-in-Bay. At the end of a daylong battle on September 10, the British surrendered to Perry. With his ships and those he had captured, Perry ferried twenty-five hundred American soldiers to Amherstburg, which was captured by the Americans without opposition on September 27. At the same time, mounted American troops moved by land to Detroit, which was recaptured on October 9 without fighting. As Dickson was organizing the Indian supplies for transportation to Lake Huron, General Proctor and his force were in a retreat up the River Thames. Lacking supplies, Tecumseh, who had urged Proctor to fight, had no option but to accompany Proctor with his confederation of tribes. Unaware of but anticipating the defeat of the British fleet on Lake Erie, Dickson had planned, with the assistance of Duncan Cameron, to move the goods overland to the Bay of Matchedash in Lake Huron.[21]

Amherstburg had been the post from which Fort St. Joseph and Michilimackinac had been supplied. Now the two islands were cut off and unsure if or when supplies would arrive. The schooner *Nancy*, originally built at Detroit for the North West Company, had been pressed into service by the British government as a supply ship. Before the Americans had captured Amherstburg, Proctor had loaded the schooner with gunpowder and ordnance stores. After the battle between the American and British squadrons, the *Nancy* was the only British ship left on the upper Great

Lakes. On the way to Michilimackinac, the *Nancy* had been attacked but escaped capture. The commander learned that she was so badly damaged that she was "unfit for the Lake" and went to Sault Ste. Marie for the winter to be repaired. Bullock therefore sent men to every settlement in the area to acquire meat, fish, and flour.[22]

Bad weather had delayed Dickson's arrival at Michilimackinac, but when he disembarked on October 22, Dickson happily discovered that William McKay had journeyed safely with the goods and had already sorted them in preparation for Dickson—any delay "would be very injurous" to the tribes. Dickson found the selection of Indian goods sent by William McGillivray, a Montreal merchant, to be excellent and felt all should "adequately support the Indians for the Winter." Included in his plans was yet another trip to the Mississippi.[23]

Before Dickson left for the interior, he and Captain Bullock consulted on the defense of Michilimackinac. After the Americans secured Lake Erie and General Proctor was defeated at the battle on the Thames, where Tecumseh also perished, there existed the possibility that the Americans might attempt to retake the island. Dickson and Bullock hoped that any

After Tecumseh was killed at the Battle of the Thames, a deputation of Indians was sent to Montreal to meet with Sir George Prevost with the intent of naming Tecumseh's successor. MISSOURI HISTORY MUSEUM, ST. LOUIS

action would not occur before the lakes froze, closing navigation. If they had the winter to prepare, they were certain that the British could "baffle any attempt of the Enemy for the next season." Dickson assured Noah Freer, Proctor's military secretary, that Captain McKay and Lewis Crawford, since they knew the country, could secure anything necessary for the supply and defense of the island. To further secure the region, Bullock detached a squad of Michigan Fencibles to be stationed at La Baye.[24]

At the end of October, Dickson left Michilimackinac with a flotilla of six boats on which were the detachment of Michigan Fencibles, Lieutenant James Pullman, Sergeant McGilpin, and twenty-six rank and file. Pullman was the officer in charge of the La Baye garrison. The Fencibles were to remain at La Baye for the winter while Dickson traveled farther up the Fox River to Garlic Island in Lake Winnebago. From there, he would conduct the business of the Indian Department until the lake and rivers were navigable.[25]

Louis Grignon and John Lawe had been appointed lieutenants in the British Indian Department, and Dickson sent written orders and corresponded with them throughout the winter months of 1813 to 1814. In his first order to Grignon and Lawe, Dickson explained that he had been ordered by Captain Bullock to procure beef, flour, and pease from the residents of La Baye for the garrison stationed in the community. Only a short time before, some farmers at La Baye began to see a profit to be made in this arrangement. Dickson had requested fifty bushels of wheat and a pair of oxen from Dominique Brunette Sr., telling Lawe "there must be no toll at the mill." But when approached, Brunette asked an outrageous price for a pair of oxen. His mode of selling wheat was "quite new & he deserves credit for his ingenuity." Dickson commented, "His offer is like selling a loaf of Bread reserving all the Crust & as much of the Crumb as he chooses to take." He told Lawe that if Brunette would sell his wheat for three dollars a bushel, Lawe should buy it; otherwise, "we shall keep our Eye on it when Hunger will make us keen." When Dickson learned that the mill was nearly stopped, he told Lawe to give the soldiers wheat and have them grind it with a hand mill.[26]

Before winter set in, Dickson visited many of the tribes. By mid-December, he had visited "all the Indians of the Rock River & a good number from the Ouisconsin." He learned that all was quiet at Prairie du Chien, but sent sixteen men to the Mississippi River, with Duncan Graham to follow, just to ensure all was well. Upon his return to his camp at Lake Winnebago, some Chippewa from the la Court Oreilles band visited Dickson, as did a number of Winnebago.[27]

Dickson was also responsible for sending supplies to Michilimackinac. Bullock had scoured enough to maintain the garrison until February, but they would be out of provisions before the lakes opened. Working with the Indians and others, Dickson filled several small boats with food. In November, he engaged Jean Vieux to bring the boats to La Baye and then on to Michilimackinac. Dickson warned Lawe to watch the Fencibles "as some of them are great thieves and have threatened to kill animals at La Baye."[28]

By the end of December, Dickson felt that most of his time was consumed sending people about the country to locate food and feeding the Indians who came to him. Writing Lawe, he said:

> I am most heartily tired of this distributing Goods and wish for the
> Spring. I hear nothing but the cry of hunger from all Quarters. I think
> if we come across an American Convoy of provisions, it will go hard
> but we shall take it.

Lawe was the keeper of the stores and what provisions there might be, so Dickson regularly wrote to him as to what goods were to be given to the emissaries he sent to the various tribes, but it was never enough. Dickson commented in a letter dated Christmas Day, 1813, "It would require a Ship load of Goods to cloathe them all."[29]

Dickson also had good news to impart to Lawe. He had received letters from Prairie du Chien. From them, he had learned that all was quiet. He speculated that Louis Honore had visited the Sac and convinced them to return to the British. When he went to La Baye to celebrate the New Year with Jacob Franks, John Lawe, and their families, Dickson further learned that Grignon had been to Prairie du Chien. Grignon shared the news that General Benjamin Howard had planned to attack the prairie, but had progressed only as far as the Des Moines River, building a fort some miles in from the river's mouth.[30]

—⊩—

Throughout January and February of 1814, Dickson, wintering at Lake Winnebago, had to contend with a lack of provisions and Indians coming to him in various states of hunger. He repeatedly asked Lieutenant John Lawe for provisions, sending trade goods as payment. From Garlic Island, Dickson maintained a concern about activities along the Mississippi and at Prairie du Chien. At the end of January, he received a packet of letters from the prairie detailing the "roguish tricks" he had long expected. These included correspondence from James Aird and Francis Michael Dease, both Indian agents for Britain under Dickson, and a report from Louis Barthe, an Indian Department interpreter. The Sioux, under the instigation of Red Wing, had attacked and killed some Chippewa along the Mississippi. Dickson felt that Red Wing had done this to prevent any Sioux coming to visit Dickson. There had also been problems between the Sac and Fox and the Winnebago, which Dickson now learned had happened because Dease had not followed his orders. The people of the prairie did not like the Winnebago. While Dickson agreed with this opinion, the residents of Prairie du Chien needed to remember "that if the Americans are not with them the obligation is due to the Puants." Dickson also questioned Joseph Rolette's patriotism, as he was selling flour at the outrageous price of ten dollars per thousand weight. By spring, Dickson speculated Rolette would have raised the flour to fifteen dollars. Dickson concluded, "If God spares my life until Spring I shall do my duty rigidly without respect to persons."[31]

But more "roguish tricks" were afoot on the upper Mississippi River. Nicolas Boilvin had pressed for an American force to ascend the Mississippi to Prairie du Chien. When this did not happen, he had written to the secretary of war that he had had a communication from the Sioux, Menominee, Chippewa, Ottawa, and Fox of Prairie du Chien. The request had come to him through Michel Brisbois. The tribes had asked that Boilvin comply with their desire to have him retake possession of Prairie du Chien and bring American traders with him. The arrival of Boilvin and the traders would be well received not only by the nations but also by the English residents of the prairie. To ascertain whether their request was viable and also to investigate the situation at the prairie, Boilvin told the secretary he planned to send two spies to Prairie du Chien. Then in the spring, General Howard and Governor Clark could "take steps necessary." Several days later, Boilvin informed President Madison of his intentions.[32]

On or about December 11, 1813, Boilvin had dispatched Louis Ribeau and J. Demonchell from St. Louis to travel to Prairie du Chien by way of Peoria, each being paid one hundred dollars to compensate for the risk they were taking. The journey did not go as planned. Along the way, they were captured by Sac friendly to the British and taken as prisoners to Prairie du Chien. The men were found to be carrying letters from Nicolas Boilvin and Nicolas Jarrot addressed to the people of the prairie. The men and the letters were brought to Dickson, who interrogated them. They willingly told all they knew, and Dickson deemed them "decent men." Having read the letters, Dickson decried them as "flaming Epistles." In them, Boilvin and Jarrot "exhorted" the residents

> to claim the protection of the great republic before it is too late & a great deal of other stuff, but their main objective is to discover whether there is any risque in their ascending the Mississippi this Spring.

Dickson sent the prisoners to La Baye, telling Lawe that the men were to be given to the charge of Lieutenant Pullman. They were not to be treated inhumanely. Rather, Pullman was to give them the same provisions as the soldiers and allow the men freedom to walk about during the day. As Demonchell was not well, Dickson requested that he be given medicine.[33]

The rest of the winter passed with the constant concern of feeding the Indians. Dickson had had serious apprehensions about the loyalty of the Potawatomi, and in mid-February six Potawatomi arrived at his camp. Dickson suspected they were spies from the Americans or the advance party of a greater number. With a band of Menominee to support him, Dickson awaited the Potawatomi's intentions. He counseled Lawe to warn the people at La Baye to be on guard against an attack by the Milwaukee Indians, for he anticipated he would be attacked. The attack did not occur. Relieved, Dickson gave the men some clothing and told the party of six not to return. He then enumerated thirty-four remarks on the bad intentions of the Potawatomi and sent them to Lawe.[34]

While Dickson remained at Lake Winnebago attempting to keep the Potawatomi at bay, he questioned whether the Sac whom he had sent to Detroit would join the Sac of whom Keokuk was now chief and turn to the Americans at St. Louis for their needs. He had heard of Red Wing's duplicity, and without any news from the Mississippi did not know the tenor of the western tribes. Dickson need not have worried. In February, at the invitation of Lieutenant General Drummond, chiefs from several of the western nations, including the Chippewa, Ottawa, and Sac and Fox, visited Quebec and received a warm welcome from Sir George Prevost.[35]

Dickson was greatly relieved when the ice began to break up and the Indians were able to spear sturgeon. Soon, he hoped, supplies would be able to come from Michilimackinac. "I will eat Bull frogs before I buy any more bad Beef at 30s and I will starve or plunder rather than be imposed on in the price of Provisions," he wrote in March to John Lawe.[36]

By early April, the Fox River was open to Lake Winnebago, and Dickson soon departed for the portage to the Wisconsin River, arriving on the twenty-third. He met with the Winnebago in an effort to "bring them to their senses & hope to do as much to others where I go." From the portage he left for Prairie du Chien worried, as he had not heard from Duncan Graham since February. He arrived within a few days, and as he had in past summers, he met with several of the residents of the prairie to learn of activities on the Mississippi. In their discussions, Dease warned him that he had heard that some Indians had declared their intentions to kill Dickson. Dease warned Dickson that "it was very improper" for him to go out at night unarmed and without having other men accompany him. His old friend, Brisbois, repeated the warning from Dease that the Indians wanted to kill him.[37]

Dickson's stay at Prairie du Chien was not long, but in his few days on the prairie he prevailed upon the many tribes of the upper Mississippi to send warriors with him to Michilimackinac. Before leaving, he dispatched Sac and Fox warriors to Rock Island on the Mississippi River. They were to guard against a possible attack from the Americans to the south. With Dickson at Prairie du Chien were gathered about three hundred Indian allies, and the tribes had promised to send more. Sensing the resolute position of the British, La Feuille, who had not traveled with Dickson to join Proctor's army, made the journey with Dickson to Michilimackinac. Also accompanying their warriors were the Dakota chief Petit Corbeau, the Menominee chief Tomah, and the Winnebago chief Lassaminie.

The British had approved a plan in which every effort was "to be made for the preservation of Michilimackinac," in order "to maintain uninterrupted our intercourse with the Western Indians." A relief force, consisting of two companies of the Royal Newfoundland Fencibles, gunners of the Royal Artillery, and a detachment of Royal Navy, arrived on May 18. They brought with them abundant supplies. Leading the men was the new post commander and senior British officer in the Northwest, Lieutenant Colonel Robert McDouall.[38]

Lieutenant Colonel McDouall, Sir George Prevost, and His Majesty's government had determined that Michilimackinac was "the life and soul" of the Northwest. Due to its position, the island had influence that

> extends and is felt amongst the Indian tribes at New Orleans and the Pacific Ocean; vast tracts of country look to it for protection and supplies, and it gives security to the great establishments of the Northwest and Hudson Bay Companies by supporting the Indians on the Mississippi.[39]

Soon after the arrival of McDouall, with the lakes open, warriors began to arrive in great numbers at the island. As in the past, the Indians needed to be fed, and McDouall soon appealed to General Gordon Drummond, the new commander of Upper Canada, to send more supplies, as those he had brought would soon be depleted. When Dickson and his band reached the island, McDouall reported that his issue of food would be for about sixteen hundred people per day.[40]

To celebrate the birthday of King George, Dickson and McDouall held an impressive and formal council with the chiefs and warriors who had come to the island to support the British. The four chiefs who had accompanied Dickson addressed McDouall. La Feuille traced the continuity of relations with the British since his father's generation, announcing that he "took the same road as my deceased Father used to take to come here." La Feuille explained that he had not "lifted the Tomahawk" through laziness or fear but "because I want strength." The Sioux had suffered much

> since the Americans have adopted us for their children; but we have the good fortune to have the Red Head [Dickson] for a friend, who in spite of the barriers which the Americans made, always found passage to come & save the Indians from perishing.[41]

Petit Corbeau requested "big guns and brave warriors to our support." He assured McDouall "that I and my young warriors have devoted our bodies to our Father the Red Head." Tomah thanked McDouall for the goods that had saved the Menominee lives. Looking at the island, he saw a "fire whose assistance gives life to all the copper coloured skins, & particularly our nation who have so often had the happiness of seeing & approaching it."[42]

Finally, Lassaminie explained that "a thick cloud hovers near our Lands, every time it approaches we go to meet it, & have succeeded so far as to drive it farther from us; but we have lost many young warriors." He then asked for "forces to fight the Enemy, and be persuaded that the Tomahawk shall always be lifted up till the period arrives that you will grant peace to the Americans."[43]

McDouall responded in a long and eloquent speech, saying he was "proud to see such an assemblage of distinguished Chiefs & Warriors." He thanked them for their loyalty and "past services" and then recounted the British victories in the conflict. McDouall counseled the warriors not to listen to the "deceitful message" of the Americans. He promised to "make up as well as I can for the disappointment [over the lack of supplies the previous winter] and to give you proofs of my esteem, and of the confidence which I place in your valor and courage." He expressed his pleasure that they had "listened to the wise councils of your friend and chief the Red Head, whose constant study is for your advantage and to do you good." He finished with the wish that the Great Spirit might give them "strength and courage in so good a cause, and crown you with victory in the day of Battle."[44]

Several days later, Dickson commented on how pleased the Indians were by the manner in which McDouall had treated them. They were, however, disappointed that the Americans had not appeared as soon as they expected. They therefore were "much inclined to meet them halfway." Little did Dickson know when he wrote Secretary Freer on June 18 how soon they would be meeting the enemy, and it would not be "halfway."[45]

# 8

## WILLIAM CLARK'S EXPEDITION TO PRAIRIE DU CHIEN

*March–June 1814*

Zebulon Pike and Nicolas Boilvin had each recommended that a fort be constructed at Prairie du Chien to secure the upper Mississippi for the United States. The presence of an American fortification would diminish the influence of the British traders among the tribes and thereby shift the Indian trade to the United States. With Great Britain and the United States now at war, there rose a greater urgency for a permanent US installation at Prairie du Chien. In their correspondence, American officials expressed a fear that Robert Dickson would unite the tribes and, using Prairie du Chien as a base, attack American settlements in Illinois and Missouri. In March 1813 Ninian Edwards, governor of Illinois Territory, had expressed his fear that the British might construct a fort at the mouth of the Wisconsin River, just below Prairie du Chien. If they did so, he felt that in two years "this [Illinois] and Missouri Territory will be totally deserted—in other words conquered."[1] With the loss of Mackinac Island, abandonment of Fort Dearborn, and surrender of Detroit in the first months of the war, all the land west of Lake Huron had again come under British control. The Illinois Country was exposed, and Governor Edwards's concerns were all the more prescient.

Zebulon Pike may have thought that he had garnered the loyalty of the Sac and Fox, Winnebago, and Sioux with whom he had met on his expedition up the Mississippi, but five long years had passed since his journey. Alliances had been confirmed and broken, and hard winters had tested the Indians' trust in their American "father." Now that war had been declared, many of the tribes living in the Northwest Territory assessed their situation and chose for whom they would fight. La Feuille presented the best explanation of the Sioux loyalty to Britain: "We live by our English Traders who have always assisted us, [and] have always found our English Father the protector of our women and children."[2]

Benjamin Howard, governor of Missouri Territory (the former Louisiana Territory) since 1810, was convinced in the early months of the war that St. Louis and Missouri were in danger of "total overthrow" by Dickson and the British-allied Indians. Howard and William Clark began to discuss details for an offensive against the tribes of the upper Mississippi and western Great Lakes. In November 1812, Howard returned to his home in Kentucky, so Clark completed the military plan. He decided he would send an army into "Indian country" as far up the Mississippi as Prairie du Chien, which Howard had described as the "Metropolis of British traders." Two armed galleys allocated to the US Indian Department would support this army. To make the plan operational, Clark and Howard had requested four thousand troops be sent to St. Louis. To supply the anticipated army, Clark purchased five hundred barrels of salted pork.[3]

Howard had left St. Louis, and as it was December and no movement against Prairie du Chien could begin until spring when the Mississippi River opened, Clark headed east. He stopped first in Philadelphia to push the publication of his book on his explorations with Meriwether Lewis. Then he traveled to his family home in Virginia to be with his wife and children.

Howard had been governor of Missouri Territory since 1810, but once in Kentucky, he made it known that he now preferred a military command. William Clark was in position to take over as governor, while Howard assumed command of the Eighth Military District, which included the territories of Illinois and Missouri. A brigadier general, Howard was to be headquartered in St. Louis. Clark received the appointment of governor of Missouri Territory on June 16, 1813, from the new president, James Monroe, and his position as agent of Indian affairs west of the Mississippi became part of that office. Clark had control over all Indian affairs and direct command of the territorial militia.[4]

William Clark and Robert Dickson now held similar positions. Each was an Indian agent for their country responsible for the well-being of the tribes of the western Great Lakes and upper Mississippi. As Dickson made recommendations to ensure the loyalty and support of the western Indians to Britain, Clark began to implement his plan to take away the control Dickson and the British traders had over the Indians. Since 1810, Clark had also been recommending that the US Army establish a garrison at Prairie du Chien, and now Clark was in a position to direct the task himself.

While in the east, previous to his new appointment, Clark had been in Washington City to confer with the newly appointed secretary of war, John Armstrong, who directed the Indian agents. Clark had met with him to discuss his proposal to convert the keelboats owned by the Indian Department into gunboats, so he could use them to convey the army he had requested up the Mississippi River. Armstrong gave his support to Clark's plan. Returning to St. Louis in the summer of 1813, Clark started to execute the two-pronged plan that he had outlined to Armstrong. First, relations among the tribes living along the Missouri River who were friendly to America needed to be strengthened, especially with the Osage. Clark would make this a priority. Once he felt the lands west of the city were under control, he would launch the armed expedition up the Mississippi River that he and Howard had been discussing for two years.[5]

In July 1813, while Dickson was bringing the western Indians to Sandwich to rendezvous with General Proctor, Clark ordered the refitting of the keelboats to begin, insisting it occur along the St. Louis waterfront. He wanted the work to be done in a very visible manner in hopes that "the hostile Indians would hear of it, and magnify its size and importance."[6] Clark also sought to neutralize the Sac and Fox, as the loss of Fort Madison had heightened fears in St. Louis. Within the Sac nation there was a division; some bands were friendly to the United States, while other bands, like the one led by Black Hawk, were pro-British. Clark knew that the friendly bands would come to St. Louis to trade. When they arrived, he attempted to persuade them to relocate west of the Mississippi River. He wanted to place them on lands traditionally held by the Osage. The loss of Fort Madison, however, made Clark intensify his plans.[7]

In 1808, the United States had built Fort Madison on the west side of the Mississippi River on the Des Moines River several miles upstream from the river's mouth. More of a fortified fur factory, when war began the post was the northernmost US garrison on the upper Mississippi. Almost from its beginning, the fort was attacked by Sac and other tribes. An 1809 attempt to storm the fort was stopped only by the threat of cannon fire. Harassment continued, then escalated with the declaration of war. More

**Military Installations in the Upper Northwest Territory**

MAPPING SPECIALISTS, LTD., FITCHBURG, WI

than a year later, in July 1813, the British-allied Sac began another siege. With Indians surrounding the garrison, the soldiers could not venture outside the walls to collect their dead and wounded or gather firewood. The soldiers burned outbuildings so they would not fall into the hands of the Sac. Then in September, the army abandoned the post, burning it as they evacuated. Now only Fort Belle Fontaine, headquarters of the Department of Louisiana, a small post on the Missouri River north of St. Louis, stood between the Americans at St. Louis and the vast force of the western Indians whose alliance with the British Dickson had secured.

While Clark hoped to neutralize the Sac, General Howard attempted to defuse any threat by the Potawatomi. In a move to protect St. Louis and the lower Illinois settlements, Howard directed an expedition in September 1813 of approximately thirteen hundred regulars and rangers of the Missouri and Illinois militias. The men traveled up the Illinois River and attacked Potawatomi villages around Lake Pimiteoui. A French village had been located along the Illinois River at the present-day site of Peoria. The previous year, troops led by Governor Edwards had arrested the residents and destroyed the village. On the site of the settlement, the soldiers now built Fort Clark, named for George Rogers Clark. The militia pursued the Potawatomi up the Illinois and Spoon Rivers with no results and then returned home. The regulars from the First Infantry remained to garrison the post.[8]

Also in September, news of Oliver Hazard Perry's defeat of the British fleet on Lake Erie encouraged Clark as much as it had dismayed Dickson. Perry's victory was followed by the death of Tecumseh at the battle of the Thames in October and the subsequent surrender of his confederacy to William Henry Harrison. With this news Clark and others thought the war would soon end. Clark therefore turned his attention from preparation for the expedition to Prairie du Chien to the release of his two-volume *History of the Expedition under the Command of Captains Lewis and Clark* and to his family, who had come west to St. Louis with the end of the threat of attack by Tecumseh and his followers.

—⊩—

Over the winter months of 1813 to 1814, while Dickson struggled to meet the needs of the western Indians for food and supplies, the threat of war escalated once again. Clark learned of "depredations" by the Osage and unsettling movements by the Sac and Fox against American settlers west of St. Louis. Clark attributed the occurrences to Dickson's influence, though in reality the tribes were upset with American settlement on their lands. Dickson himself had escalated the tension, instructing an Indian Department officer "to get the Indians to drive them down again" if the Americans should venture up the Mississippi River toward Prairie du Chien. He also predicted that "St. Louis might be taken this spring with 500 or 600 men."[9]

Through Clark's correspondence, it can be seen that Robert Dickson had become his nemesis. Clark wrote to Armstrong, "Dickson, the principal British Agent, has been this winter with the Socs [sic], Wild Oats [Menominee] & Winnebagoes; and is now on the upper part of the Mississippi no doubt using his influence with those tribes to aid the British as usual." A St. Louis newspaper columnist added to the fear: "For the last six months it has been no unusual thing for our wives and children to start from their sleep under dreadful imagination that he [Dickson] was thundering at their doors."[10]

Clark had conceived of the plan to have a military force secure Prairie du Chien. He had secured permission from Secretary of War Armstrong to adapt boats for carrying men and provisions up the Mississippi. Now he wished to know who would lead the expedition. From his letters to Secretary Armstrong, it is obvious Clark thought himself to be the best choice for directing and leading the men. So Clark began to condition Armstrong to select him. Presenting his first line of reasoning to have himself appointed leader of the expedition to Prairie du Chien in what would be a stream of letters to Armstrong and others, Clark wrote to the secretary of war in early February 1814 detailing his knowledge of the frontier:

> Permit me to observe that early in the Spring, is the time that
> Indians form their War parties and set out on their War excursions.
> . . . [T]here can be no doubt that a part of those tribes will remain
> hostile until we are in possession of Mackanack, the Streights of
> St. Maries, the upper Mississippi, and a post established at Prairie
> du Chien.[11]

He continued to show his expertise by describing Prairie du Chien, pointing out to Armstrong that the prairie "has been a very important point for the British for the last two years, past, where large numbers of Indians [were] collected for reinforcing their Armies in upper Canada." He repeated that Prairie du Chien should be garrisoned by a military force, "as a very important point for the U. S. either in peace or War."[12]

Having argued the importance of Prairie du Chien and the need for a fort, Clark began to angle for the appointment to lead the expedition to Prairie du Chien. He lamented that General Howard was required "for the good of the service" to leave St. Louis before he could carry out his plans for the upper Mississippi. But Clark wished to point out that the troops under his command were "sufficient to take possession of the upper Mississippi as high as the falls of St. Anthony and also build a Fort at Prairie de Chien." Clark felt the keelboats he had had refitted with cannons would "give entire Security, both for Transporting Troops and Supplies." Indeed, by February the keelboats were almost finished. According to Clark, the largest of the boats could carry a four- and a six-pound cannon and several howitzers. One hundred men could be accommodated on that boat, able to "fight without incommoding the oarsmen."[13] Clark concluded by saying that since General Howard had been ordered to Detroit and Clark knew of no other officer with Howard's capabilities, Clark requested Armstrong the favor "to inform me, to whome the government has, or will Confide the protection of those frontiers."[14]

By the end of March, Clark had not received a reply to his query. It is probable that Secretary Armstrong could not give him an answer, as the First Infantry had been recalled from the region. Enlistments had ended, and the regiment had been "reduced to a Shadow." Recruitment was necessary, and there were not enough men in the Missouri Territory to fill its ranks. Armstrong was not convinced of the need for an expedition to Prairie du Chien and conveyed to Clark that General Howard believed that the tribes would not "prosecute the War."[15]

Having heard nothing definitive, Clark again presented his argument in a letter dated March 28. He began by demonstrating that, as he was in situ, he could gather up-to-date, pertinent facts. He had received information "from different sources, and from the Indians themselves" that Dickson had taken five large boats filled with ammunition and goods into Green Bay and across the country to the Mississippi "and at this time is raising a large Indian force." Clark assured Armstrong that he could not be misled, as he knew that the "authority was respectable" who brought him reports. Therefore, Clark felt "Compelled . . . to flusterate [sic] the hostile plans of the enemy." In a veiled challenge to Armstrong, he assumed that he could "rely on the Genl Government to support me in my plans &c."[16]

Once again Clark pressed for an answer as to who would lead the expedition. Major General Harrison, who had regarded the threat to Illinois and St. Louis as exaggerated, had ordered Howard to Detroit instead. Clark explained that the forces at Fort Clark would keep Dickson and the British-allied Indians from descending the Illinois River, but that would leave the Mississippi undefended "from its source to this place." Colonel William Russell, who commanded the regular force that was to protect the west, was sick in Vincennes, so there was no one authorized to "Call on the force of the Country" and defend St. Louis.[17]

As he wrote his letter, Clark's thought process evolved from presenting a military situation to making a decision based on the conditions, which he now saw as pertaining to Indian affairs, instead of simply a military consideration. Therefore, in the fourth paragraph of his letter of March 28 to the secretary of war, Clark wrote that he felt it his duty "to adopt such measures as will be best Calculated to effect the object of defense &c," and thereby appointed himself in charge of the planned expedition to Prairie du Chien. He then told Secretary Armstrong what he was going to do.[18]

As governor and head of the territorial militia, Clark decided to raise about 150 men for two months. He felt he would need to pay at least seventy-five cents per day to attract men "suited to the Service." As soon as he had the requisite number of men, Clark would send them up the Mississippi River in three of the armed keelboats. One keelboat would patrol the river from St. Louis to the Des Moines River and intercept any war parties the men might encounter. The other two boats, which were larger, would "scour the river as high as Prairie de Chien." In addition, Clark surmised that the men in the two larger armed boats would be able to destroy "any fleet of small Boats or Canoes which they may meet with," and destroy any caches of arms and ammunition they might find en route and at Prairie du Chien. Clark explained that he already had "provision necessary for the enterprise." Then he rationalized, as Indian agent for the West, he would charge the cost of powder and lead, and the wages for the men, which Clark estimated to be between four thousand and six thousand dollars, to the Indian Fund. To Clark, this was appropriate as the purpose of the enterprise was to "prevent the progress of hostile views of other Tribes—and also to detect unlawful Trade, and influence among the Indian Tribes." Though Clark had begun his letter by "expressing apprehensions," he ended by informing Armstrong of his intentions to proceed with the plan.[19]

Traveling by water up the Ohio River and then across the Appalachian Mountains by land, Clark's letter did not reach Armstrong until one month later. Reading Clark's letter, Armstrong plainly saw that what Clark proposed was a military event, and no matter what Clark said, it did not pertain to Indian affairs. As the commanding superior of both Indian Agent Clark and General Howard, Armstrong responded. He told Clark that General Howard was about to resume his military duties at St. Louis. Therefore, the arrangements Clark had outlined were to "necessarily be submitted to his judgment & decision." In other words, Clark was to wait until Howard arrived in St. Louis, and then discuss all actions with Howard, who would then decide if the expedition up the Mississippi River to Prairie du Chien (and beyond) would be ordered.[20] But Clark didn't wait for a reply. Instead, he issued his own orders. He was heading with the American militia to take Prairie du Chien.

—ıı—

The reply to Clark from Secretary Armstrong was written on April 30 and may not have left Washington City by the time Clark launched his venture up the Mississippi River to Prairie du Chien. His decision to proceed without waiting for a reply from Armstrong may have been advanced by the arrival in St. Louis of Major Zachary Taylor with a detachment of sixty-one men of the Seventh US Infantry under his command. Colonel Russell had sent Taylor's detachment to bolster the defense of the frontier. Clark learned from Taylor that Howard had been ordered back to St. Louis, but when he would arrive was unknown. Clark and Taylor discussed Clark's plan. Taylor deferred to the governor, so Clark decided to use the men of the Seventh Infantry to attack and secure Prairie du Chien. It was assumed that Major Taylor would be in command of the men.[21]

So in the spring of 1814, Clark prepared to initiate his military campaign up the Mississippi River to Prairie du Chien. Although Clark felt Green Bay and Mackinac were important, as "[t]he British will not relinquish the Indian Trade, unless we possess the northern lakes & passes," he focused on Prairie du Chien. Once Prairie du Chien was secured, then Green Bay and Mackinac would be vulnerable. Additionally, to bolster Clark's justification for attacking Prairie du Chien, the community was Dickson's headquarters on the upper Mississippi.[22] After a year's preparation all was ready.

Before the operation to Prairie du Chien could proceed, an illness in Taylor's family forced the major to return to Vincennes. With no junior officer in his detachment, on April 29 Taylor ordered Lieutenant Joseph Perkins to take command of his detachment of sixty-one regular troops. Lieutenant Perkins was part of the Twenty-fourth Infantry Regiment. Captain Walter Wilkinson had reassigned Perkins from St. Genevieve to St. Louis to open a recruiting rendezvous, and Perkins had arrived in St. Louis just five days earlier. Major Taylor countermanded Perkins's orders, directing Perkins to lead the detachment of regulars up the Mississippi and follow Governor Clark's instructions.[23]

On May 1, Lieutenant Perkins boarded the largest of the gunboats; on board were the sixty-one regulars from Taylor's command. Captain Frederick Yeiser of the St. Louis militia commanded the vessel. The expedition also included another armed boat and three barges. The 140 Missouri militiamen who had answered Clark's call for sixty-day volunteers traveled in these craft; Captain Yeiser and Captain John Sullivan had command of the militia troops. Among the militia officers were lieutenants George Hancock Kennerly and James Kennerly, brothers who were first cousins of Julia Clark, the governor's wife. The men had christened the lead boat of the flotilla the *Governor Clark*.[24]

Three days after the armed boats and men left St. Louis, Clark wrote to Secretary Armstrong. In the letter, Clark explained that the expedition, of which he had "the honor" of informing the secretary, had "moved, and is at this time above the frontiers." Not only was the expedition in motion, but Clark had also decided to accompany the troops, as he "thought it would be best." Clark would travel overland and join the flotilla. Once all had arrived at their destination, he would "if practicable (of which I have no doubt) build a fort at Prairie du Chien and leave a Company of 61 men of the 7th Regiment, and an Armed Boat under Comd. Lt. Kenerly for the defense of that point." He went on to explain that the men Taylor brought to St. Louis to protect the frontiers he had ordered detached to the expedition.

He had no doubt that with his force of two hundred men, he would easily take control of Prairie du Chien, convince the Indians not to fight, and "flusterate the plans of Mr. Dickson." Once more Clark raised the specter of Dickson uniting the tribes to descend upon the Missouri frontier and support British forces on the Great Lakes.[25]

Back in February when Clark first attempted to persuade Armstrong to authorize the expedition, he had recommended that the US fur factory, originally at Fort Madison and now located on the Missouri River, be moved to Prairie du Chien. Clark's suggestion was a confirmation that the war on the frontier was being fought for reasons different from those for which war on the Atlantic Ocean and the eastern Great Lakes was fought. Along the Mississippi River, economic dominance over the Native population drove all actions. With the government-subsidized factory at Fort Madison gone, another needed to be established on the upper Mississippi. If located at Prairie du Chien, the fort and factory, along with the presence of Nicolas Boilvin as an Indian agent, would finally give the United States control of the farthest reaches of the Northwest Territory and the riches it offered.

Once the expedition had arrived at Prairie du Chien, the immediate action Clark proposed would demonstrate to the Indians the power of the United States over the British traders. As the first step in crushing the British traders at Prairie du Chien, Clark told General Howard he would "take possession of the establishment of the old Mackinack Company, and make such additions as will give the place Sufficient Strength."[26]

Clark had conveyed his plans to Secretary Armstrong on May 4, writing Howard the following day that he was sure that Armstrong would support the "contemplated establishment" and send all the troops he could spare to reinforce the fort. Confident in his assumption, Clark left St. Louis the next day. Nicolas Boilvin and his family accompanied Clark. Though unable to live securely at Prairie du Chien, Boilvin was still the agent to the Sac and Fox. With the security provided by American troops, Boilvin could finally return to all he had left behind in 1812. He planned to meet with some of the chiefs once he arrived on the prairie. The boat carrying Clark and Boilvin overtook the armed boats before the vessels had reached the Rock River.

General Howard arrived in St. Louis on May 8 to find Clark and the

## Prairie du Chien, ca. 1814

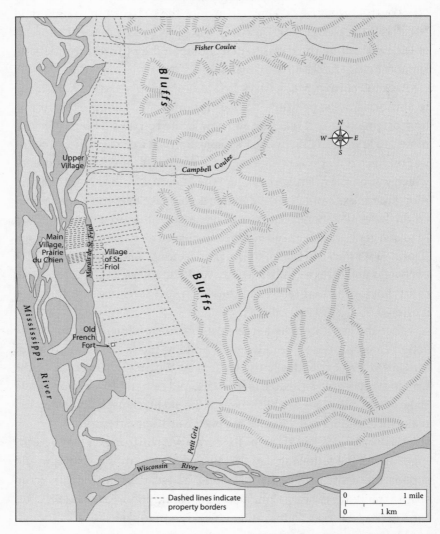

Fisher Coulee

Bluffs

Upper Village

Campbell Coulee

Main Village, Prairie du Chien

Village of St. Friol

Marais de St. Friol

Bluffs

Old French Fort

Mississippi River

Petit Gris

Wisconsin River

N W E S

--- Dashed lines indicate property borders

0 ___ 1 mile
0 ___ 1 km

MAPPING SPECIALISTS, LTD., FITCHBURG, WI

men gone. A week later, Howard wrote a report to Armstrong of his assessment of the frontier. To explain Clark's absence and movement, Howard enclosed copies of Clark's correspondence. He informed Armstrong that he and Clark had not discussed Clark's actions, but Howard did support Clark. Howard and Clark were of the same opinion that establishing a garrison at Prairie du Chien was of "much importance." In his letter to Howard, Clark had asked for military support, but this Howard was unable to provide. Howard therefore made a request of Armstrong, although he stated it as a recommendation: that four companies of regulars should be sent to him so that he could reinforce the soon-to-be new post at Prairie du Chien and the existing Fort Clark. Howard was convinced that as soon at the fort was built, the garrison "will be assailed as soon as they [the British agents] receive notice and can embody the Indians." He laid out the argument that support was needed because the post would be located six hundred miles north in "Indian country" and could easily be cut off from supplies and support. He also pointed out that the militia had enlisted for only sixty days, and once their enlistment was up, Lieutenant Perkins and his sixty-one men would be left at Prairie du Chien with "no officer to assist him."27

As Howard contemplated the entire American situation on the frontier, the flotilla advanced up the river. High water and strong winds made travel slow. The flotilla passed Black Hawk's village. Black Hawk was not at his village when the Americans arrived, but he was told the soldiers "appeared friendly, and were kindly treated by our people." The first resistance to the Americans occurred near the mouth of the Rock River. A band of Sac and Fox fired upon the boats. After a heavy return from the gunboats, the band sued for peace. This Clark granted, provided the Sac and Fox fight against the enemies of the United States, especially the Winnebago. Further up the river, at the Spanish Mines (those worked by Julien Dubuque), another band of Fox fired upon the flotilla and were pushed back. Clark believed that they too would be willing to ally themselves with the United States, if the influence of the British was destroyed.28

Learning of the approach of the US forces, Captain Dease called upon the Fox and Sioux to oppose the Americans as they attempted to land at Prairie du Chien. This the chiefs refused to do. With no support, then, Dease and the militia left the prairie, and most of the residents abandoned their homes to disappear into the surrounding coulees and bluffs. Clark and his command landed at Prairie du Chien on June 2 with no opposition.29

The vessels having touched shore in front of the Main Village, Clark's first order fulfilled his promise to General Howard. The regulars under command of Lieutenant Perkins marched to the buildings used by the

Michilimackinac Company as their depot in Prairie du Chien and secured the structures without any resistance. The regulars and the Missouri volunteers proceeded to create a barracks within the Michilimackinac Company buildings. In taking over the company's property, the Americans were also confiscating the personal property of Francois Bouthellier, who had rented his home and warehouses to the company. Stowing their supplies, the soldiers immediately enclosed the structures with defensive works. Here they would stay until the construction of a fort had been completed.[30]

As the soldiers went about their work, Clark took a few men to Robert Dickson's home. With Dickson gone and his wife and children probably secure with her brother's family where they lived along the St. Peter's River, the house was unprotected. Clark ordered the men to enter the building and conduct a search. They confiscated Dickson's papers, which reportedly were contained in a number of trunks. These papers included correspondence between Dickson and Dease, letters between other officers in the British Indian Department, and speeches between the Winnebago and Sac and Fox. Clark reported that the papers documented the delivery of presents to the Indians. The Niles' Weekly Register would later sensationalize the documents saying that the papers proved that Dickson was a "hairbuyer," paying Indians for human scalps.[31]

Not all the residents of the prairie had fled with the arrival of the Americans, and so through them word was sent to the people in hiding that they would not be molested by the Americans, and they should return to their homes. Most did, although several of the more prominent traders remained absent. Henry Munro Fisher was in a delicate position. He held an American commission as a captain of militia for Illinois Territory and justice of the peace, yet he had signed the petition sent to Michilimackinac in 1813 in which the men avowed their loyalty to Great Britain, asking the British for troops to protect and support Prairie du Chien. Fisher's situation the summer of 1814 was so untenable that he left the village, taking with him his two oldest sons, Henry and Alexander, and Charles, a son of Michel Brisbois. Fisher left his youngest son, George, and his daughter, Genevieve or Jane, with her uncle and aunt, Michel and Dometille Brisbois. Fisher's second wife and infant daughter went to Mackinac Island to stay with the wife's family. Arriving in Canada, Fisher received an appointment as quartermaster of the British Indian Department.[32]

Joseph Rolette probably left the prairie at this time, too, choosing where his loyalty lay. A month later Rolette was at Mackinac helping to organize volunteers to return to Prairie du Chien and attack the US forces. Others who lived and traded at Prairie du Chien had already received commissions in the British Indian Department. Duncan Graham, Michel Brisbois (the son), Joseph Renville, and Jean Baptiste Cadot became lieutenants, and Antoine Brisbois, Colin Campbell, and Louis Honore became interpreters.[33]

—ıı—

Clark spent several days investigating the community and meeting with Indians encamped in the vicinity. On June 5, Clark selected the site for the new fort and gave Perkins orders as to how it should be fashioned. Construction of the American fort on the prairie began the following day, with the work being done by the regulars and the Missouri volunteers. The site Governor Clark selected for the fort was a slightly raised, round mound situated about three hundred feet behind houses within the Main Village. Though Pike had recommended a site south of the prairie and on the west bank of the Mississippi River for the construction of a fort, Clark chose a location more politically expressive than militarily strategic. The mound was centrally located in the Main Village. It would stand on the village lot claimed by James McFarlane and just behind his home. Standing atop the mound, one looked at the back walls of not only McFarlane's home but also the homes of Robert Dickson, Joseph Rolette, and Henry Munro Fisher. Just to the south stood the Michilimackinac Company buildings and the residences of Michel Brisbois, Jean Baptiste Faribault, James Aird, and other traders. In this position, the Americans within the fort could monitor and control all movement in the Main Village with special attention to the homes of the British traders, and they would be able to see anyone attempting to land along the riverbank in front of the village.[34]

By the nineteenth of June, Lieutenant Perkins had the construction of the fort so far advanced that he moved into it. Perkins ordered some of the cannon carried on the barges to be mounted within the fort. He reported that a six-pounder protected one blockhouse and a three-pounder had been sited in the other blockhouse. In his report to General Howard, Perkins said nothing more about the physical layout of the fort. A contemporary newspaper account and the reminiscence of Thomas G. Anderson,

a British trader who operated out of Prairie du Chien and who would organize a company of volunteers to assist in the attack on the American
fort, better defined the fortification. According to Anderson, the fort was
triangular in shape with one blockhouse at the north. Seventy feet of pick-
eted wall made of oak connected the second blockhouse to the south. A
wall of ten-foot-high pickets angled out to the west from each blockhouse
and joined in a point that faced the river. Earthworks were thrown up
outside the walls, and further out *chevaux-de-frise* added another line of
protection. Since many of the men assigned by Major Taylor to Lieutenant
Perkins were from Kentucky, the new post was named Fort Shelby in honor
of Isaac Shelby, governor of Kentucky.[35]

To protect the fort even further, Clark ordered the gunboat commanded by Captain Yeiser moored in the river directly off the front of
the fort. On board were fourteen cannon and a number of cohorns. The
seventy to eighty men on board were to man the guns and provide the
rowing power to propel the boat, keeping it in a strategic position should
the American fort be attacked.

Whatever his misgivings regarding Clark's actions, Howard saw the
need to maintain the new American fort. On June 20, Howard requested
Secretary Armstrong send troops to be stationed at Prairie du Chien. The
company under command of Lieutenant Perkins was on loan. If problems
arose in Indiana or Illinois, the men would have to return. As Howard explained, if he needed to bring more troops to Prairie du Chien, he would
be forced to abandon Fort Clark, "which is much more important for the
immediate protection of the frontier." General Howard wanted the "post
maintained and supported" but reinforcements had to be sent to Prairie
du Chien "to produce the effect contemplated in its establishment." With
insight, Howard warned,

> Rest assured that the Garrison will be assailed as soon as they [the
> British] receive notice and can embody the Indians, the situation
> of this Garrison will be extremely dangerous, both as respects its
> defense and receiving supplies unless the force I mention is immedi-
> ately sent on.[36]

—||—

Upon disembarking with the American forces, Nicolas Boilvin had walked to his home and the Indian Agency building that he and his family had been forced to flee two years previously. With Boilvin were his wife and three children. They found their home ransacked and personal possessions gone or broken. Even so, with the Americans in control of the prairie, Boilvin optimistically believed he could continue his work among the Sac and Fox and the Winnebago. He expected to again make his home at Prairie du Chien.

Glad to be back on the prairie, Boilvin was unhappy with Clark. Boilvin later reported to Armstrong that Governor Clark had placed himself in charge, directing not only the construction of a fort but any other American activity at Prairie du Chien as well. Boilvin wrote:

> I was at Prairie du Chien under such great subordination to Governor Clarke [sic], superintendent, that I was obliged to await his orders and do nothing what so ever without orders from him. I remained helpless, without authority except to turn over to him all the tribes of the region submissive to his control for the time.[37]

In the few days that Clark remained at Prairie du Chien, he and Boilvin spent time in council with members of some of the tribes who were visiting the prairie. Boilvin stated that at these meetings, Clark gave the tribes false promises. The tribes needed food and ammunition, the latter so they could hunt for food. According to Boilvin, the chiefs tried to explain to Clark their desperate situation, saying, "If the English come we shall be obliged to go over to their side or perish since they have supplied our wants." They asked for Boilvin's support. Boilvin wrote to Armstrong, "I believe it is within my power to bring back all these nations if you would only favor me with a single answer." Boilvin accused Clark of being one of the "gentlemen" who were "immortalizing themselves in an uncivilized land."[38]

Whether at one of these meetings or in a separate situation, there occurred two incidents that undid any good influence Boilvin may have accomplished while talking with the chiefs. Tete de Chien, a Winnebago chief, would later arrive at Mackinac telling a story of atrocities committed by the Americans. He told Colonel Robert McDouall, the British commander at Mackinac, that when the Americans arrived at the prairie, they had accosted eight Winnebago. Showing kindness, the Americans offered them food. While the Winnebago were eating, the United States troops opened fire on the men, killing all but one, who escaped. Tete de Chien added that later, Governor Clark invited four Indians, unaware of what had happened, to meet with him in friendship. He placed them in a log structure and then had them shot through the gaps between the logs. Among the dead were Tete de Chien's brother and the wife of La Feuille. This had occurred while La Feuille was participating in the conference at Fort Michilimackinac that Dickson and Lieutenant Colonel McDouall had called. Boilvin did not mention this incident in his report to Secretary Armstrong. However, news of the incidents spread to the Potawatomi. Gomo, a Potawatomi chief, reported to Thomas Forsyth, the US Indian agent at Peoria, that Governor Clark's men had killed two Winnebago at the mouth of the Wisconsin River. Two other Indians who had come to trade told Forsyth that "Clark's Army" had killed six Winnebago.[39] After he returned to St. Louis, Clark would offhandedly report to Armstrong, "Twenty Winnebago men taken prisoner at Prairie du Chien made their escape in the dark of night, from a Strong Guard under a heavy fire, several of them wounded & dead."[40] The truth of what happened is still unknown.

—II—

Having accomplished his goal of securing the prairie for the United States, Governor Clark took leave of Prairie du Chien on June 7. He may have commandeered the Michilimackinac Company buildings, confiscated the correspondence of Robert Dickson, and ordered the construction of a fortification, but he did not accomplish what he had told Armstrong was his purpose for the expedition. The expedition to secure Prairie du Chien had done nothing to diminish Dickson's influence among the tribes of the region or persuade the tribes to be disposed to establish friendly relations with the United States.

Clark left the prairie for St. Louis in the smallest of the gunboats confident of his success. He left the two larger gunboats, which included the *Governor Clark*, at Prairie du Chien. Also remaining behind were Lieutenant Perkins and the sixty-one regulars who would man Fort Shelby. Placed in duty under Perkins were Captain George Kennerly, Clark's aide-de-camp, and Lieutenant James Kennerly of the militia. Captain Yeiser and Lieutenant Sullivan also remained with most of the companies of militia that they commanded. Each man was in charge of a gunboat; the boats were to defend the fort if attacked. The militiamen would assist the regulars in the completion of Fort Shelby. The work would be far enough along that the men would be able to move into the fort on June 20.[41]

On June 13, Clark triumphantly arrived at St. Louis. He boasted the fort had been built at Prairie du Chien, and the garrison anxiously awaited "a visit from Dickson and his red troops." The *Missouri Gazette* reported that Clark and his friends gathered for a celebratory dinner at William Christy's Missouri Hotel, where they toasted "the late expedition [which] has cleansed [Prairie du Chien] of spies and traitors."[42]

As the fort progressed toward completion, many of the Missouri volunteers wished to return home. The sixty days of service for which they had enlisted had expired. So, late in June, Lieutenant Sullivan, his company, and thirty-two men from Yeiser's command left the prairie in the smaller of the two gunboats. Yeiser and the rest of his company agreed to stay on the *Governor Clark* until a reinforcement of regulars and Missouri Rangers would relieve them.

With the arrival of Lieutenant Sullivan in St. Louis, Clark reported to Secretary Armstrong that nothing of importance had occurred at Prairie du Chien since he had sent a letter to Armstrong from that place. As Armstrong knew, General Howard had ordered a detachment of rangers and regular infantry to the prairie who were to arrive about the twenty-fifth of July. This was all that Howard could spare; he had to keep Fort Clark fully staffed, as he considered Fort Clark more important than Fort Shelby for the protection of the frontier. Howard reported to Armstrong, "[T]he Savages are weekly attacking and attempting to assail the frontier," and enumerated the people killed in Illinois and between the Mississippi and Missouri Rivers north of St. Louis.[43]

Also in his letter to Armstrong, Clark boasted that because of "the arrangements" he had made at Prairie du Chien, the Sac and Fox were no longer hostile to the United States. While the Winnebago, Menominee, and Kickapoo were still hostile, Clark did not consider them a threat in the Mississippi valley. He also felt Dickson's influence with the Sioux had been diminished, and Mr. Boilvin, still at Prairie du Chien, would further secure it. Once more, Clark recommended the US fur factory be moved to Prairie du Chien.[44]

Although Clark reported at the end of June that Howard had ordered a detachment in support of Fort Shelby, the detachment did not leave until July 4. On that day, Major John Campbell left Capais Grais (Cape au Gris) with a command of forty regulars and sixty-four rangers, under the command of Lieutenants Stephen Rector and Jonathan Riggs, loaded into armed boats. With Campbell and the infantrymen were sutlers and women and children. Rector and Riggs each commanded a boat, each carrying rangers and supplies for the men at Prairie du Chien. Capais Grais lay above St. Louis on the west bank of the Mississippi River across from the mouth of the Illinois. A small log fort had been built there by Missouri militia and in 1814 was under the command of Captain David Musick.[45]

On July 13, eighty miles below the Rock River, Campbell met a party of Indians with a packet of correspondence for Governor Clark. They had left Prairie du Chien several days earlier. They reported that the garrison had been completed and everything was quiet. Five days later, further up the river, a party of nine Sac met the boats. They were carrying a white flag with a request that the Americans come to their village. At the mouth of the Rock River, five other Sac escorted Campbell to the village. Campbell continued and about one mile up the river found Black Hawk and about 150 warriors waiting for him, along with women and children. Black Hawk greeted Campbell, asking if he had any presents from his "Father." Campbell replied that the gifts would come only if the Sac fulfilled their promise to war against the Winnebago. Black Hawk replied that he had made no such promise "and that his Father was drunk if he said so."[46] But Black Hawk had no ill intentions toward the Americans. As he later recalled, "We had no intention of hurting them, or any of his party, or we could have easily defeated them." The chief then poetically related to Campbell that "the Mississippi was a broad and straight road and the people of the United States should meet with no obstructions in traveling it." Campbell's party stayed with Black Hawk's band for the day and then returned to the barges to resume the journey to Prairie du Chien.[47]

More than a month had passed since the American forces led by Governor Clark had landed at Prairie du Chien. Since then not only had Tete de Chien carried stories to Mackinac of the happenings on the prairie, but some of the residents of the village had also followed the Fox-Wisconsin waterway to Green Bay and crossed Lake Michigan to Mackinac Island. The British response General Howard had feared was about to happen.

# 9

# The Battle for Prairie du Chien

*July 1814*

Some of the men who had left Prairie du Chien at the arrival of the American force commanded by William Clark reached Michilimackinac on June 21. They immediately sought Lieutenant Colonel Robert McDouall and relayed to him the details of all that had occurred at the prairie, impressing upon him that General Clark had arrived with six or seven very large boats carrying three hundred men.

Already at Michilimackinac were fifteen hundred to sixteen hundred Indians. Some had come on their own to guarantee the protection of the island and in anticipation of fighting the Americans. Included were the three hundred chiefs and warriors from the "Countries adjoining La Prairie des Chiens" that Robert Dickson had brought to the island. McDouall had gathered them together on June 5 in celebration of the king's birthday. In his speech, McDouall had thanked them for their past service and especially their loyalty "in hastening to the defence of the Island when threatened by the enemy." McDouall updated them on the progress of the conflict. He encouraged them not to listen to American "stratagems, which is meant to sow dissention among the tribes," and stated he was "highly pleased that you have listen to the wise councils of your friend and chief the Red Head."[1]

The Indians were still encamped at Michilimackinac when the men from Prairie du Chien arrived. According to McDouall, upon hearing the report of the men, "they felt themselves not a little uneasy at the proximity of the Enemy to their defenseless families." But upon the arrival the following day of the Winnebago chief Tete de Chien, their unease turned to a restless need for action. Tete de Chien provided more information on what had taken place after Clark and the Americans secured Prairie du Chien, telling his story of the American atrocities to his tribespeople to McDouall and the Indians. He then begged for assistance to take revenge upon the "deliberate and barbarous murder of seven men of his own nation." When those gathered heard that William Clark had ordered the American troops to shoot the Winnebago, "the sentiment of indignation & desire for revenge was universal." The chiefs argued for leaving for the prairie immediately so that they could be with their families to protect all from unwonted capture and killing as had happened to La Feuille's wife and Tete de Chien's brother. Once their families were safe, they vowed to drive the Americans from their lands.[2]

General Robert McDouall, British commander of Fort Mackinac, 1814–1815. IMAGE COURTESY OF STANREAR MUSEUM

McDouall quickly assessed the reports and immediately saw the need to dislodge the Americans from Prairie du Chien. Clark had invaded the heart of the western country occupied by the many Indian nations who were friendly to Great Britain. McDouall had two choices: he could organize a force to attack the Americans at Prairie du Chien or he could take no action and leave the tribes to the American forces, essentially ending the British connection to them. The latter was unacceptable. As McDouall reported to General Drummond, if the Americans were allowed to remain and in time settle at Prairie du Chien,

> [b]y dint of threats, bribes, & sowing divisions among them, tribe after tribe would be graned over or subdued. . . . Nothing could prevent the enemy from gaining the source of the Mississippi, gradually extending themselves by the Red River to Lake Winnipeg from whence the descent of Nelson's River to York Fort would in time be easy. The total subjugation of the Indians on the Mississippi would either lead to their Extermination by the enemy or they would be spared on the express condition of assisting them to expel us from Upper Canada.

McDouall determined to give the tribes encouragement and assistance to retake Prairie du Chien, even though it weakened his position at Michilimackinac. The continued loyalty of the tribes of the upper Mississippi was vital to the British military and economic position in North America.[3]

With this prescient assessment of the future, McDouall examined his position at Michilimackinac and came to the conclusion that he could allow some of the tribes to leave for the prairie and still be able to defend the island if an American force from Detroit should make an attempt to regain Michilimackinac. The two tribes most affected by the American presence at Prairie du Chien were the Sioux and the Winnebago, and McDouall determined that he could part with their warriors. Likely the decision was pragmatic; McDouall realized that he would not be able to force the Sioux and Winnebago to remain at Michilimackinac, as they were insistent on returning home and could leave of their own volition. Instead, by incorporating the tribes into his plan, he ensured their assistance at Prairie du

Chien. McDouall also recognized the strategic importance of Prairie du Chien. A permanent American force at the prairie would place La Baye and Michilimackinac in danger. If it remained in American hands, Clark could reinforce the fort and then use the prairie as a base to mount an attack on La Baye. If La Baye fell to the Americans, Michilimackinac could then be attacked from the west.

Though McDouall felt he could protect Michilimackinac without the Sioux and Winnebago, he knew he could not spare any of the men of the Royal Newfoundland Regiment who had just arrived. He therefore turned to the men who had the most vested interests in keeping the prairie in British hands—the traders. He selected three men for the expedition: Joseph Rolette, Thomas G. Anderson, and Pierre Grignon. Rolette and Anderson organized their trade from the prairie, and Rolette and his family resided in the Main Village. Grignon lived at La Baye but visited the prairie as part of his trading concerns. McDouall also needed the community on the Fox River committed to his plans, so a member of the Grignon family was an advantageous choice. McDouall appointed each man a captain of volunteers and ordered each to raise a company, which would then be under their command.[4]

Anderson later recalled that he enthusiastically exclaimed, "We must go and take the fort." With his appointment, Anderson went up and down the major thoroughfare of the island, seeking recruits, and estimated that by sundown he had more than eighty volunteers. Having recruited his company, Anderson created a uniform for himself. He donned a red coat, which he embellished with a pair of epaulettes, stuck a red cock feather in the band of the round hat he wore, and finished his attire with the addition of "an old rusty sword." He named his company Anderson's Mississippi Volunteers. Joseph Rolette engaged men for his company at the same time as Anderson. A couple of the men who joined were traders, but most who joined both companies were clerks and engagés. Anderson's recollections had improved with time, for McDouall reported that between them, Anderson and Rolette raised sixty-three men in the course of two days. Grignon computed that Anderson's and Rolette's companies each numbered about fifty men. The two companies were armed and clothed from the stores held at Michilimackinac.[5]

With the Sioux and Winnebago poised to return to the Mississippi and two companies raised, McDouall held several councils with the Indians. He found they continued to be enthusiastic and "never was more zeal or unanimity shown amongst them." This state McDouall attributed to Tete de Chien, whom McDouall found to be "scarcely inferior to Tecumseh, & I doubt not will act a distinguished part in the Campaign." Tete de Chien requested two favors of McDouall. First, he requested "one of their Fathers big Guns to strike terror into their Enemy's." The appeal for a cannon had been made many times by the chiefs. McDouall agreed to let the force borrow a three-pound brass cannon, one from the arsenal of artillery that McDouall had brought to the island from York. He did not think that the cannon would be of any value in the capture of the fort at Prairie du Chien, but he considered its presence on the campaign a way to encourage the Indians. So that the cannon could be fired without injury to anyone, McDouall ordered Sergeant James Keating of the Royal Artillery to accompany it. McDouall then ordered a corporal and twelve men of the Michigan Fencibles attached to the force. Lastly, McDouall honored Tete de Chien's other request, that an officer of "their Fathers" be chosen to lead the campaign. McDouall thereby appointed Major William McKay the commander of the expedition, promoting him to the local rank of lieutenant colonel.[6]

William McKay was familiar to the Indians and the Canadians. He had entered the fur trade as an employee of the North West Company, rising to partner. He had traded along the Menomonee River, wintering awhile with the Grignon family before moving on to Lake Winnipeg. Having retired from the trade, when the war began, McKay offered his services to the British. He helped in the capture of the American garrison at Michilimackinac and the organization of the Corps of Canadian Voyageurs, moving military and supplies to fortifications in Upper Canada. In January 1814, he was appointed captain of the newly organized volunteer unit of Michigan Fencibles. McDouall expressed his utmost faith in McKay's ability to lead the expeditionary force. He praised McKay as being "determined yet consiliatory[,] well acquainted with the language & mode of managing the Indians & familiar with the place intended to be attacked." Acceding to both of their requests, the chiefs told McDouall that "they had not a wish ungratified—that they & their young Men would die in defence of their Gun."[7]

Lt. Colonel William McKay, 1816, by Levi Stevens. MCCORD MUSEUM, MONTREAL M17684

Dickson would not join the campaign, as he was needed at Michili-mackinac, but other members of the Indian Department were included in the force. Lieutenant Graham acted as second in command, with Louis Honore and Jacques Porlier assisting. Michel Brisbois Jr. would interpret for the Winnebago and Joseph Renville for the Sioux. Dickson watched over these preparations and believed that the tribes participating in the expedition were in good hands; now he had to make sure that there were Indians available for the defense of Michilimackinac. Dickson ordered all the lieutenants and interpreters of the department who remained at Michilimackinac to take a count of the Indians on the island, specifying those who were armed and unarmed, and asked to be informed of all ar-riving Indian canoes. Dickson remained on the island to await the bedding, Indian presents, and provisions that were to be shipped from Lachine, a common hub for departing and arriving trading expeditions near Mon-treal. All on the island and at Prairie du Chien would need these goods before the onset of winter.[8]

—II—

The campaign to retake Prairie du Chien had been organized and supplied in a week's time. McKay and the force sailed from Michilimackinac on June 28, the fort guns firing a salute at their departure. The men of the Fencibles and Rolette's and Anderson's companies, as well as the munitions, moved forward aboard three barges, small open vessels that had been built the previous winter. One barge had a platform constructed near the prow and here the three-pound cannon had been mounted. The Sioux and Winnebago traveled in their canoes. About six days later, the convoy entered the mouth of the Fox River.[9]

At La Baye, the force halted. Informed of the purpose of the expedition, "such was the zeal displayed, that the force was immediately doubled." Pierre Grignon raised his company of thirty men from the ranks of the local militia, which included many older men. Peter Powell and Augustin Grignon were appointed lieutenants. Jean Jacques Porlier, the son of Jacques Porlier, received a commission of lieutenant in the Michigan Fencibles. Lieutenant Pullman, who commanded the Michigan Fencibles stationed at La Baye, also joined the expedition. There was enthusiasm for the campaign among the Menominee, and about seventy-five warriors led by three chiefs joined the Winnebago and Sioux, as did a party of about twenty-five Chippewa and Menominee. Three more barges were secured to transport the men and additional provisions, and then all moved up the Fox River. At the portage, more Menominee and Winnebago attached themselves to the force. Before arriving at the mouth of the Wisconsin River, the Sioux from St. Peter's joined the group. McKay estimated his command to be about 650 men, of whom 120 were Michigan Fencibles, Canadian Volunteers, and officers of the Indian Department. The rest of the force was composed of the Indian warriors.[10]

By July 16, the force was close to the Mississippi River. McKay ordered a halt at an old Fox village on the Wisconsin River about twenty-eight miles from Prairie du Chien. He then dispatched Michel Brisbois Jr., Augustin Grignon, a Sioux, and a Winnebago to proceed to the prairie and reconnoiter the American position. They were to locate one of the residents and bring him to McKay to obtain intelligence. The men left in a canoe and paddled to Petit Gris, a ferrying point on the river about five or six miles from Prairie du Chien. There they left the canoe and walked overland, without encountering anyone, to the settlement. It was evening

Augustin Grignon was one of a multi-generational family of fur traders at Green Bay and Kaukauna. He served as a lieutenant in the company that his brother, Pierre, formed in July, 1814. WHI IMAGE ID 4170

when Michel arrived at his father's house a few hundred feet south of Fort Shelby. He mounted a fence on the property to get a better look at one of the American gunboats. Some of the men on the boat noticed "his inquisitive observations," one firing a shot that passed between Brisbois's legs. Michel and Augustin left the village and crossed over the slough to the old Indian trail that stretched the length of the prairie. They quietly walked northward and entered the home of Antoine Brisbois, a British sympathizer, located about three miles from the Main Village. They asked Antoine to come with them and led him to the place where they had left their canoe. There they awaited the arrival of McKay.[11]

McKay and the force appeared at Petit Gris the following morning "when the sun was about an hour high." With Antoine able to provide the details, McKay learned that the Americans had built Fort Shelby "on a height" behind the houses in the Main Village. There were two block-houses armed with six pieces of cannon and staffed by sixty to seventy men including officers in the fort. Lying at anchor immediately in front of the fort was a seventy-foot gunboat the Americans had named *Governor Clark, Gun Boat No. 1.* On the gunboat were fourteen pieces of cannon—six-pounders, three-pounders, and cohorns. Seventy to eighty men were stationed aboard the gunboat and remained, as Colonel McKay observed, "perfectly safe from small arms while they can use their own to . . . great advantage."[12]

Informed as to the situation on the prairie, McKay led the force down to the mouth of the Wisconsin River, then turned north. The men familiar with the Mississippi directed the boats through the backwaters and among the numerous islands to the landing place below the old French fort. Quietly, the canoes touched shore, and the barges drifted into shallow water and were secured. They had reached the prairie unperceived about ten o'clock on July 17.[13]

—⊦⊢—

It was a Sunday and the American soldiers were engaged in various diversions. Joseph Crelie had lent his horse and wagon to one of the officers, and he and others were about to enjoy a pleasure ride through the country. Boilvin had ordered his hired man, Sandy, to go to the common and select a heifer, as Boilvin wished to have some fresh meat for his meal that day. On his way across the prairie, Sandy spied men with red coats moving toward the Main Village. Seeing many red coats and the dozen flags carried by the Indians, he knew it was a British force. Sandy carefully returned to Boilvin and told him there were "lots of red cattle" and invited Boilvin to come with him so he could show him. Boilvin went, saw what Sandy had seen, and hastened back to his house. He informed the American officers, and then went to his house, packed up his family and important belongings, and boarded the gunboat. The alarm raised, all of the remaining residents of the prairie left their homes. Some, including Joseph Crelie, sought safety within Fort Shelby. Most, however, ran to outlying places on the prairie. In later years, both Crelie and Augustin Grignon stated that if McKay and the force had arrived an hour later, they would have found all the American officers away from the garrison.[14]

The British and their Indian allies whom Sandy had seen moving across the prairie were Rolette and Anderson positioning their companies. McKay had directed them, with the Sioux and Winnebago, to take a position above Fort Shelby. McKay, with the Fencibles, Grignon's company, and Menominee and Chippewa, spread out below the fort. McKay established his headquarters in the remains of the old French fort located on the south end of the prairie. Having positioned his men, McKay performed one of the gentlemanly protocols of war. At half past twelve, he sent Captain Anderson under a flag of truce to Fort Shelby. Anderson carried a written invitation from Colonel McKay to Lieutenant Perkins.[15]

July 17th 1814.

Sir,

An hour after the receipt of this Surrender to His Majesty's Forces under my command, unconditionally. Otherwise I order you to defend yourself to the last Man, the Humanity of a British Officer obliges me (in case you should be obstinate) to request you will send out of the way your women and children.

I am Sir

Your very Hble. Servt.

W. McKay

Lt. Col. Comg. the Expedition

Lieutenant Perkins politely responded,

Fort Shelby July 17th 1814

Sir,

I received your polite note and prefer the latter and am determined to defend to the last man.

Yours &c.

Jos. Perkins

Capt. Comg. United States Troops[16]

Having received Perkins's response, McKay planned not to attack the fort until the following morning at daylight, as it was already afternoon. The Indians argued against such inaction. Faced with this pressure and recalling that in past conflicts while waiting for fighting to commence, the Indians had sometimes wandered from camp in search of food, McKay decided to begin instituting maneuvers at once.[17]

Several traders in the expedition had homes and families at Prairie du Chien. These traders engaged some of the men from the prairie during the fur-trading season. Most of the residents raised crops and livestock on the prairie, a good proportion of these crops providing food for the men who spent the winters at posts on the northern rivers. In many ways, most of the residents of the prairie supported the British. Only a very few, like Crelie, declared themselves to be Americans. It was therefore in McKay's best interest to prevent the Indians from harming the residents and their property.

McKay ordered that firing commence, the companies maintaining their positions above and below the fort. As the companies of volunteers and the Fencibles ranged on the prairie and not on the island where Fort Shelby stood, their firing had little effect, barely reaching the earth-embanked pickets that connected the blockhouses. The Americans in the fort returned the British fire, but even the shot from the American six-pounder did not reach the position held by Anderson's company. Only the Indians ventured into the Main Village. Taking cover behind houses, they kept

*Defense of Fort Shelby,* pencil sketch by Cal N. Peters, ca. 1939. COURTESY OF VILLA LOUIS HISTORIC SITE

up a constant musket fire upon the fort. McKay later assessed the Indian participation as "perfectly useless," but Anderson recalled that on this day, the Indian firing cut down the American flag that flew over the fort and wounded two soldiers.[18]

Without moving from their positions, the British initiated another tactic. Someone, either McKay or the Indians, urged that the three-pounder be brought into play. The Fencibles conveyed the cannon forward and "brought it to bear" upon the American gunboat, the *Governor Clark*. Again, a very safe position was maintained, the British keeping the cannon about a half mile from the gunboat. The first shot was a blank; Grignon felt it was "intended as a war-flourish or bravado." After that, live rounds were fired, and the gunboat returned the fire. Because of the distance, "the firing upon the boat by the cannon, and the firing by the guns or cannon from the boat, was generally ineffectual." Under the cover of the fire, though, Pierre Grignon, part of his company, and several Menominee were able to board two of the boats and row to an island in the Mississippi River opposite the *Governor Clark*. They intended to annoy the American gunboat and perhaps force it closer to shore by firing upon it. This tactic proved successful. The Governor Clark shifted anchor and moved from the middle of the channel nearer to the western shore of the Main Village island.[19]

With Grignon upon the island, McKay ordered the British cannon to slowly advance toward the gunboat, firing from each new position. In the course of three hours, Sergeant Keating directed the firing of eighty-six rounds. The Americans returned fire, discharging the cannons from the gunboat and Fort Shelby, along with musket fire. Anderson remembered that one shot from the American gunboat hit the dirt and rolled between the wheels of the cannon carriage. It was a three-pound ball and seemed to say, "'Will you return us this ball, sir?' 'Yes,' we replied; and loading our gun with it, shot it off.'"[20]

While Grignon's company and the Michigan Fencibles, with Sergeant Keating in the lead, focused on the *Governor Clark*, the rest of the Canadians and Indians, led by McKay, kept up an irregular firing of muskets upon Fort Shelby. Too far distant, the shooting made little impact. McKay ordered the men to advance across the Marais de St. Friol, a slough that separated the Main Village from the rest of the prairie. Some took up position

This mural was painted by Cal N. Peters as part of a WPA grant to the City of Prairie du Chien and can still be seen at the city's town hall. *Showing the attack by the British, July 19, 1814, on American Fort Shelby,* mural by Cal N. Peters, ca. 1940. COURTESY OF THE CITY OF PRAIRIE DU CHIEN

behind the houses and, protected from the guns of the fort, increased their firing. To the north of the fort, there were no houses and few trees, so Rolette, Anderson, and the Sioux and Winnebago remained about a quarter of a mile away from the fortification walls. According to Grignon, whenever Rolette saw the flash from an American cannon he would shout, "Down, my men!—Down!" which Grignon considered "rather un-military."[21]

With the *Governor Clark* forced close to shore, the British cannon finally hit its mark, with either one or two of the shots piercing the *Governor Clark* below the waterline. The gunboat sprang a leak. Captain Yeiser, who commanded the boat, ordered the anchor line to be cut, and the *Governor Clark* began to drift downstream. Seeing this, the Americans in Fort Shelby called out, ordering the gunboat to stop. When this did not happen, Perkins ordered that a shot be fired over the bow to induce the gunboat to drop anchor.

As the current pulled the *Governor Clark* downriver, the gunboat passed the position held by the British cannon. Sergeant Keating ordered the cannon turned and fired upon the gunboat. It was hit twice on the side and once in the stern, but the current soon carried the gunboat beyond the reach of the cannon. Both Grignon and Anderson later criticized McKay

## The Battle of Prairie du Chien

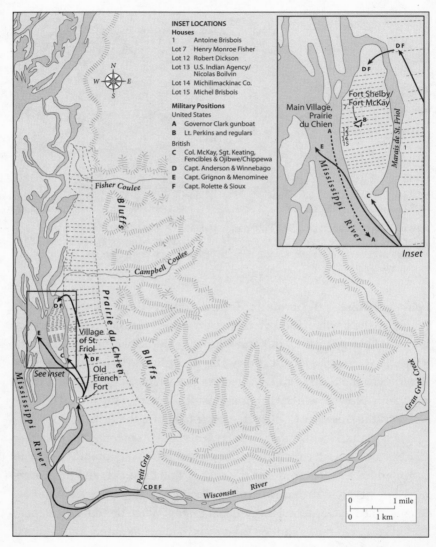

**INSET LOCATIONS**

**Houses**

| | |
|---|---|
| 1 | Antoine Brisbois |
| Lot 7 | Henry Monroe Fisher |
| Lot 12 | Robert Dickson |
| Lot 13 | U.S. Indian Agency/ Nicolas Boilvin |
| Lot 14 | Michilimackinac Co. |
| Lot 15 | Michel Brisbois |

**Military Positions**

United States

**A** Governor Clark gunboat
**B** Lt. Perkins and regulars

British

**C** Col. McKay, Sgt. Keating, Fencibles & Ojibwe/Chippewa
**D** Capt. Anderson & Winnebago
**E** Capt. Grignon & Menominee
**F** Capt. Rolette & Sioux

*Inset*

MAPPING SPECIALISTS, LTD., FITCHBURG, WI

for not ordering Grignon's men to follow the *Governor Clark*, believing they might have captured it. McKay explained in his report to McDouall that to pursue the gunboat, his men would have had to follow the *Governor Clark* in small barges from which they could not have boarded the gunboat.

Additionally, he had only one cannon, and he was not about to leave his men unprotected by sending the cannon downriver.[22]

At the mouth of the Wisconsin River, Yeiser ordered the boat to be docked by an island. It was leaking so badly that had he not stopped to repair the shattered wood, the gunboat probably would have sunk. In the meantime, McKay sent an Ioway and two Sac off with a canoe in which they carried four kegs of gunpowder. They were to bypass the American gunboat and head for the rapids of the Rock River. The three men were to gather the Sac and give them the gunpowder. McKay felt the gunboat would have to slow at the rapids and possibly tie up for firewood. When this happened, the Sac could shoot at the gunboat and harass the Americans.[23]

The following day was the eighteenth of July. Though McKay and his men had succeeded in forcing the *Governor Clark* to leave Prairie du Chien, the Americans under Lieutenant Perkins still held Fort Shelby. The British were low on cannonballs. McKay and his officers spent much of the day in counsel. They resolved to assault the fort. Toward evening, McKay assembled the leading chiefs and explained the plan. When the Indian allies were informed of this plan, the Winnebago chief—Sar-sel, or The Teal—replied with hesitation. He recounted how the Winnebago had assaulted an American fort with the Shawnee many years ago. That offensive failed, and they did not wish to resort to the same strategy. He suggested, instead, they mine into the fort from the riverbank and blow up the garrison. McKay replied, "Go at it." After spending much of the evening digging, they had progressed only twelve to fifteen feet, so the Winnebago gave up on the effort.[24]

Some of the Indians had collected cannonballs "which the Americans had by their short shots, scattered about the prairie without effect." Of these, some were three-pound shot and could be used in the British cannon. Others were useless as ammunition because of size, but still had value, as they were made from lead. In all, the British had only six rounds of shot remaining. By the next day, a small furnace was set up, and the men began to melt the lead cannon shot. Some bricks were hollowed out to make a mold, and the men cast a number of three-pound leaden balls. Other men threw up two breastworks, one within 700 yards of the fort and the other within 450 yards. With the renewed munitions and breastworks in place, McKay determined to mount an assault on Fort Shelby.[25]

As this was being accomplished, McKay had another idea. A few of the rounds of cannon shot were iron. He ordered the village blacksmith to heat the shot red hot. With shot now heated in the blacksmith's forge, McKay spread his troops out in front of Fort Shelby behind the breastworks. About three o'clock in the afternoon, McKay told Grignon

> to go around and specifically direct the interpreters to order the Indians not to fire on the fort till the cannon should commence playing the hot shot and the fort should be set on fire; then to use their muskets as briskly as possible.

McKay marched to the first breastwork. The first hot shot was brought forward. As it was about to be placed into the British cannon, a white flag "was put out from the fort."[26]

Two days earlier, Lieutenant Perkins had helplessly watched the *Governor Clark* float away. On it were munitions and supplies for the men within Fort Shelby. At the time, Perkins had "no idea that she had gone off and left us." By the evening of the nineteenth, with no gunboat to resupply their store, the Americans had expended most of the ammunition for their six- and three-pounders. And that was not their only trouble. When the Americans built Fort Shelby in early June, they had dug a well that served their needs. Now, however, it was mid-July and the water level in the well had dropped. Perkins ordered that it be sunk deeper, but in the course of the excavation the well had collapsed. The men were now without water. Seeing that McKay was about to fire the fort, Perkins had "thought it best to capitulate on the best terms I could." He consulted with the other two officers in the fort, James Kennerly, aide to General Clark, and George Kennerly, lieutenant of the militia. They concluded that surrender was the best option.[27]

Perkins composed a note, which he gave to George Kennerly, who left the fort under the white flag. Perkins wrote,

Fort Shelby
July the 19th 1814

Sir,

I am willing to surrender the garrison and Troops under my

command, provided you will save and protect the officers and men, and prevent the Indians from ill treating them.

> I am respectfully
> Your obt. Hum. Servt
> Joseph Perkins
> Capt. Comd. U. S. Troops[28]

Upon seeing the flag, McKay had issued strict orders to the Indians not to fire on the Americans. If they did so, they would be fired upon by the British troops. Receiving Perkins's conditions for surrender of the fort, McKay prepared his written response.

> Old Fort Prairie du Chien
> July 19th 1814

Sir,

> I will thank you to prolong the hour to march out of your Fort till eight O'clock to-morrow morning when you shall march out with the Honors of our Parade before the Fort[,] deliver up your arms & put yourself under the protection of the Troops under my command—

> I am Sir
> Your obedt. Humble Servt
> W.McKay
> Lt. Col. Comg. Expedition[29]

Fort Shelby now secured, McKay reconsidered his decision not to send Grignon in pursuit of the *Governor Clark*. He dispatched Grignon with an officer and twenty-six men to pursue the gunboat and "observe her motions."[30]

The formal surrender of Fort Shelby by Lieutenant Perkins to Lieutenant Colonel McKay occurred on the twentieth of July. At the capitulation the previous day, McKay had placed a strong guard within the fort and withdrawn all arms and cannon. Prior to the formal surrender, McKay had given exacting orders to the Indians that they were not in any way to harm the Americans. He then ordered the regulars and volunteers to keep the Indians in check. Nevertheless, one of the Winnebago peering into the fort saw a soldier and made a motion to him of a desire to shake hands. The soldier stuck his hand out through a porthole upon which the Winnebago cut off one of his fingers for a trophy. There was also an incident when the Americans marched from the fort for the surrender. A Sioux attempted to strike one of the soldiers, but a son-in-law of La Feuille knocked him down.[31]

No other confrontations happened and the formal surrender occurred. The American flag was lowered, McKay noting that though the standard was riddled with musket shot, the American eagle had been untouched. The British flag was then raised over the fort. The men were not immediately paroled, and it is assumed they stayed in the fort under guard until they left the prairie. McKay reported that the surrendered force included a lieutenant of a US regiment, a militia captain and a militia lieutenant, three sergeants, three corporals, two musicians, fifty-three privates, and one commissary. Lieutenant Perkins confirmed this number in his report of the events at Prairie du Chien. Perkins also noted that four men were claimed by McKay to be British subjects and removed.[32]

All the arms, munitions, and supplies in the fort were taken as spoils of war. These included an iron six-pounder mounted on a garrison carriage, an iron three-pounder on a field carriage, three swivel guns, sixty-one small arms, four swords, a field carriage for the six-pounder, ammunition, twenty-eight barrels of pork, and forty-six barrels of flour. The British force that was to remain at Prairie du Chien would use all of these.[33]

Lieutenant Colonel McKay submitted an extensive report, dated July 27, to Colonel McDouall on the events of the four days in July 1814 that would come to be known as the Battle of Prairie du Chien. In the report, he complimented every officer and interpreter under his command. He commended Joseph Rolette for his coolness in action running down from the upper end of the village "thro' the heat of fire" to receive orders. He especially praised Rolette for all he did in "preserving the citizens from being quite ruined by pillaging Indians." McKay found Captain Anderson to be indispensable in keeping everything in order during the action, but particularly in all the help he gave Sergeant Keating in following the cannon and transporting the ammunition. All of the lieutenants, whom McKay named along with Captain Dease, acted "with that courage and activity so becoming Canadian Militia or Volunteers." While all of the interpreters

*Surrender of Fort Shelby to Captain Anderson, July 20, 1814*, pencil sketch by Cal N. Peters, ca. 1938. COURTESY VILLA LOUIS HISTORIC SITE

assisted, McKay pointed out the Sioux interpreters, St. Germain and Renville, "absolutely prevented their Indians committing any outrages in the plundering way." Commissary Honore kept an exact account of provisions so none was lost. The Michigan Fencibles "behaved with great courage, coolness, and regularity." And of Sergeant Keating, "too much cannot be said for him for the fate of the day and our successes are to be attributed in a great measure to his courage and well managed firing." McKay was not as complimentary of his Indian allies and was especially harsh on the Winnebago, recounting their pillaging and stating he really had no desire to give them their presents.[34]

McKay recommended that if the British intended to retain the fort at Prairie du Chien, reinforcement of fifty regular troops would be a necessity, as would a large quantity of ammunition for the cannon and arms. Pork would also have to be procured, but as the harvest would soon be in, flour would become available in a month and a half. He based his recommendation on his opinion that an attack "may undoubtedly be looked for from below." He frankly told McDouall that if "four or five of these

Floating Block Houses" such as the *Governor Clark* came up the river, the present force could not repulse an attack "unless for particularly favored by providence than before." If he heard that an American force appeared anywhere between Fort Madison and the prairie, he would move his men downriver and attack .[35]

Displaying his ability as a military commander, McKay was correct in his assessment that the United States would be sending a force to strengthen the American presence at Prairie du Chien. Unknown to McKay, Captain Campbell and his men had reached the Rock River about the time Lieutenant Perkins had requested terms of surrender. Campbell and two officers commanded three "Floating Bock Houses" as McKay feared. The attack "from below" was only two days' travel from Prairie du Chien.

# 10

## AMERICAN ATTEMPTS AT RELIEF AND BRITISH SUCCESSES

### *July–September 1814*

The first day of the attack on Fort Shelby, Colonel McKay had focused on the *Governor Clark*. In the face of the cannon fire, to the dismay of Lieutenant Perkins, the captain aboard the gunboat ordered the vessel's anchor cable cut, and the *Governor Clark* drifted downstream to lay in the shelter of an island so damages could be repaired. Unable to spare the men to follow the gunboat and attack it, McKay had decided to turn to British allies down the Mississippi River.

The evening of July 19, one night before the formal surrender of Fort Shelby to the British, the canoe sent down to the Rock River from Prairie du Chien by McKay and manned by two Sac and one Ioway arrived at Black Hawk's camp. Only hours before, the camp had seen Major John Campbell and his American contingent off to the prairie. Now, the men in the canoe informed Black Hawk that the British had come to Prairie du Chien and captured the American fort. The six kegs of gunpowder sent with them were to be used by Black Hawk's band to attack the *Governor Clark* at the Rock River rapids. They invited Black Hawk to "join them again in the war, which we agreed to." Black Hawk collected his warriors, and that evening they left their village, walking overland in an attempt to catch up with the American boats. Black Hawk later stated, "If we had known the day before, we could easily have taken them all, as the war chief used no precautions to prevent it."[1]

In the meantime, Campbell and his men continued their journey up the river, totally unaware of the events that had transpired at Prairie du Chien. The convoy stayed encamped on the shore about four miles above the Rock River, waiting for a wind that would help them pass through the fourteen miles of rapids above Rock Island where the Rock River entered the Mississippi River. On the morning of the twenty-first, a wind had arisen, so the men poled the barges into the river. They had only gone three miles when the wind strengthened and pushed the barge in which Campbell rode close to the shore, where it grounded. To lessen the weight of his boat, Campbell ordered the lead and musket balls to be unloaded and transferred to the other barges, and all got under way once again. They soon entered the rapids. About this time, the Sac arrived at the Mississippi. Black Hawk saw the barges halfway up the rapids, "all sailing with a strong wind." The wind had increased to such an extent that again Campbell's barge became separated from the others. Fearing that his boat would be dashed to pieces on the rocks, he ordered it poled toward shore. While they were attempting this change of course, the wind and churning water pushed the barge so hard against the shallow river bottom that it became impossible to dislodge it.[2]

Black Hawk saw his opportunity. About thirty minutes after the barge grounded, he and his band attacked, killing the two sentinels Campbell had posted on shore, along with another soldier. The barge stuck fast, Campbell ordered the men "to defend her to the last extremity, which they did for two and a half hours." Campbell later reported that the boat was so near the bank that the Sac were "able to fire in at our port oar holes." In the course of the fight, Black Hawk prepared flaming arrows and, after a few attempts, succeeded in setting the sail, which lay unfurled on the deck, on fire.[3]

The other two barges had been ahead of Campbell's barge. Hearing gunfire and seeing smoke, Lieutenants Rector and Riggs determined to turn back. It took almost an hour to turn around and tack against the wind to return to Campbell's aid. Once there, Campbell ordered Lieutenant Rector to "fall along side" his burning boat. Doing so, the wounded were transferred to the boat commanded by Lieutenant Rector as the Indians commenced their attack. The combined weight of the many people on board caused the boat to take on water through the oar holes, so the provisions stowed on Rector's barge were thrown into the river. In the course of directing the movement of people, Campbell was wounded. The other barge, commanded by Lieutenant Riggs, attempted to draw near and help, but the anchor would not hold. The wind was driving the boat toward shore, so Riggs commanded the cable be cut, and the current pulled the barge downstream. Finally, some of Campbell's men were able to pole Rector's barge back from shore, and the current pulled the soldiers and wounded away from the Sac.[4]

Black Hawk's men boarded the grounded barge, put out the fire, and began a search for plunder. Riggs, who had been providing cover fire for Rector off shore, wanted to salvage Campbell's barge. A skirmish over possession of Campbell's barge continued "until half an hour by Sun" when the wind died. Unable to bring off the boat, Riggs finally left and turned downriver. Now unhampered by gunfire, Black Hawk searched the boat, finding several cannon, barrels of clothing, and canvas lodges. These he distributed to the warriors. They disposed of the dead and then walked to a Fox village below Rock Island. There they erected the lodges and hoisted the British flag.[5]

As Riggs's boat left for St. Louis, the *Governor Clark* passed the Sac encampment, heading downriver. The gunboat maneuvered to provide support and protection for the two barges. The young warriors sprang to follow the boat, firing at it, but did little damage. The sight of the *Governor Clark*, however, confirmed the account of the British capture of Prairie du Chien. That same day, Black Hawk saw Pierre Grignon with a company coming down the Mississippi in pursuit of the American gunboat. Although they had drawn close enough to the *Governor Clark* to shout demands for surrender, Captain Yeiser had ignored the British. Grignon continued to follow in hopes that the gunboat would get stuck in the rapids. Yeiser navigated the *Governor Clark* safely through the rapids, though, so Grignon and his men turned back to the prairie.[6]

When McKay learned of the attack by Black Hawk and his warriors on the barges, he called it "one of the most brilliant actions fought by indians only since the commencement of the war." He now felt there was little danger of attack by the Americans for the present. But he thought another attempt would be made in the fall or early spring. He dispatched some men and a barge to recover the cannon that had been salvaged from Campbell's boat, for they could be mounted within the fort at Prairie du Chien. Black Hawk met McKay's men when they arrived at the site of the burned barge. The men complimented Black Hawk and his warriors on their bravery. After feasting and dancing, the men loaded the cannon onto the barge. Black Hawk gave the men from the prairie documents he had rescued from Campbell's vessel. They left one cannon and three men with Black Hawk, promising to return soon with "a large body of soldiers." The British had initiated the first phase of setting up a defensible position in case another attempt should be made to send a force to Prairie du Chien. Black Hawk appointed warriors who were to spy and keep watch for any movement on the Mississippi.[7]

—⊩—

The combined taking of Fort Shelby by the British and attack upon the troops General Howard had sent to reinforce Lieutenant Perkins was reported in the *Niles' Weekly Register* in August. The editor concluded with the grim speculation that all the American men left in the fort at Prairie du Chien "were probably massacred." These two events were "probably the commencement of *Dickson's* operations [to attack St. Louis]" (original emphasis). To Americans, Dickson still seemed so great a threat that an incident in which a Sac spoke to Clark was transformed into a violent confrontation. The editor asked his readers, "How will the English government and their agent Robert Dickson appear to the world, when it is announced that *he* suborned a Sac warrior to assassinate governor Clark while in council at Praire de Chien" (original emphasis).[8] In fact, neither speculation of massacre or assassination was true. Dickson remained at Michilimackinac, and McKay was looking forward to joining him. He complained of the heat at Prairie du Chien, which had reached 98 degrees one day, saying, "I could not live six months in this very warm climate." He was putting the fort in order to make a "good state of defense." As soon as the boat he had sent to the Rock River for the cannon returned, he would leave for Michilimackinac.[9]

McKay had planned to keep the prisoners at Prairie du Chien as hostages in case an American force came to the prairie and attempted to retake the fort. He threatened that if this happened and the Americans fired one shot, he would give the prisoners over to the Indians. In the interim, however, he still had to feed the American soldiers, which, as he acknowledged, would deplete his provisions. He could send them as prisoners to Michilimackinac, but the size of a guard needed to convey the Americans would leave him "quite destitute of resources."[10]

McKay had to anticipate that another force would be coming from St. Louis. With no other option, then, he determined to send Lieutenant Perkins and the soldiers to St. Louis. They were to leave on July 28, escorted by Michel Brisbois Jr. and a small group of men. McKay furnished a boat and provisions for the trip, and they embarked at the end of July. Brisbois and his men accompanied the American prisoners as far as the Rock River. Brisbois went to the Sac village just above the mouth of the river and consulted with the four hundred to five hundred Sac who lived there. The Sac agreed to let the Americans proceed down the river. At the rapids, the British escort disembarked. Perkins and his men continued on and arrived at St. Louis on August 6, "all in good health except the wounded who are likely to recover."[11]

There was more to get in order at Prairie du Chien than the return of the American soldiers. From the first arrival on the prairie, McKay had difficulty controlling his Indian allies, especially the Sioux and Winnebago. Prior to the attack on Fort Shelby, the two tribes had been placed north of the fort. While waiting for action to commence, they had shot some horses and cattle grazing in the common that belonged to the residents. Some Winnebago looted the homes to the point of taking "the coverings off their Beds & leaving many without a second shirt to put on their backs." When the Winnebago began to enter the houses within the Main Village, McKay had ordered Captain Dease and the Prairie du Chien Militia to keep guard over the homes. This prevented the militia from joining McKay and those stationed below the fort. The Indians' unrest may have been what made McKay determine to initiate the attack on the fort after Perkins had refused to surrender the garrison. Then, after the surrender of Fort Shelby and unable to garner the spoils of war, the Winnebago "swarmed among the settlers," plundering whatever they desired. A few warriors went into the fields and cut down the green wheat.

One evening a few days after the surrender, news came to the village that some Indians were killing cattle, some of which belonged to Joseph Rolette. Hearing this, Rolette announced that he was going to find the Indians. Joseph Renville, interpreter to the Sioux, heard Rolette make the comment and followed him to the Sioux camp. Arriving there, Rolette "invited the Sioux to go with him," recommending the Sioux take their guns and "take away the meat the Puans [Winnebago] had and fight with them." At that moment, Michel Brisbois passed by, and Renville pulled him in, saying, "Let us go and stop this business." Renville knew that if the Sioux attacked the Winnebago, there would be fighting among all the tribes at the prairie. In the end, Renville and Brisbois were able to calm Rolette; they convinced the Winnebago to give the meat to McKay.[12]

But McKay knew he needed to appease the Winnebago, as they were British allies. To prevent any more damage, McKay gathered the tribes and distributed presents. Most then left for their homes; about one hundred Sioux, Lac Courte Oreilles, and Winnebago remained. Once the majority of the tribes had gone and order had been established, McKay reported, "The Inhabitants have all come forward and taken the oath of allegiance and are now doing duty on parole or otherwise as required."[13]

—⊪—

Whether by his design or at the request of the troops, by August 1 the British fortification at Prairie du Chien had been named "Fort McKay." By this date, the residents of the prairie attempted to return their lives to some normality and resume the work the season demanded. Some of the men from La Baye who had volunteered under Pierre Grignon requested that they be allowed to return home. Their families awaited them, and it was time to harvest the crops they had planted in the spring. Joseph Rolette had business to attend to at Michilimackinac to prepare his store of trade goods for the wintering posts he operated. McKay gave Rolette and the men from La Baye permission to depart, although Rolette was called on for one last duty. He was to convey four men to Michilimackinac. They were the British whom McKay had found among the American force when Perkins surrendered Fort Shelby. Two were British deserters. Two were "bad subjects" who had joined the Americans when they arrived at the prairie; one had been "particularly active in this abuse" of "deprecating the British Character." Lieutenant Perkins, in his report, listed the British deserters as Richard Marion and John Brown and the other men as Francis Liekee and Peter Parrish. Rolette agreed to complete this responsibility but asked that McKay submit his request to McDouall for a discharge from service.[14]

Rolette left the prairie for Michilimackinac on or about August 1. When his boat hove in sight of the island village, the residents crowded the shore awaiting news of what had happened at Prairie du Chien. According to August Grignon, the following dialogue occurred between the residents of the island and Rolette.

> Capt. Rolette, what is the news?
>
> "A great battle – a sanguinary contest," responded Rolette, with an air of great solemnity and importance.
>
> How many were killed?
>
> *None!*
>
> How many were wounded?
>
> *None!*
>
> "What a bloody contest!" vociferously shouted the crowd, as they escorted the hero from the boat to the garrison.[15]

Joseph Rolette wished to return to his life as a trader, but Thomas G. Anderson desired to remain within the military through the end of the war. On August 10, Lieutenant Colonel McKay departed the prairie to return with four others to Michilimackinac. When McKay left, the garrison numbered about 120 Michigan volunteers and militia. The Sac, Fox, and Kickapoo had gone. Petit Corbeau had gone with his band of Dakota Sioux to distribute the presents he had received at Michilimackinac. He would be at his village, but "in readiness at a moment's notice if wanted here." He intended to return with his band and winter on the upper prairie. La Feuille, with about fifty Dakota warriors, remained as a guard.[16]

Colonel McKay had had three captains of volunteers under his command while at Prairie du Chien. Pierre Grignon had found William McKay to be "a fine looking, tall, well proportioned man, but was regarded as strict, and sometimes severe over those in his employ in the Indian trade." There is no record of Joseph Rolette's opinion of McKay. Though McKay had praised Anderson's ability during the assault on Fort Shelby, Anderson later developed a dislike of McKay. Although he commended McKay in a letter to Colonel McDouall as "an undaunted and able commander" whose "judicious management" made the capture of Prairie du Chien possible, in later life he accused McKay of being drunk at his headquarters while others were engaged with the Americans and incapable of making decisions. No one else made that accusation of McKay; perhaps Anderson balked at McKay's strictness and position or wished to inflate his role in the capture of Fort Shelby. As McKay prepared to depart and Grignon and Rolette returned to their business pursuits, he had only two choices as to whom to place in command of the garrison: Thomas G. Anderson or Captain Pullman of the Michigan Fencibles. McKay chose Anderson.[17]

—ıı—

On assuming command of Fort McKay, Anderson pictured himself. "I am now, on a smaller scale, a Wellington—commanding all around me." In mid-August, Prairie du Chien was by no means secure, but Anderson would demonstrate the organizational skills for which McKay commended him. Anderson determined to create order and discipline. Daily he had the men drill with their muskets and practice firing the cannon and swivel guns. With periodic arrivals of gunpowder from Michilimackinac, Anderson made sure this continued. He would brook no defiance and often had men confined in irons for refusal to stand guard duty or for drunkenness. The lack of provisions for the men proved a difficulty. Flour was greatly needed for rations. Even with the destruction by the Winnebago, the wheat harvest looked to be good, so Anderson assured McDouall that flour could be acquired from the residents of the prairie. As the fort's stores dwindled, Anderson ordered the off-duty volunteers to help with the harvest when threshing began in mid-August. Many of the farmers on the prairie had horse flouring mills to grind the wheat. Many of the mills needed repair, so Anderson promised the farmers "every assistance."[18]

While some of the volunteers worked in the fields, Anderson detailed others to make repairs to the garrison and enlarge the physical structure of the fort. A new well was dug, platforms were constructed on which the swivels and three-pounders were mounted, and the area between the blockhouses was expanded. Besides overseeing the maneuvers and construction, Anderson met with the various Indians who arrived at the

Thomas Gummersal Anderson, ca. 1850, by William Sawyer. Anderson, a Prairie du Chien resident and British supporter, raised a company of volunteers and assisted in the capture of Fort Shelby, afterward becoming commander of the garrison. COURTESY OF MARGOT MADDISON-MACFADYEN

prairie, taking over Boilvin's house for these small councils.[19]

Though in command of Fort McKay, Anderson, like McKay, was to receive all orders for conduct and action from Lieutenant Colonel McDouall at Michilimackinac. Fort McKay was under his jurisdiction. Confronted with an American naval squadron under orders to retake Mackinac, McDouall did not communicate with Anderson until the end of August. To maintain a flow of information to Michilimackinac, Anderson employed Lieutenant Pierre Grignon. On August 21, McDouall wrote to Grignon that La Baye was to be "an intermediate point of communication between Fort McKay and this Island [Mackinac]," and Grignon was to do everything for the "good of the service" and the advantage of the two posts. If Grignon should learn that Fort McKay was to be attacked, he was "with the most indefatigable exertion" to collect as many Menominee and Winnebago as possible and "repair to his [Anderson's] assistance" with provisions. To support Michilimackinac, Grignon needed to obtain flour, and if that was not possible, then wheat. Finally, he and the Menominee must be prepared to help defend Mackinac Island.[20] So, both Anderson and McDouall depended on Grignon. Until the end of British control of Prairie du Chien, Grignon spent many days paddling and trudging between La Baye and Prairie du Chien.

In mid-August, delegations of two or three Fox started coming to Prairie du Chien. They told Anderson that the Americans were "coming up." Then three young Fox arrived with a pipe. The Sac had sent them as emissaries to tell Anderson that the Americans were on their way up to Prairie du Chien in barges. Three different couriers had seen the barges on the Mississippi above Cape au Gris. The young men told Anderson that the Sac requested him to bring his force to the rapids and meet the enemy at that point. Of this meeting, Anderson recorded in his journal, "I cannot put faith in this report." He believed that the Sac and Fox were telling him a story so that he would give them more guns and ammunition, and that the story had been concocted by the Fox and the Sioux chief Red Wing to get the British away from Prairie du Chien so that they could destroy the fort.[21]

Anderson had met with Red Wing soon after he had taken over command of Fort McKay. Red Wing told Anderson he would not fight against the Americans even though "all the blood in my heart is English." When Anderson continued to press him, Red Wing told Anderson how he had seen the future three times in a dream. Pointing to the lion on the British peace medal, Red Wing said,

> This lion, like our tiger, sleeps all day; but the eagle who is the most powerful of all birds, only sleeps at night; in the day time he flies about everywhere and sees all on the ground. He will light on a tree over the lion, and they will scold at each other for a while; but they will finally make up and be friends, and smoke the pipe of peace. The lion will then go home, and leave us Indians with our foes.[22]

Several days later, Lieutenant Duncan Graham returned to Prairie du Chien. He had been down the Mississippi. The Americans had left a gunboat secured to the riverbank a few miles above the site of Fort Madison, and Anderson had sent Graham in an attempt to bring the boat up to the prairie. If this could not be accomplished, he was to burn the boat to prevent the Americans from recovering it. Graham reported that as he was about to leave from the Rock River to go and destroy the boat, two young

Sac couriers arrived from a Sac town on the Missouri River. They reported that some French gentlemen from St. Louis sent word to the Missouri Sac to inform the Sac on the Rock River "to be on their guard, as the Americans were to leave the Illinois on the 4th inst., in a strong detachment, to cut off the Sauks."[23]

With Graham's report, Anderson decided there must have been some validity to the accounts brought to the prairie by the Fox. He called together all the officers on the prairie to share the information Graham had brought and to ask their opinion as to what should be done. As a response, "they universally agreed that it was absolutely necessary to send a small detachment, not only for the preservation of the post, but to retain the Indians in our favor." So, even though Anderson found it "most inconvenient," he thought it was his duty to send an expedition to the Sac. Lieutenant Graham was placed in charge of the force that included thirty men from the garrison at Fort McKay, about fifty Sioux, forty-five Fox, and sixteen Winnebago. They would travel on the Mississippi and were armed with a brass three-pound cannon commanded by Sergeant Keating, and two swivels for which Lieutenant Michel Brisbois Jr. and Sergeant Colin Campbell were responsible. Before the expedition embarked, interpreter Renville left the prairie for the Sioux country to ask for assistance from La Feuille and Petit Corbeau. According to Graham, the Sac had already sent word to the Winnebago, and he estimated about twelve hundred warriors would be assembled at the rapids by the time the men from Prairie du Chien arrived. [24]

The British expedition left Prairie du Chien on August 27 and arrived at the Rock Island rapids two days later. At that moment there was no danger from the Americans, but as Graham pointed out, "Our coming here has given more satisfaction to the Sauks than if all the goods in the King's store in Mackinaw had been sent them." Graham explained to Black Hawk and the others the intention of the expedition, and he was informed that those at the rapids would "stand by us to the last man." He found them "animated to meet the Enemy." Graham still had no details as to how many American barges were coming up the Mississippi or the number of men they would be carrying. So, he had the Indians maintain a constant lookout and set up their line of defense on Rock Island. To him, the island was "the best place for defense that I know on the Mississippi." He assured Anderson that "we cannot be surprised on the least notice of their coming."[25]

—⊩⊩—

As the British and Sac lay in wait for the arrival of the Americans, other events had transpired on the American side. Although it was true that a confrontation was not far off, the British were unaware of the true nature of the American offensive, which had been in the making for the past several weeks.

As late as August 1, General Howard was unaware of what had happened to Lieutenant Perkins and the men under his command. Howard had in hand the reports submitted by Major John Campbell and Ensign Riggs on the failure of their attempt to reach Prairie du Chien and relieve the men in the fort, but he was still unaware the British had succeeded in taking the fort. Clark had given him a copy of the report from Captain Yeiser as to how he was driven from Prairie du Chien by a large British and Indian force, leaving Lieutenant Perkins to defend Fort Shelby with only sixty men. Based on this report, Howard fully believed that Perkins and his men were still in defense of Fort Shelby. Howard found that the "situation of this Command is deplorable not only from the smallness of it" but the fact that he did not have the means to support a garrison so far removed from St. Louis. Therefore, he informed the secretary of war, "I have determined to make an effort to bring the Command away." He realized he would be leaving the mid-Mississippi vulnerable, but he had to make the attempt or "leave upwards of Sixty of our men to perish inevitably." To rescue Perkins and bring the men back to St. Louis, Howard planned to organize a command of about four hundred men to travel in fortified boats. Howard requested instructions as to what to do if the expedition he was to send to Prairie du Chien failed. Should he try again, and if so, what aid could he expect from the secretary? If the men Howard supplied were to fail in their mission, he did not have the resources to raise a large enough force to march by land to Prairie du Chien.[26]

About two weeks later, Howard finally received from Clark a copy of Lieutenant Perkins's report. Informed of Prairie du Chien's capture and Perkins's safe return with his men to St. Louis, Howard was still determined to organize an expedition up the Mississippi. Instead of Prairie du Chien being the objective, however, Howard decided to advance a two-pronged attack against the Sac along the Missouri and Mississippi Rivers.

The frontier along these waterways and their tributaries suffered daily harassments from the Indians. Howard's military offensive would target the Sac bands who lived along the Missouri at the mouth of the Grand River and those whose villages lay along the lower reaches of the Rock River.

On August 22, Howard ordered Major Zachary Taylor to lead a force of rangers and militia upstream to the Sac villages at the mouth of the Rock River. In a tactic often used to fight elusive Indians, Taylor was ordered to "destroy the villages." Howard explained the next part of the plan to the secretary of war:

> He will, after effecting or failing to effect the object at that place, drop down to the Des Moines and erect a fort which must be maintained until further orders can be sent.

Taylor collected his force at Fort Cape au Gris. With few regular soldiers available and Perkins's company unavailable, as they were still on parole, Taylor set about raising volunteers. Nelson Rector raised a company of Illinois volunteers, as did Samuel Whiteside, a noted Indian fighter. A company of Missouri Rangers was added, so that Taylor's command amounted to 334 men. On August 28 they headed up the Mississippi in eight fortified gunboats. At the same time, Howard sent another expedition under the command of General Henry Dodge of the Missouri Militia up the Missouri River.[27]

When Taylor and his command reached the Rock River on September 4, they had not yet seen any trace of the Indians, and they had no idea that Black Hawk's Sac warriors were lying in wait for the American forces. The men who waited were equally unaware of Howard's new offensive against the Sac; they were under the impression that the Americans were attempting to take Prairie du Chien once more. Another blow was soon dealt to the Americans: after only a few days upon the river an outbreak of measles had occurred on the boats, rendering many men too sick to fight.

At their arrival at the mouth of the Rock River, the Sac and the other Indians made an appearance in "considerable numbers" along the east bank of the river. Some then crossed behind the gunboats to the west side. As the gunboats sailed past the mouth of the river, Taylor realized that his vessels were too large to tack into the Rock River and advance to the Sac villages. He decided to continue up the Mississippi. As they proceeded, he noticed a great number of horses on a large island opposite the river mouth and on the western shore. He considered this a ruse by the Indians to attract the boats and ignored the ploy. Unable to follow the plan outlined by General Howard, Taylor devised his own strategy. He would have the gunboats pass the nearest Sac village as if the objective of the expedition was Prairie du Chien. Doing this, Taylor could view the shore to locate a landing that gave him the best advantage to bring his artillery to bear on the villages. He also hoped that a party of Indians would approach his gunboat with a flag, since he proposed to raise a white flag. He could then bring them to council; at the council he would learn the situation at Prairie du Chien and the number of Sac in the area, but more to the point he could retaliate for "their repeated acts of treachery." If the Indians did not show a flag but attacked, Taylor would draw the Sac some distance from their villages. Then in the night, his men could leave the gunboats, advance to the villages, and "destroy them."[28]

Lieutenant Duncan Graham had sent eight Sac downriver to see if they could learn anything about the expedition of which the Missouri Sac had warned their brothers, and on the evening of September 3 the "discovery party" had returned. Based on the number of gunboats and men, Graham concluded the convoy's destination was Prairie du Chien. Knowing the Mississippi well, Graham believed the rapids marked the only place to attack with an advantage. He moved some of the Sac and most of the warriors from the other tribes to the west side of the island in the Mississippi and established a position at the narrowest point of the channel, "determined to dispute the road with them inch by inch." He watched the eight fortified gunboats tack up the river, noting that four of the vessels were equal in size to the *Governor Clark*. The boat in the lead was flying a white flag as it approached the head of Credit Island.[29]

Then, as had occurred with the flotilla under the command of Major John Campbell, the weather turned. The wind shifted to blow down the river, and rain, thunder, and lightning broke over the boats. Taylor described it as blowing "a perfect hurricane quarterly down the river." The boats could go no farther. To prevent them from foundering or drifting onto the sand, Taylor ordered the gunboats to tie up in the lee of a small island covered with willows just east of the northern tip of Credit Island.

He posted sentries and waited for the dawn. Graham had sent the women and children from the Sac villages to safety on Credit Island. The men were to stay at the village and only cross to the island if the Americans attempted to land. The cannon and swivels Graham placed under the protection of the Sioux in case there was a need for retreat, and they promised "they would rather be killed to the last man than give up the guns."[30]

In the night, one of the sentinels was killed, so Taylor took down the white flag and raised a "bloody" flag in its place. Graham understood that now Taylor would fight, giving no quarter. Graham and his men had repositioned the guns on a high point on the west side of the Mississippi. With the sign for no quarter, as day broke, Graham ordered the Sac to fire upon one of the boats. In return, Taylor ordered his men and cannon to open fire, but all troops were to remain on board. The British cannon and swivels repeatedly found their targets, so Taylor ordered his men to get into formation and "drum" the Indians from the island. As the American Rangers went ashore and proceeded through the willows, the Sac crossed to Credit Island. The cannons on the gunboats commanded by Whiteside and Rector fired upon the Sac with little effect. Rector moved farther down, which opened his boat to direct fire from the British cannon and swivels.[31]

Repositioning their arms, all the American gunboats were now exposed to the British artillery. The gunboat commanded by Lieutenant Hempstead was shattered "considerably." Taylor then ordered all the gunboats to retreat in an orderly manner down the river. Graham and his men continued to fire, reposition, and fire the cannon at the American boats "as far as the ground would permit us to drag the guns; but they soon got out of our reach." In all, the engagement lasted only an hour, and Graham estimated that of the fifty-three shots from their artillery directed at the American gunboats, only three or four did not pierce the wooden sides and superstructures protecting the men and cannon.[32]

The American gunboats continued downriver for at least three miles, then pulled to shore. Graham thought they might be building breastworks from which to make a stand. But Taylor only wanted to repair the boats as best as possible and tend to the wounded. Noticing that the Indians had followed, Taylor collected all the officers under his command. With only 334 effective men to fight, he asked whether they thought there was any prospect for success. The men expressed the opinion that they were outnumbered three to one and would be incapable of destroying the Sac villages. Taylor therefore ordered the gunboats to pull up their anchors, hoist sails, and move southward.[33]

Taylor reported he could have destroyed the Sac villages if the enemy had not been supplied with artillery. Once again, Sergeant Keating and the brass three-pounder had made a difference. Graham praised Brisbois and Campbell for their execution with the swivels; however,

> [i]t is to the skill and courage of Serg't Keating, on whom everything depended, that we owe our success and no praise of mine can bestow on him what he deserves.[34]

Small band after small band of Sac and Sioux from the Rock River returned to Prairie du Chien, each relaying stories of the action against the enemy directed by Lieutenant Graham. Anderson had reported to McDouall of his decision to send Graham to the Rock River and the requests sent to the tribes to support Graham. Anderson begged to remark that the upper Mississippi was in a critical situation. He stated that Robert Dickson was absolutely needed at the prairie, as was the reinforcement of troops that Lieutenant Colonel McKay had requested. But Anderson had not received any communication from McDouall since McKay had departed from the prairie and placed Anderson in charge of the garrison. No news had been received from Dickson or Michilimackinac. This likely raised concerns at Prairie du Chien.[35]

—⊩—

Lieutenant Colonel Robert McDouall had been sent to Michilimackinac for a greater responsibility than command of the British force on the island. The British had lost control of Lake Erie in the battle of Put-in-Bay in September of 1813, which effectively cut the British supply line between Montreal and Michilimackinac. A new route had been established from York to Nottawasaga Bay and a naval base opened in Georgian Bay, from which Mackinac Island and the surrounding countryside could be supplied and reinforced. These initiatives were crucial to maintaining the British presence in the Northwest and preserving alliances with the American Indians. In May 1814, McDouall had arrived at Michilimackinac with the

Royal Newfoundland Fencibles and the Royal Artillery, ordered to keep the island in British hands so that the flow of goods and thereby Indian support continued. He had barely arrived when Tete de Chien and the traders from Prairie du Chien brought their reports of American takeover of the prairie. Faced with the Americans at his western door, McDouall had sent McKay with what little he could spare to Prairie du Chien, with successful results. The rest of the garrison, along with Robert Dickson, the Menominee, and other tribes he could retain, were needed for the protection of Michilimackinac and the straits.

As McKay's force left for the prairie, Captain Arthur Sinclair of the United States Navy had been ordered to seize control of the upper lakes by recapturing Mackinac and destroying the British naval presence on the lakes. Less than a week after the British retook Prairie du Chien, Sinclair and his fleet arrived off Mackinac Island. His force included two sloops and two schooners, on board which were 750 men from three regular army regiments, 250 Ohio militia, and several artillerymen. Lieutenant Colonel George Croghan, a nephew of William Clark, commanded the contingent. Sinclair had already destroyed the abandoned British post at St. Joseph Island and raided an outpost of the North West Company on the St. Mary's River. To face this force, McDouall had about 300 men, of which 100 were local militia, and an Indian contingent of about 350. As McKay advised McDouall that he needed to send reinforcements to Prairie du Chien if he wished to keep the prairie out of American control, McDouall faced an American force that outnumbered his force two to one. He would not write to Anderson with instructions for the command of Fort McKay until August 21.

The American ships fired upon the island for two days. Most of the shot fell harmlessly as the British blockhouse stood too high for the naval guns to reach. Dense fog stalled the attack. On August 4, Croghan decided to land a force and work his way through woods to attack the blockhouse. Rather than wait to be attacked, McDouall led a small number of militiamen in the fort and outlying blockhouse. He left the main body of his force to man the breastworks that faced the American line of advance. In the second battle for Mackinac Island, the British-allied Indians led by Dickson played a major role. A band of Menominee under Tomah maintained a position on the left flank of the British. Part of the American force, under

Major Holmes, had been sent to turn the flank and charge the fort. At a signal, the Menominee voiced their war cry and opened fire. Tomah's men stopped the advance, killing Holmes and the second in command. Leaderless, the Americans fell back in confusion. Croghan sent more regulars, but they faced a withering fire from the Indians. Croghan ordered a retreat, the Americans returning to the ships. In one day of fighting, the British military and its Indian allies had retained the island.[36]

They were not yet out of the woods. The USS *Tigress* and USS *Scorpion* continued a blockade of Mackinac Island, preventing the much-needed provisions from arriving at the fort in hopes of starving the garrison into surrender before the following spring. In addition to supplies for the fort, the season was drawing near for the arrival of the presents and goods for distribution to the western tribes. If the blockade was not lifted, the fort would be forced to surrender. This would also cut off support for Fort McKay and the western Indians and lead to the loss of the upper Mississippi and Britain's Indian allies.

At both La Baye and Prairie du Chien, the tribes were gathering in an-

Lt. Colonel Robert McDouall commissioned this painting, *Michilimackinac on Lake Huron,* by William Dashwood, around 1820. It shows the captured American vessels *Scorpion* and *Tigress.* MACKINAC STATE HISTORIC PARKS COLLECTION

ticipation of the arrival of Robert Dickson with their presents. They were foraging in the fields and eyeing the residents' cattle. The blockade had to be lifted. So, on the night of September 3—the night before the battle of Credit Island—four boatloads of British and Indians led by Captain Andrew Bulger and Robert Dickson set out from Mackinac Island. They slipped alongside the *Tigress* and boarded the schooner. After a brief but bloody battle, the British force captured the ship in five minutes. The British then ran the *Tigress* alongside the *Scorpion* and captured it. The western lakes were once again open, and orders for provisions and Indian presents could safely be sent from Montreal.

The British victories at Prairie du Chien and the Rock Island rapids, coupled with the successful defense of Michilimackinac, reasserted British preeminence in the western lakes and upper Mississippi. Rumors abounded in St. Louis and the Illinois Country about the British and Indians coming down to attack "our frontiers." Some had heard that the British were building at fort at Green Bay. Others said tribes were massing at La Baye and Milwaukee to assault Fort Clark. Now, only Fort Independence protected St. Louis. Thomas Forsyth, US Indian agent to the Sac and Fox, calculated that the British could raise three thousand to four thousand Indians, not including the Sioux and the tribes along the Missouri River. If the reports he had heard were true—that Spain had joined Great Britain in the war—then he feared the Spanish could come down the Missouri and the British down the Mississippi and Illinois. If this happened, "indiscriminate massacre must take place."[37]

# 11

## TENSIONS AT FORT MCKAY

*September 1814–January 1815*

American attempts to gain control of the western lakes and upper Mississippi had failed in the face of the British–Indian alliance. Each American force had been pieced together by a mix of regulars, rangers, and militia. While the same was true of the British forces, the tribes—especially those present at the Rock River and Mackinac Island—had proved to be invaluable. The advance of Taylor up the Mississippi and Dodge up the Missouri had united the Sac, who throughout the conflict had wavered in their allegiance. The victory of the British–Sac force at the battle of Credit Island drew unallied bands of Indians to join the British alliance and made existing tribal alliances more assured of the power of the British. With the death of General Howard on September 18, the Americans were without a commander. The time was opportune for the British to push into Illinois.

Most of the bands of Sioux that had participated in the attack on Taylor's gunboats had returned to Prairie du Chien, but instead of going to their villages, they agreed to wait at Prairie La Crosse to see if they were needed to fight the Americans. Dakota Sioux chief Petit Corbeau, however, insisted on camping at Prairie du Chien. He told Anderson that when the Americans were at the prairie, they had sent tobacco to each village to induce the Sioux to join them. They had not sent tobacco to his village, as "they knew him to be too good an Englishman to be induced to join them." While Petit Corbeau found this action to be an honor, the Americans meant it as an insult, and he planned to retaliate. He and his band "intended to hunt Americans all winter."[1]

Little by little Anderson learned of the loyalty of other tribes. Forty Yankton Sioux from the Des Moines River had arrived at the Dakota Sioux chief La Feuille's village "destined for the war-path." Winneshiek, the elder Winnebago chief, arrived at Prairie du Chien with a pipe and a belt for the Sioux. He assured Anderson that he only wished to ask permission to winter on Sioux lands that lay between the Mississippi and Rivieres des Sioux and not go to war with the Chippewa. He also planned to "request all Indians of what nation soever, to join hands, and not allow an American to come this far."[2]

The morale of the Indian allies was high. Some were gathering on the prairie, awaiting an order to advance, while others, like Petit Corbeau, were eager to take action on their own. But all expected to be supported with guns, ammunition, and food in any undertaking. Periodically, gunpowder and tobacco arrived at Prairie du Chien from La Baye, but little else arrived for the support of the garrison and western Indians. Anderson had sent what he could spare as presents to the Missouri bands of Sac, but his store of meat, flour, and other goods was dangerously low. When Lieutenant Graham and his detachment returned victorious from the Rock River, Anderson rewarded the Indians who accompanied him with "a good deal of bread, and some wheat," which further depleted the stores. The Winnebago at Prairie du Chien, needing more than bread, raided and drove off oxen belonging to Joseph Rolette again. Even though men in Rolette's company saw this happen, they did not stop the Winnebago. Anderson could not condone this action or others might do the same, so he sent Lieutenant Brisbois to the mouth of the Wisconsin to confiscate what might remain of the oxen. Brisbois returned with some dried beef and tallow, which Anderson then gave to his men. The Winnebago expressed surprise, as they had expected to be brought back to the prairie and confined in the fort for their actions. Perhaps Anderson thought it would be unwise to punish the Winnebago for what everyone needed.[3]

In small numbers, almost daily, Indians arrived at the prairie asking for food, which Anderson obliged as best he could. By September 21, Fort McKay had only two more days' worth of rations. Anderson went onto the prairie to talk with the residents to purchase flour, but could procure none. He therefore ordered Captain Dease to assemble all the residents in front of the fort the following day and appealed to them to try to produce more flour. As many of the men were required to do duty to protect the prairie, they explained that a lack of horses, mills, and time prevented them from grinding the grain. The demands of the Fencibles in the fort far exceeded what the residents annually produced for their own needs. And even if the horse flouring mills were fully functional, Anderson demanded flour faster than they could produce. The residents promised to furnish what they could spare, but they had to feed their families and reserve part of the harvest as seed for the following season. Hearing this, Dease chose to supply the Sac with ammunition rather than flour.

Antoine Brisbois had decided to use his connections to locate provisions. In late September, he arrived at the prairie with a boatload of corn. Some of the volunteers refused to take the corn for their rations. For this Anderson pulled them out of the ranks, took away their guns, and forbade anyone to provide them with food or give them shelter. He ordered the officers of the Indian Department to tell the Indians that if any of the rebellious volunteers were found beyond the prairie, the Indians were to bring them back dead or alive. Finally, Anderson exempted the inhabitants from working at the garrison so they could thresh wheat. To the "starving Indians" he distributed gunpowder and tobacco. Anderson wrote, "Robert Dickson's arrival is much wished for by all ranks and colors."[4]

The repulse of the Americans at Mackinac Island and the capture of the *Tigress* and *Scorpion* had returned the western lakes to British control. More important than the military victories, these actions opened the lakes so that the much-needed provisions could reach Michilimackinac. When news of the taking of the American schooners was relayed to Montreal, provisions, goods, and Indian presents that had been in the storehouses of Josiah Bleakley were quickly loaded onto canoes. On September 10 a brigade of canoes left Lachine for Michilimackinac, where it was assumed Dickson had returned after the capture of the *Tigress* and *Scorpion* and was waiting to oversee the distribution of the Indian presents. Included in the brigade were sixteen large canoes and one small one filled with bags of flour, kegs of pork and salt and spirits, cases of guns, bags of shot and kegs of powder, and tents. Ten additional canoes transported one hundred bales of Indian presents that consisted of strouds, blankets, calicos and cottons, handkerchiefs, sewing implements, awls, flints, and fire steels. The men also loaded into each canoe corn, grease, pork, flour, guns, powder, and shot.

Another brigade of canoes departed Lachine for Michilimackinac on the twenty-second of September. Alexander McKenzie was in charge of these canoes, of which eleven contained one hundred bales of dry goods, five bales of tobacco, flour, pork, salt, peas, Indian corn, tallow, guns, powder, and shot. The Indian presents had been placed in separate canoes and contained much the same merchandise as in the previous brigade, as well as ribbons, silk, garters, garnets, and "10 Cases Chiefs Guns 10 ea: & 1 Blanket of 2 ½ pts."[5]

Yet a third group of canoes was set to travel to Michilimackinac. These had been loaded at Montreal and placed in the charge of Jacques Porlier of the Indian Department. Twelve canoes departed on September 12, but the thirteenth canoe had been detained, as its cargo had not yet arrived. It awaited the delivery of "medals, silver works, and Flags." As these items were presents for the chiefs, General Sheaffe ordered the canoe to stay behind. The rest departed for Michilimackinac under Porlier's guidance. With him, Sheaffe had sent written orders as to the distribution of the Indian goods.[6]

Some of the bales of Indian goods in the brigades had been marked with the letter M. These goods were for the Indians usually supplied with presents by the commander of the military post at Michilimackinac. When the presents arrived at the post, they were to be distributed under the direction of the commanding officer

in such a manner as shall be most conducive to the benefit of His Majesty's service, for in confirming the Indians in their attachment to this Government, or reclaiming such of them as from any Misfortune or Circumstances may be wavering.

The goods marked I were intended as presents to the western Indians who were "under the agency of Robert Dickson, Esq, and especially such tribes as furnished warriors under his directions or by his orders." Under no circumstances were they to be opened at Michilimackinac. They were to be stored until Dickson or William McKay could transport them to La Baye or the place most proper for the presents to be distributed "conducive to the benefit of His Majesty's service as above said." Colonel McDouall was to aid in every way possible the conveyance of the presents to La Baye by furnishing bateaux or canoes as well as Michigan Fencibles to man the boats. These men were then to be under Dickson's or McKay's command. Both McDouall and Dickson were given a "peremptory and special instruction" that the goods were to be distributed with "the strictest impartiality." The British high command in Montreal understood the importance of the Indian allies in past military actions, and they were determined to impress all with the paramount need to preserve the alliance.[7]

William McKay, having returned to his duties in the Indian Department, had continued on to Montreal after he left Prairie du Chien at the end of July. As the canoes filled with provisions for the forts and Indian presents were pushed from the banks of the St. Lawrence River and guided upstream, it was McKay who remained behind to wait for the medals and flags. Finally on September 21, this important cargo arrived, and McKay began his voyage to Michilimackinac. McKay caught up with Porlier and the other canoes on September 26. Indicating that he had instructions for Robert Dickson from the commander of the British forces, McKay proceeded westward telling Porlier to follow "with the utmost expedition."[8]

McKay touched the shore of Mackinac Island on October 9 and immediately went in search of Robert Dickson. When he could not find him, McKay walked to the fort to report his arrival to Captain Bullock. He informed Bullock of his mission and orders from Sheaffe. As Dickson was not at Michilimackinac—he had gone to York, the military headquarters for Upper Canada—McKay required the assistance of the military "to proceed to la Baye and the Mississippi with the goods and presents he had with him as well as those coming on with Mr. Porlier." The twelve canoes under Porlier's direction arrived on the nineteenth and twentieth of October. Per the orders from General Sheaffe, all the goods marked M Porlier turned over to John Askin Jr., who now operated the Indian Department store on that island.[9]

Though only mid-October, winter had already come to Mackinac Island. There was nearly a foot of snow on the ground, and the small brooks were completely frozen over. Captain Bullock offered McKay every assistance assigning boats, men, and provisions to meet all the needs to travel as far as Prairie du Chien to distribute the goods. The boats were loaded with bales, bags, and kegs marked *I* and the special presents for the chiefs. Just as everything was ready for departure, Dickson arrived back at Michilimackinac. McKay, feeling he may be needed in the great effort that stood ahead, offered to accompany Dickson to La Baye and the Mississippi. Dickson appreciated McKay's offer, but told him that he had with him several officers and interpreters. With them, he could distribute the goods and presents to the Indians "according to the desire and wishes of Government." Instead, Dickson requested of McKay a greater service: to return to Lower Canada and report to the commander that Dickson greatly needed instructions. Dickson wanted to receive, "by express, as soon as possible," instructions as to

> what the Government wished him to do in respect to the Tribes of Indians next spring, that for the present he was quite at a loss how to act, that in the meantime he would endeavour to do for the best.

Dickson was aware of the desire of many of the tribes to attack the Americans, especially after the success at Credit Island. Not only had the chiefs and their warriors voiced their intent at Prairie du Chien, but also others had been to La Baye seeking powder and ball, as "the other Indians called for them to meet the enemy who were on their way to build a fort at Chicago."[10]

Additionally, Dickson knew of the hardships that the western tribes faced. From La Baye, Louis Grignon had written Dickson an imploring letter at the end of September. Though Pierre Grignon informed Dickson of the situation with and behavior of the Indians, Grignon was "commencing to be very anxious," having heard nothing from Dickson. Fifteen lodges of Indians had encamped at La Baye "waiting resolutely for you," while others were "assembling all around." Not sure that Dickson would receive his message before he left Michilimackinac, Grignon also wrote to John Askin Jr. In that letter, Grignon frankly stated,

> The country around here is very much devastated. About 100 cattle since spring, in connection with the Indians, have done great harm

to the crops; several fields are entirely bare in their finest parts. . . .
The Indians have stolen at their leisure not finding any one to oppose
them.

Faced with these realities, as superintendent and agent to the Indians of
the west, Dickson desperately needed instructions from the British command. Was he to prepare the tribes for an assault upon the Americans in
Illinois and St. Louis in the spring? If so, how was he to provide for them?[11]

After sending McKay on his way to York, Dickson had left Mackinac
Island with six bateaux loaded with the Indian presents. With him was a
detachment of Michigan Fencibles consisting of a lieutenant, twenty-six
men, and fourteen Canadians whom Dickson had brought from York. In
front of the small fleet of boats paddled the interpreter Joseph Roc. He was
to go ahead and announce to the tribes at La Baye and on the Mississippi
that Dickson and the presents were on their way. Not knowing the state
of the harvest at La Baye, Captain Bullock sent Pierre Grignon in advance
to the Green Bay community to obtain flour. He hoped it could be sent via
the boats that returned to Michilimackinac.[12]

By early November, Dickson had arrived at La Baye. Not only did he
find Menominee, Winnebago, and families from other tribes awaiting
him, but the angry citizens of the community also confronted Dickson
and the officer who had traveled with him from Michilimackinac. Their
grievances pertained to loss of livestock and crops for the past two seasons.
Throughout the winter of 1813–1814, from his headquarters on Lake Winnebago, Dickson had written time and again to John Lawe asking him to
obtain flour and beef from the residents of La Baye. In the spring of 1814,
Sioux, Winnebago, and Menominee chiefs and their warriors had passed
through La Baye on the way to the council called by Dickson and McDouall
at Michilimackinac. In July, the expeditionary force for Prairie du Chien
led by McKay had stopped at La Baye for several days to acquire provisions
for the journey to the Mississippi. The small force of Michigan Fencibles
under Lieutenant Pullman stationed in the old fort at La Baye had been
pulled for defense of the Mississippi and then stationed at Fort McKay. In
the months that ensued, as at Prairie du Chien, tribes had come to La Baye
in search of food. Left with no military presence, the residents could not
prevent the Indians from killing cattle and cutting or trampling wheat. All

of this had taken a toll on La Baye and its residents. With representatives of the British government and military enforcement now at La Baye, the residents demanded their injuries and losses be addressed.

—ıı—

When the men and boats left Michilimackinac, another officer, Lieutenant Andrew Bulger of the Royal Newfoundland Regiment, had accompanied Dickson. Bulger had participated in many of the major engagements of the war, most recently the repulse of the Americans at Mackinac and the capture of the *Tigress* and *Scorpion*, the latter cause leaving him wounded. The British command at York must have acknowledged McKay's assessment that Fort McKay be reinforced, for Dickson had returned to Michilimackinac with a company of Michigan Fencibles. He also carried an appointment for Lieutenant Bulger. On October 17, Bulger was appointed to the command of Fort McKay with the rank of captain, superseding Captain Anderson. Anderson would remain at the post, serving under Bulger. The command gave Bulger the authority to have "exclusive direction of all operations on the Mississippi." Having fought together in the defense of Michilimackinac and the capture of the American warships, Dickson and Bulger would now be in a closer association at La Baye, preparing to deal with the residents' petitions and what waited for them on the Mississippi. Lieutenant Graham joined them on November 9. Roc had reached the Mississippi and informed Anderson of the arrival of Dickson, and Anderson in turn had sent Graham with a detachment to meet Dickson and assist with the transportation of the provisions to Prairie du Chien.[13]

With two officers of the Indian Department present, Captain Bulger convened a court of inquiry on the thirteenth of November. The officers would hear testimony from the residents of La Baye on their claims of losses "from depradations committed on their property by the Indians." Thirty-nine men appeared before the court. Each testified individually, submitting itemized lists of the horses, cattle, oxen, and hogs killed or lost. As each testimony corroborated the testimony previously heard, the court believed the statements to be substantiated. A committee was appointed to affix a value upon each animal, and the court deemed the valuation fair. The claims were then submitted to Lieutenant Colonel McDouall. The testimony, along with what he saw of the community with his own eyes, overwhelmed Bulger. He wrote to McDouall not to expect La Baye to supply Michilimackinac with wheat as the place was "in a state of famine." The "devastations" by the Indians had "impoverished the settlement." Unless the British opened a store at La Baye from which the Indian families could receive provisions, they would continue to kill the cattle as often as their need required. If the slaughter of the farm animals was to be allowed to continue, the British would "have to abandon the place altogether."[14]

Bulger also sympathized with the plight of the tribes. He told McDouall that the quantity of ammunition sent from Montreal for Dickson to distribute was only about one-fourth of what was needed by the western Indians. In the past, the tribes planted corn in the summer and had the traders to resort to if the crops and winter hunting were poor. This year, because of "being so often called from their homes" to fight for the British, they would entirely depend upon hunting to provide for their families. But the powder, ball, and guns Dickson had at his disposal were insufficient. There were twenty thousand persons under the protection of the British in this region. As Dickson, Bulger, and others of the Indian Department traveled to the Mississippi, they would be distributing presents and goods first to the Menominee, then to the Winnebago and others along the route. Bulger feared that there would be little left for the "Saulks in particular, who have given such striking proof of their zeal in the cause, & who received scarcely anything last year." He found the assemblage of Indians at La Baye when he arrived "a most distressing sight; men, women, & children, naked and in a state of starvation." He feared there would be nothing for the Potawatomi who were on their way to La Baye. He impressed upon McDouall the absolute necessity that more gunpowder be sent immediately to the region.[15]

Dickson and Bulger pressed westward through the Fox River rapids to the portage. The morning they left the portage, they found the Wisconsin River to be filled with floating ice. All the Indians they met were in want of provisions. Dickson handed out what he could, but they "appeared to be struck with consternation when they saw the small portion of supplies allotted to them." Between the weather conditions and having to eat food to which he was not accustomed, Bulger suffered more than he had ever suffered during the course of "my whole life before." Though Dickson helped Bulger all he could, tension began to develop between the two men. In particular, Bulger felt Dickson did not fully appreciate the authority

McDouall had granted him. Neither knew that this tension would be the beginning of a long rivalry between them. They finally arrived at Prairie du Chien on the thirtieth of November.[16]

Serving with the Royal Newfoundland Fencibles since 1804, Bulger was conversant in the standards expected at British garrisons. After one month at Prairie du Chien, Bulger found "everything"—from the accounts maintained by Anderson to the unfinished state of the fort structure—"in such a confused state." Bulger did say that he was convinced Anderson did "everything for the best," but he was "totally unacquainted with the rules and customs of the service." Faced with what he saw, Bulger feared for the future of the British at Prairie du Chien. Anderson had had men working on improving Fort McKay from the time he assumed command to the day Bulger arrived on the prairie, yet the barracks were a "mere shell," the guard house open, no sentry boxes built, the gate out of order, and the blockhouses only partially erected. There was no magazine or store, and the well still did not provide enough water. Bulger employed workmen from the community to finish the barracks, but the rest could not be completed for some time. All building materials, but for wood, needed to be sent from Michilimackinac. Yet to send men from the garrison up the rivers for wood put them at risk of being attacked by roving bands of US-friendly Indians. Bulger expected an attack in the spring. When he

A undated sketch of Fort McKay, found in the papers of Andrew Bulger. WHI IMAGE ID 42230

received a report brought by a Sioux who had escaped from St. Louis that Americans accompanied by Missouri Indians planned an attack by land and water on Prairie du Chien, Bulger made a dismal assessment. In the present state of the fort, he wrote McDouall, if it were ever to be threatened by an American force, "It could never hold out, and the best thing to be done, if we fail in keeping the Enemy down the rapids—would be to blow up the Fort & make our escape in the best manner we could."[17]

In August, McDouall had told Anderson to allow the Green Bay Volunteers to return home. When Joseph Rolette returned to the prairie, he brought the forms for their release and the funds for their pay, which he had advanced. Rolette had also advanced money so that the Michigan Fencibles could receive their pay. Bulger found this arrangement unsatisfactory, for Rolette was issuing scrip that could only be exchanged at his store. Instead, Bulger issued scrip that could be exchanged with any trader or merchant who forwarded it to the commissary at Mackinac. The commissary would reimburse the traders for goods issued to the soldiers. Finally, Bulger instituted a regimented command at the post, assigning specific duties to each officer.[18]

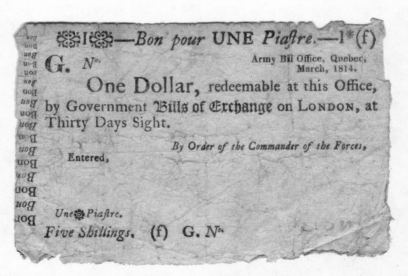

The men of the Michigan Fencibles, British Indian Department, and various volunteer militias who served during the War of 1812 were paid with army bills, or *Bon*. WISCONSIN HISTORICAL MUSEUM N6139; WHI IMAGE ID 118610

As to the prairie itself, Bulger disabused McDouall of the picture he had painted of a "plentiful country":

> This country, Sir, is without resources; it cannot support 20 men, much less than 60. The Inhabitants are miserably poor, ruined by the depredations of the rascally Puants & other Indians, they have now actually nothing left. Nor are there 10 head of cattle in the whole place, whereas it formerly could boast of near 400 head.

While at Michilimackinac during August, Rolette, besides offering to advance money, had entered into a contract with McDouall to provide game, deer, and, if possible, beef for the men stationed at Fort McKay. Learning this, Bulger opined that Rolette had set about to secure the contract in order to fill "his pockets with Gov't money." However, Bulger also believed that Rolette had done all he could to live up to the agreement and should not be punished. Bulger told Rolette to continue to provide what he could, as the conditions of the country made it difficult to find game and for him to stop "would have been the ruination of us."[19]

Then, against orders, Rolette attempted to find meat using the warriors of the Gens de la Feuille Tiré (Gens des Feuilles or Wahpeton) Sioux, who were known to be friendly to the Americans. Rolette sent Louis Champagney and Antoine Dubois, his brother-in-law and the nephew of La Feuille, to begin negotiations with the Gens des Feuilles. The two men were returning to the prairie with one of the warriors. During the night of December 8, the warrior took the British men's muskets and shot them. Champagney lived about three hours. Though wounded, Dubois buried him, surrounding his grave with gunpowder so wolves would not disturb it, and then walked the twenty-four miles to the prairie. He died four days later. Bulger immediately dispatched about eighty men of the Michigan Fencibles, volunteers, and militia and about a dozen Menominee under the command of Duncan Graham to arrest the Sioux warrior. Finding he had fled his village, Captain Graham brought in a chief of the Gens de la Feuille Tiré as a hostage and confined him in the fort.

Learning that Rolette had sent powder and ball to the Gens de la Feuille Tiré contrary to the wishes of Anderson, La Feuille, and Petit Corbeau, Bulger opened a "court of enquiry" to investigate the affair. Bugler told

Rolette that sending ammunition was an impropriety. Motives aside, Bulger stated that if Rolette had sent the supplies to the Indians without the consent of Captain Anderson, then Rolette was to blame for the deaths of Champagney and DuBois. More importantly, Bulger informed Rolette, he would have been "acting in opposition to, and setting the constituted authorities of the Government at defiance, which . . . never can be countenanced." Rolette's defense was that Anderson and Lieutenant Brisbois had never told him *not* to send ammunition to the Gens de la Feuille Tiré. Bulger sent Rolette's explanations on to McDouall asking him to make his own judgment. Bulger ended his report with the speculation that La Feuille would cut off this band of Sioux and that La Feuille and Petit Corbeau would attack and destroy it. The imprisonment of the young Sioux proved an easy way for Bulger to solve the issue, unlike other problems that soon arose.[20]

—⊣⊢—

In the course of the four months in which Anderson had commanded the garrison, he had men refuse to obey orders, shirk guard duty, get drunk, and reject rations of corn and bustard meat. He had punished each infraction with a day or two of incarceration. Dissatisfaction among the Michigan Fencibles and the Mississippi Volunteers with military life continued after Bulger arrived at the fort. On the last day of 1814, the discontent of several privates of the Michigan Fencibles turned mutinous.

As had happened in the past, when the soldiers were called to parade drill, some did not follow orders and others returned the sergeant's orders with rude comments. On December 31, while at drill, the sergeant issued orders, and in response, the men laughed at him and cursed in French. Bulger had told the sergeant major that if any man talked or laughed again, he was to be placed in arms. On that day, Private Antoine Bonnain took no notice of the orders directed his way. The sergeant ordered him to fall out and go to the guardhouse. When he did not do so, the sergeant attempted to remove Bonnain's musket, at which Bonnain struck the sergeant on the head with his gun. The sergeant of the guard was called, and he ordered two men to take Bonnain to the guardhouse. The two privates refused and chaos broke out. All the men broke ranks, taking Bonnain to the barracks for safety. They placed men at the door with drawn knives and bayonets and swore that anyone who attempted to take Bonnain would be killed.[21]

Bulger was called and, observing the state of the garrison, saw "the necessity of taking strong measures to subdue them." Bulger immediately summoned a drumhead court-martial for Bonnain. The court ordered him tied to a gun and flogged. Bulger then ordered the sergeant to go down the ranks with him and point out the men who had been most active in the mutiny. These he confined in the guardhouse with rations of bread and water. Some bragged to Bulger that they were not afraid of him and had helped shield Bonnain. That was enough for Bulger. He announced to all the troops that they were subject to the articles of war and punishment would be dispensed. Horrified with "the troubled state of this country," as evidenced by the killing of Champagney and Dubois and the revolt of the Fencibles, Dickson requested that Captain Bulger immediately declare martial law. Bulger responded, and martial law took effect from that day forward. All civil and military officers as well as all civilians were now under his governance.[22]

By British regulations, the conduct of the men at Fort McKay fell under the definition of "Conduct tending to excite Mutiny & disturbance among the Troops." Bulger therefore convened a garrison court-martial on January 2, 1815, with Captain Anderson, Lieutenant James Pullman, and Lieutenant James Keating appointed officers of the court. In the first case, Private LaSeur Dupuis was found guilty for refusing to take Bonnain to the guardhouse and sentenced to three hundred lashes. In the second, Private Hypolite Senecal was brought before the court-martial accused of using a weapon to prevent anyone from taking Bonnain to the guardhouse and also found guilty, with the same sentence. The entire garrison was then assembled to witness the punishment of the privates. The sentences were reduced to one hundred fifty lashes each. According to Dickson, the punishment had a startling effect on the men, "and they begin to look like soldiers."[23]

Button of the Royal Artillery, ca. 1814, recovered at Prairie du Chien. COURTESY OF MARY ELISE ANTOINE

While Bulger dealt with the unruly garrison, tensions on the prairie troubled Dickson. Throughout the fall and early winter,

This cartridge box was found at the site of Fort Shelby, decoration added later. COURTESY OF MARY ELISE ANTOINE

Indians had continued to arrive with expectations for needed provisions and powder. On the journey with Bulger from La Baye, four hundred pounds of powder had been lost from Lieutenant Pullman's boats. After sending powder and provisions to the Sac, by January Dickson had expended almost all the goods and ammunition he had brought to Prairie du Chien. He rhetorically questioned Lawe, "What shall we do in the Spring if not timely supplied?"

Dickson had questioned Rolette's loyalty in April 1813. Now, having witnessed the trouble with the Gens des Feuilles and the rebellious nature of the Fencibles, combined with other events "which have since come to my knowledge," Dickson felt compelled to act. On January 2, while on parade at Fort McKay, Robert Dickson charged Joseph Rolette "with treasonable practices against Our Sovereign Lord the King." The charges were "seditious words & discourses tending to excite insurrection against his Majesty's Government—also illicit illegal and dangerous conduct towards the Indians his Majesty's allies." Dickson requested that Bulger call a military court of enquiry.[24]

The following day, January 3, Bulger proclaimed a "Military Court of Enquiry for the security of His Majesty's Possessions" so that Rolette's actions "could be examined and enquired into." The court convened the fifth of January with Bulger presiding and Anderson, Pullman, and Keating once again serving as officers of the court. For the entire day they listened to testimony. Robert Dickson, as the prosecution, addressed the court first. He stated he found it painful to charge Rolette with so serious a crime as high treason, since he was long acquainted with Rolette and knew his family had "distinguished themselves in the service of their country." He then stated his case against him.[25]

In his opening statement, Dickson explained that when he had arrived at Prairie du Chien in the spring of 1813, he held councils with the various tribes. In these councils, he found the conduct of some different from what he had expected. He cited La Feuille's refusal to go to Michilimackinac and the refusal of the Sioux to go fight at Sandusky, causing other Indians to leave, which he felt led to the fall of Amherstburg and Detroit. Since then, he had been "endeavouring to trace what could have given rise to such a conduct on their part." Only with the events of the last days had he come to realize the cause: Rolette's seditious words at the home of Michel Brisbois, for which he had already been pardoned. Dickson began by questioning Rolette about the events that had occurred in Brisbois's home. Dickson then called Captain Dease to support the contention that Rolette had made statements that could be construed as spoken against Britain. Dease testified that Rolette's statement, combined with his contacts with the Sioux by marriage and trade, had caused the state of confusion in the upper Mississippi in the spring of 1813 and that by the spring of 1814 had led the Indians to declare their intentions to kill Dickson. Next, Jean Baptiste Faribault testified that he had heard Rolette say that Dickson was not fit to hold the position he had as agent to the western Indians, assuming more authority than his commission permitted. He stated that Rolette bragged, "I do not fear that he will impose upon me, I think he is aware of the power I have with the Sioux nation." Finally, Dickson called Joseph Renville, interpreter for the Sioux, and questioned him about the event a few days after the surrender of Fort Shelby, when some Winnebago were about to kill cattle owned by Rolette. Dickson elicited testimony to show that Rolette had ordered the Sioux to kill the Winnebago if they took his cattle. Only the intervention of Lieutenant Graham's men had stopped him. The final questions Dickson posed to several witnesses pertained to the letters Nicolas Boilvin had sent to the prairie in February 1813 asking the residents to support the Americans. Dickson wanted an explanation of Rolette's response when reading the letters, the supposition being that Rolette supported the Americans.[26]

Acting in his own defense, Rolette then cross-examined some of the witnesses Dickson had presented and presented witnesses of his own. He did not ask any as to whether the person had ever heard him speak against the British government. Rather, he elicited the information that the 1813 inquiry had found that Rolette had spoken without thought and the charges declared void and unfounded and the documents destroyed. To each witness he cited an incident in which Rolette had asked that person to do something. He asked, "[D]id I not recommend to you to enroll yourself in the Company of Volunteers?" Or "Have you known that I have always recommended to Wabasha's Band to listen to Mr. Dickson as their Father and their protector & that I have always spoken to the Inhabitants in favor of the English Government?" To these and similars questions he received, "Yes." Rolette then mounted his defense. He addressed the issue of the letters from Boilvin by saying he had given Graham all the supplies he would need on his journey to bring the letters to Michilimackinac. At the same time, he had sent tobacco to Renville to invite the Sioux to come and defend the prairie. He then assailed Dickson, stating that if Dickson feared for his life in the spring of 1814, the fear was of his own doing. He had spent the winter at Lake Winnebago and given many goods to the Potawatomi, who were attached to the Americans, instead of keeping them for the tribes of the Mississippi, who were "an impediment to the Americans."[27]

The court then withdrew to deliberate. They delivered an opinion that the charges had not been proved and acquitted Joseph Rolette. The court stated it could not "refrain from noticing the unwillingness betrayed by the Evidences for the prosecution" and stated that the testimony given by Captain Dease and Roc, the interpreter, was "self-contradictory."[28] Bulger later wrote to McDouall, "I think the charges would not have been brought forward at all, if Mr. Dickson & Mr. Rolette had not quarreled." He felt the object of the accusations was "to ruin the man, and not the good of the Country." Bulger was already frustrated by Dickson's attempts to supersede his authority; now he was angry. But before he could take action against Dickson, another matter arose.[29]

No sooner had this court been dismissed than Bulger had reasons to impanel another. On January 6 chiefs and other men of the band Gens de la Feuilles Tiré arrived on the prairie with the man they said had killed Champagney and Dubois. They surrendered him to Bulger requesting that he might suffer death for his crimes. He was also being offered as atonement for all the band had done in the name of friendship with the Americans. Bulger assembled a court-martial headed by Robert Dickson and composed of seven officers of the Indian Department and Mississippi Volunteers. The court charged Chunksah of the Gens de la Feuilles Tiré with the murders of Louis Champagney and Antoine Dubois. Joseph Renville and Duncan Graham were called to testify. Each had spoken with Dubois before he died. In their conversations, Dubois had identified Chunksah as the man who had shot him and Champagney. Then Corbeau Francois, a chief of the band, testified that Chunksah had murdered both men. In his own defense, Chunksah insisted it was his brother who had committed the killings. The court found Chunksah guilty. Chunksah was summarily executed in front of the assembled garrison and militia. Afterward, two chiefs of the Gens de la Feuille Tiré sat in council with Bulger. They brought and laid at his feet American medals and flags they possessed. In the name of the band, the chiefs promised fidelity to the British and renounced any contact with the Americans.[30]

As agent to the western Indians and commanding officer of Fort McKay, respectively, Robert Dickson and Andrew Bulger were the two most powerful British in the upper Mississippi. If fidelity between Britain and not only an enemy tribe but all the tribes was still possible, then surely Dickson and Bulger could reconcile their own growing differences. Or could they?

# 12

## NEWS OF PEACE

*January–April 1815*

While Bulger's actions with the garrison and the Gens de la Feuille Tiré may have seemed harsh and uncompromising, they had impressed the residents of the prairie. Several days after the execution of Chunksah, forty-four men wrote a letter in which they expressed their gratitude to the British. Having addressed their correspondence to Captain Bulger and Robert Dickson, Bulger declined to receive the letter. Someone wisely rewrote the missive, addressing it to Bulger only, and presented it to him with an apology for the error. This Bulger deigned to receive. The inhabitants thanked Bulger for the protection he had brought to "His Britannic Majesty's subjects." They thanked him for the justice he had brought to the "savage territory" and they hoped to live peacefully from then on. They concluded by asking permission to express "our zeal, courage and loyalty toward our Sovereign." Bulger graciously replied that it gave him great pleasure to learn that what he had done "for the preservation of good order and tranquility" had met with the approbation of the inhabitants of Prairie du Chien. He was also flattered to hear the sentiments of loyalty toward the king and promised to pass them to Lieutenant Colonel McDouall.[1]

While Bulger did inform McDouall of the letter he had received from the residents of the prairie, he was far more concerned about the fact that the letter had originally been addressed to him and Dickson. Bulger then indulged in a complaint that Dickson's vanity would not allow him to acknowledge that Dickson was under Bulger's command. Rather, Dickson wanted people to believe that Bulger was under him. He decided to put Dickson in his place. In front of the officers of the garrison and the Indian Department, Bulger reprimanded Dickson on the conduct of the officers of the Indian Department over the past few months and demanded he wait on Bulger. He told Dickson that he, and not Dickson, had control of all the resources of the country—and he planned to exercise that control.[2]

The scarcity of provisions and Dickson's insistence that the Indians be fed from the stores at Prairie du Chien caused relations between the two men to continue to deteriorate. Any communication they had was conducted by writing very formal letters to each other, though Dickson's house stood only about two hundred feet west of Fort McKay. There had long been contention between the Indian Department and the British military. Deputy Superintendent General William Claus always maintained that the Indian Department should possess sole jurisdiction and authority over Indian affairs. The British military found this position difficult to accept, particularly as the large expeditures and distribution of presents to the Indian allies came from army supply stores. The problem of authority over provisioning the Indians was finally settled in the fall of 1813. By a "General Order Affecting the Awards of Presents to the Indian Warriors," the Indian Department was told to cooperate with His Majesty's officers. The conflict between Dickson and Bulger was part of a much larger disagreement over authority.[3]

With the authority of the General Orders, in mid-January, Bulger began a campaign to control the Indian Department and diminish the influence Dickson had among his men and the tribes. Bulger told the inhabitants of the prairie that they could no longer exchange flour for grease, meat, and other foods with the Fox. When Dickson questioned this restriction, Bulger told him this was the only means to preserve provisions for the troops. He told Dickson that the Indians had received the supplies he had for them and therefore "they must support themselves." When Dickson inquired whether corn and flour would be coming from Michilimackinac, Bulger shrugged the question off, declining to answer. He cut the rations that were issued to the Indian Department staff at Prairie du Chien in half. When Dickson questioned this, Bulger cited the figures he had maintained since his arrival. He told Dickson that the department had already drawn 4,654 rations of corn and flour, when they really could have existed on 900 rations, as this was all the officers and interpreters needed. Dickson explained that there were men engaged as voyageurs for the department, and the rations had included the provisions he had given to the fifteen hundred Indians who visited him on the prairie. He fed them and gave them provisions so they could return home. Dickson asked, "Could I allow them to die of hunger?" He reminded Bulger that had he not given the Indians the food they needed for themselves and their families, "we could not depend on a single man to assist us in the spring, and you are well aware that the safety of the country hangs on their fadility [fidelity] and attachment."[4]

The two men continued their written debate, neither budging from his stance. In his letter of February 6, Bulger posed a question to Dickson:

> Do you, or do you not, recognize my authority as Commanding offi-
> cer of Fort McKay, and on the Mississippi, to control the resources of
> the Country, and direct the expenditures of every Department?

He then issued an ultimatum.

> If you do not, then either you or I must be removed from this country,
> for I will never serve her upon such terms.

Dickson humbly wrote a response acknowledging that he recognized that Bulger had the authority to control the resources of the country and direct expenditures. He wished the opportunity to talk with Bulger and do away with any misunderstandings.

> Rest assured Sir, that I shall consider this as the happiest day of my
> life, in finding the friendship and esteem I have always entertained
> for you firmly reestablished.

But whatever friendship the two men may have had now ceased. Before even receiving Dickson's letter, Bulger had written to Lieutenant Colonel McDouall voicing his complaints about Dickson. Feeding on each other, letter by letter McDouall and Bulger further disparaged Robert Dickson.[5]

Dickson, on whom the British government had relied as early as 1793 for his knowledge of the upper Mississippi and its Indian residents, who by 1811 the American generals and territorial governors had credited with the ability to unite all the tribes of the upper Mississippi, and whom Sir George Prevost appointed agent and superintendent for the western Indians, now had, according to McDouall, "fallen like Lucifer, never to rise again."[6]

Weekly, sometimes daily, Bulger wrote of his complaints about Dickson to McDouall. McDouall responded in long, rambling letters, each successive letter giving Bulger more authority to weaken Dickson. McDouall explained that he had selected Bulger to command Fort McKay because he had been "long in the army," and Dickson faced not only Bulger but also the position of officers in the British army who would support each other against the incursion of their authority by a civilian officer of the Indian Department.[7]

At the end of February, McDouall sanctioned and confirmed Bulger as commander of Fort McKay and ordered that the Indian Department on the Mississippi be subject to and under the orders of Bulger.

> The Agent & Superintendent of the Western Indians together with the Captains, Lieutenants, and Interpreters thereof, will therefore receive their instructions from Captain Bulger and govern themselves accordingly. . . . [T]he Indian Department on the Mississippi is subject to and entirely under the orders of Captain Bulger.

Bulger would now put the Indian Department in order, which heretofore had been a "scene of inextricable confusion." He was to convene a court of inquiry to ascertain how the officers of the Indian Department had been paid, and Dickson was to submit "correct and accurate statements in Triplicate" detailing how the funds advanced to him had been spent. McDouall promoted Thomas Anderson and Francis Michael Dease to captains in the Indian Department.[8]

McDouall read with "equal astonishment and indignation" the transcript of the inquiry regarding the charges Dickson had made against Rolette and concluded that it was an "Iniquitous conspiracy against the life of an individual I have ever scarcely heard of." Rolette's only fault was "culpable flippancy of the tongue, which leads him into scares—tho' he means well." The garrison at Prairie du Chien depended on Rolette, as he still had the contract to obtain game and beef for the troops. Therefore, McDouall told Bulger to reconcile the differences and "let the only rivalry be, who shall do most for the Public good."[9]

On the first of March, McDouall sent another letter to Bulger, enclosing an order to be delivered to Dickson if Bulger thought it was warranted. McDouall thought that Dickson could remain at the prairie as long as Bulger found "his assistance & services beneficial . . . and conducive to the general good." If, however, Bulger felt that Dickson would do anything to be "an impediment or hindrance" to any measures or orders Bulger issued, he was to deliver the enclosed order without delay. The order commanded that Robert Dickson depart for Michilimackinac immediately, stopping at Green Bay on his way in order to "make every arrangement to expedite the departure of the Folleavoines [Menominee] and Winnebaggo Indians." In one order, McDouall had demonstrated his authority over Dickson while also acknowledging his dependence on Dickson's power to keep the tribes allied to Great Britain. Now his order of dismissal was in Bulger's hands.

While the letters between McDouall and Bulger moved up and down the Fox-Wisconsin passage, Dickson continued his efforts to acquire provisions for the tribes. He sent Joseph Renville to winter among the Sioux at his home on the Mississippi River. Duncan Graham left with what provisions Dickson could give him for the Rock River Sac. Dickson wrote to John Lawe for tobacco and gunpowder, telling him to sell his horse if need be, for "I am in want of Cash." He asked Lawe to "take care of the poor people I have recommended to your Care." If there was no trouble from the Americans, Dickson planned to go to Michilimackinac "& a little further," in hopes of procuring adequate supplies. Perhaps as an allusion to Bulger— or as evidence that Dickson didn't see him as a threat—Dickson mentioned to Lawe that he also had "a few trifling matters to put in Order."[10]

—‖—

With the lakes and rivers frozen, no one at Michilimackinac, La Baye, or Prairie du Chien had received any news of the war from the Eastern Seaboard since December. Many, though, had been aware that negotiations

between representatives from the United States and Great Britain to end
the war had begun the previous August. When talks opened, both countries made very specific demands. With the collapse of Napoleon's regime
in France, the British could direct more troops for service in North America, and their demands became more specific. As pertained to the Indians,
the British commissioners pointed out that Britain had not induced the
Indians to attack Americans; rather,

> The Indian Nations having experienced, as they thought, oppression
> instead of protection from the United States, declared war against
> them previously [Tecumseh's rebellion] to the declaration of war by
> that country against Great Britain.

The British commissioners felt the United States had not fulfilled the article in the 1783 Treaty of Paris that ended the American Revolution in which
the United States agreed to protect the Indians. Therefore, Great Britain
could "interfere on their [the Indians'] behalf in the negotiation for peace."
The commissioners stated that Great Britain wished peace with the United
States, but they had been instructed not to pursue peace

> unless the Indian nations are included in it, and restored to all the
> rights, privileges, and territories which they enjoyed in the year 1811,
> previous their commencement of the War.

The boundaries of the Indian lands would be set in further discussions,
and both parties would agree "not to purchase the lands occupied by the
Indians within their respective lines of demarcation."[11]

In this requirement that land be maintained for the Indian nations, the
British commissioners were considering only the Northwest Territory.
That included what is presently northwest Ohio, the northern half of Indiana, most of Michigan, northeastern Illinois, and all of Wisconsin except-
ing the Sac land south of the Wisconsin River. The British also demanded
that the United States have no naval force on the Great Lakes and that the
British would have transit rights to the Mississippi River in exchange for
the continuation of American fishing rights off Newfoundland.

None of the demands were acceptable to the US commissioners. As to including an article in the peace agreement pertaining to the Indians, the commissioners responded:

> [T]he United States will admit of no line of boundary between their Territory and that of the Indian Nations because the natural growth and population of the United States would be thereby arrested. . . . They will not suppose that the British Government will avow as the basis of their policy towards the United States the system of arresting natural growth within their own Territories for the sake of preserving a perpetual desert for savages.[12]

In February, McDouall learned of the failure of the negotiations, which he communicated to Bulger in a letter dated February 25, enclosing a newspaper that gave all the particulars. He said the principal cause of the failed talks was the "question relating to the Indians." It was up to the northwestern British command to address this. He ordered Bulger to announce the position of the British in Grand Council with the Indians "with all the éclat & effect which you can give it." He also enclosed a speech that Bulger could amend if he wished. Anything Bulger said had to be "calculated to inspire," noted McDouall, adding that he was to "leave no means untried to excite their enthusiasm & perseverance. . . . Pay your court to *every one* that has influence with them, & engage them in promoting & encouraging them in the right disposition" (original emphasis).[13]

Assessing the position of the British in the Northwest, McDouall then delivered a long lecture to Bulger on the need to maintain the garrison, telling him that "to abandon it [Fort McKay] would be infinitely worse, than if we had tamely acquiesced in its conquest." To abandon Prairie du Chien would occasion the loss of Mackinac Island and "ultimately place the Canadas in jeopardy." Additionally, to abandon the prairie would exasperate the Indians and make it even more dangerous. But if the garrison were to be forced from Prairie du Chien, McDouall gave Bulger instructions as to how it should be accomplished.[14]

In March, the ice on Lake Michigan began to thaw. With the change in weather and no clear news of peace, McDouall began to plan the spring campaign. The time had come to campaign southward. He wrote to Lieutenants Lawe and Grignon at La Baye, directing them to assemble eighty to one hundred Menominee and Winnebago warriors and bring them to Michilimackinac. He also requested that Grignon send as much flour as could be had from the residents to the island. Askin then wrote Lawe with a warning that McDouall would not tolerate any killing of cattle or destruction of property by the Indians, and he suggested Lawe inform the chiefs of this before they came to Michilimackinac.[15]

About this time Bulger and Anderson left the prairie for La Baye. Few provisions had come to Prairie du Chien, so Bulger decided he would go to the bay, traveling "400 miles, in the depth of winter through a wilderness," to see what he could procure. Arriving at Green Bay, he called all the traders and inhabitants of the settlement to gather and addressed them collectively, saying, "You have now an opportunity of testifying to the world whether you are sincere in your professions of loyalty and attachment to His Majesty's Government." Bulger had heard that "there still is a considerable quantity of wheat, as well as ammunition, in this place," which he accused the residents of hoarding so that they could sell at exorbitant prices. He went on, exhorting them to show their loyalty, saying that their fate hung upon the ammunition, and therefore they were to sell it at a moderate price. He acquired a "considerable quantity of Gunpowder, and other articles," but was sorry to find that the Menominee and others were not anxious to go to Michilimackinac "and leave their families starving as they did last winter." The hesitancy of the Menominee Bulger blamed on Dickson for assuring them they would receive provisions from the British. Now that the Indians "had been reduced from a dependence on our promises," Bulger found that their belief in the British was shaken, "if not entirely alienated." Again, he cited Dickson as the cause for the lack of faith. Bulger critically stated that "unlimited power such as Mr. Dickson said he possessed, ought never to have been given to the head of a department." Since Lieutenant Colonel McDouall also held the position of a superintendent in the Indian Department, Bulger exempted him from his comments.[16]

John Lawe was caught in the middle. Lawe and Dickson were longtime friends and had worked together in the Indian Department, attending to the needs of the tribes from La Baye to the upper Mississippi River. Now McDouall and Bulger commanded the Indian Department. Askin knew the temperament of McDouall, so he discreetly sent Lawe advice not to engage with him over Dickson. In contrast, their mutual friend Duncan Graham unloaded all his frustrations about Dickson's situation on Lawe. Graham had returned to the prairie on the twenty-third of February. He informed Lawe of the expedition led by Henry Dodge against the Missouri Sac and Fox. With many of the tribe killed, the result had been to bring about one thousand five hundred Sac, Fox, Ioway, and Kickapoo to the Rock River, all ill-disposed to the Americans. They had brought a rumor that the Americans would again try to advance past the rapids and attack Prairie du Chien. Graham shared his only thought on this possibility:

> If they come, I hope they will be well supplied with provisions—in
> that case we may all not die with hunger. Should they over-power us,
> they will give us something to eat.

Graham went on to document the reports of Indians dying of hunger for want of ammunition and the two thousand Indians soon to arrive at the prairie for a council with not a pipe of tobacco or shot of powder to give them. Graham asked Lawe if he would rather be a "doorkeeper in hell" or part of the Indian Department. But, to Graham, the great calamity to befall the prairie was "party spirit."[17]

Returning to the prairie, where, no matter how wretched the conditions, there had always been friendship, Graham now found a coolness and taking of sides between the officers of the garrison and the Indian Department. He wrote Lawe:

> [It] has caused Mr. Dickson more trouble of mind than anything he
> met with since the beginning of the war. . . . Three months of this
> Winter have made him look ten years older.

Graham surmised that the discord was caused by one person who had spent the winter "sowing the seed of discord everywhere[, e]ven those under whose roof he has been hospitably treated." The main object of "this sneaking puppy was to undermine the whole [Indian] Department." Graham would not put this person's name in the letter. In addition to the fracture among the officers, Graham told Lawe that the residents of the prairie had been distressed by an order from Bulger to deliver one-fourth of all their wheat to the garrison. In relinquishing the wheat, they had given up the seed they had put by for spring sowing: "Hard times—two ruffles with no shirt—plenty of land and no wheat." Graham fully felt that if the inhabitants had the means, "they would all abandon the place."[18]

Having received dispatches from General Drummond at York, McDouall continued his plans for the spring campaign, placing Colonel McKay at the head of the Indian force at Michilimackinac and telling Bulger that "here the enemy must be beat, or all fails." He promised to do for Bulger "what is possible." But he also warned that "all these warlike preparations may suddenly be put to a stop," for in mid-March, he had received a handbill from Montreal that a Treaty of Peace had been signed at Ghent on the twenty-fourth of December. Suspicious of the truth of the report and eager to move on the Americans, McDouall shared with Bulger the plan outlined by General Drummond:

> They find the Indians at the head of the Lake, a useless burden, that they cannot feed. They have in view to send them to the Mississippi; thinking perhaps that with your assistance, you could take St. Louis, & that on their whole route, havoc & desolation would mark their progress.[19]

Information in hand, Bulger prepared to return to Prairie du Chien. He ordered Jacques Porlier to drill the Green Bay militia and have them ready to march whenever orders were given. He planned to send Dickson and the Indians up the Mississippi where there would be "an abundance of fish and fowl," thereby saving provisions and removing Dickson from the garrison. When needed, he would order their return. He told Joseph Renville to remain with the Sioux and to "endeavour to prevent any of them from coming down" to the prairie until he sent for them. Some Sac he would keep at the fort. "The fort itself," he asserted, "shall never fall into the Enemies hands."[20]

When he arrived at the prairie, Bulger sent Captain Anderson to request the Great War Belt that Robert Dickson possessed. Dickson refused to give the belt to Anderson, as it was the wampum belt Sir George Prevost had given to Dickson to hold before all when he spoke to the western tribes, representing the union between the tribes and Great Britain. Confronted with this latest refusal, Bulger wrote Dickson a letter of reprimand. It may have been at this point that Bulger decided to present Dickson with the order that McDouall had written on March 1 in which he ordered Dickson to proceed immediately to Michilimackinac. Two days later, Dickson wrote his friend John Lawe, saying, "I would long ago have wrote you fully but for obvious reasons have deferred it untill I see you." He stated he had been treated with ingratitude by "the agents of Government" for some time, "but in a short time will put all to rights." He never again would have to serve under McDouall, whom he called "a weak vain & foolish man." He was leaving the vast country in which he had served with no regrets but "for the poor people of the department whom I esteem & love." He sympathized with Graham, who was about to return to the Sac, but as Dickson was more fully aware than McDouall, an end was in sight. Rumors of peace stirred the prairie, and Dickson had received "the glorious news" for himself.[21]

Knowing that Dickson would soon be leaving the prairie, Bulger wrote a letter to Lawe that he headed "Private and Confidential." Bulger informed Lawe that Dickson would soon be at La Baye, so he wrote, "I must give you one piece of advice, which I trust you will attend to." Reminding Lawe that he had given him authority to purchase any article that might be needed "for the public service," Bulger told Lawe that this did not mean that Lawe could purchase anything that Dickson ordered. Lawe was not to make any purchase after Dickson arrived at La Baye, for "my name must not be shown for any thing Mr. Dickson may choose to purchase." Bulger signed his letter, "Believe me Yr sincere friend."[22]

The animosity between Bulger and Dickson did not seem to affect relations with the tribes and bands of Indians friendly to the British. With the spring thaws in full force and the rivers opening, more and more Indians came to the prairie prepared to participate in an offensive against the Americans. The first week of April, more than twelve hundred warriors of different tribes were encamped on the prairie "fully equipped for war." Bulger knew he had another thousand in reserve to the north. He remembered, "Upon no other occasion in the course of war had so choice a body of Indians been arrayed under the British flag." He gathered all of the Indians at the prairie in the council house and read them a speech, concluding with the announcement that "it had been decided to carry on the war in the vicinity of St. Louis." At this, each chief stood up, one after another, promising "hearty support and cooperation to make the expedition a success."[23]

To ensure that the planned expedition to St. Louis had the support of the Indians not present at the council, Bulger gave commands to officers in the Indian Department. On April 8, the same day Bulger issued Dickson his orders to leave, Bulger ordered Captain Graham and interpreter Guillroy to the Sac on the Rock River to learn the Americans' intentions. Guillroy was to "animate and encourage" the Sac and see what he could learn about the enemy's movements on the Mississippi. When translating the speeches that Graham carried, Guillroy was to impress upon the Sac that "it is *solely on their account* that the war is now carried on" (original emphasis). As their Great Father, the king, promised, the conflict would not stop "till the Indians are restored to their rights, and their future independence preserved." But they also had to do their part to aid the British. As for the Sioux, Renville was to interpret the speeches Bulger had given to Robert Dickson. Like Guillroy, Renville was to emphasize that the war was now carried "solely on account of the Indians." Bulger impressed upon Renville "to say everything likely to confirm their attachment to us."[24]

—⊣⊦—

Within a few days, war parties were sent down the Mississippi to a point of rendezvous on the Rock River in advance of the main body of soldiers and Indians. In the hopes of discouraging another attempt of attack from St. Louis, Bulger sent out several Indian war parties to attack American settlements below the Rock River. But the main British force never left Prairie du Chien. On April 16, a messenger sent by Lieutenant Graham disembarked at the prairie with a dispatch. At the very cusp of the British spring offensive, peace had come.[25]

The first persons to be confronted with the facts of peace were Graham and the Sac at the Rock River. Below the Rock Island rapids, a large band of Sac spied the *Governor Clark* on its way to the prairie. Heeding what had been said in Bulger's speeches, the Sac fired upon the gunboat, killing a ranger. After a short engagement, the Sac withdrew, perhaps at the command of Captain Graham. Major Taylor Berry, commander of the gunboat, anchored the *Governor Clark* off the mouth of the Rock River. Flying a white flag, Berry found Graham at the Sac village. Graham boarded the gunboat, and Berry presented to Graham the news of the peace agreement signed between Great Britain and the United States. Shocked by the news, Graham told Berry this was the first he or the Sac had heard of the peace. Berry questioned this and said, as their two countries were now at peace, Graham should inform the Sac that hostilities with the Indians were to end and keep them from attacking Americans. Graham expressed his respect to Berry but stated he was not able to control the Sac. Berry requested the release of Americans held prisoner by the Sac, but Graham politely explained this could not be done until he received instructions from Captain Bulger commanding Fort McKay. Graham promised Berry he would send an express to Prairie du Chien the following morning with news of the peace.[26]

Berry had presented two documents to Graham. One was a note from William Clark in which he enclosed a copy of the *National Intelligencer* containing the text of the Treaty of Ghent. The other was an order from Colonel William Russell stating that hostilities should cease between the countries and with the Indians. The dispatch, prepared by Colonel Russell, now commander of the Eighth Military District of the United States and the man appointed to convey news of peace to the western tribes, carried a threat that if the Indians should attack, this action would be considered a violation of the peace. The Indians would then have forfeited their rights and immunities and would be left to make a separate peace "on such terms as the American Government may grant them."[27]

Rumors of peace had been circulating for months, and Lieutenant Graham's dispatch confirmed the truth to the men of the prairie: the signing of the treaty had taken place in December just as Bulger's newspaper had reported. The ninth article of the treaty was the most pertinent to the situation on the prairie. The article stated that the United States and Britain would put an end to all hostilities with the Indian tribes with whom they might be at war; they were to restore to these tribes all the rights and privileges to which they were entitled prior to the war, provided the tribes agreed to desist from all hostilities against the United States. In a letter to William Clark received in March, Secretary of War James Monroe stated, "It is incumbent of the United States to execute every Article of this Treaty with perfect good faith. They wish to be particularly exact in the execution of the Article relating to the Indian Tribes."[28]

Monroe had appointed Clark, Governor Ninian Edwards, and Auguste Chouteau commissioners to conclude a treaty with the tribes that had warred against the United States. Clark was to notify the tribes on the Mississippi that peace had been concluded and inform them of the stipulations of the treaty. Clark gave that duty to Colonel William Russell, who prepared three dispatches announcing the conclusion of peace. He ordered fortified boats up the Illinois, Mississippi, and Missouri Rivers to carry the message to the tribes, and it was the gunboat sent up the Mississippi, the *Governor Clark*, that had carried the news to Graham and the Sac.[29]

Black Hawk may have been present at the attack on the *Governor Clark*, or he may have left this village after listening to Jean Guillroy interpreting the speeches Bulger had sent with Graham. Either way, Black Hawk arrived at Prairie du Chien before the messenger sent by Graham, and thus was unaware that a state of peace was in effect between Great Britain and the United States. Some of the Sac chiefs had sent Black Hawk to Prairie du Chien to affirm their loyalty to the British. On April 18, now informed of the peace, Black Hawk sat in council with Bulger. Black Hawk had brought with him the wampum belt he had received in 1813 from Robert Dickson. He repeated what he had been told: the Indians were to unite to preserve their lands and make war against the Americans, who threatened to destroy them all. If all tribes would join against the Americans, he stated, "You shall find your lands as they formerly were." That is why the Sac had fought. Now Black Hawk saw "the time drawing near when we all shall change colour," but he assured Bulger that Sac lands were still red and would remain red. The war club given to him by the "Great Father at Quebec" was still red.[30]

Black Hawk wanted something from the British in return for the loyalty of the Sac; he asked for a cannon so his people could live in safety. He rationalized that if his people had "one of your large guns," the women could hoe the ground and plant corn "unmolested," and the young men could hunt for their families "without dread of the Big Knives." Bulger replied that the British had put the war club in their hand for "their own good," and when the time came to bury the war club their "Great Father" would tell them. The following day, Bulger responded by presenting Black

Hawk with a coat and pistols "as a mark of friendship for you, and as an acknowledgement of your fidelity and attachment to the King."[31] This was all Bulger could offer Black Hawk.

Despite a hard winter and the lack of supplies and ammunition, once spring arrived most of the Indians of the Northwest continued to maintain their allegiance to the British. They were still determined to prevent the Americans from taking their lands, so that as Black Hawk stated, the women could hoe the land and plant corn and young men could hunt for their families.

# 13

## PEACE AND ITS AFTERMATH

### *April–August 1815*

Although he was now aware that peace had been proclaimed and the Treaty of Ghent signed, Lieutenant Colonel McDouall had not received official word from his superiors in regards to the future of Forts Mackinac and McKay. McDouall communicated weekly with Captain Bulger. He did not know the terms of the peace but had concerns about Article 9, which would have the greatest impact on the Indians.[1]

By the first of May, McDouall still had not received a personal dispatch from General Drummond, but on that day an American vessel from Detroit arrived at Mackinac Island and presented him with a copy of the terms upon which the two countries had agreed to peace. McDouall was told there was to be a mutual restoration of all forts and places taken on either side, and he was to take immediate steps for the evacuation of Michilimackinac. The fort and island were to be restored to the United States on the same day as the Americans would return Amherstburg to Great Britain. The proposed date for the mutual restoration was May 20. McDouall had assessed the dilapidated state of St. Joseph, where the British force would relocate, and therefore communicated to the American commander at Amherstburg that he would "be prepared to restore this Island agreeable to my instructions" on July 10.[2]

McDouall had received communication from Drummond's aide-de-camp just before the arrival of the American vessel and in that communiqué were orders regarding the British garrison at Prairie du Chien.

Drummond had ordered "that no time be lost in getting rid of all Provincial Establishments" at that post or in giving it back to the Americans. Thereby, McDouall ordered Bulger to

> take instant & immediate steps to carry this order into effect, which, however, unpalatable & unexpected is nevertheless in strict conformity to the Treaty recently concluded.

Receiving more details of the terms of the treaty, McDouall understood the one article expressly stipulated that the Indian nations "were to be on the same footing as before the war." McDouall deduced that if everything were to be restored to the conditions in place when the Americans received Fort McKay, "they must evacuate the same and retire to the boundary of 1812."[3]

Since he believed all was to be at prewar status, McDouall gave Bulger very specific directions as to what was to be done at Fort McKay. Bulger was to remove and bring back to British territory all the public stores. The guns captured with the surrender of Fort Shelby had to be restored to the fort. Bulger was to evacuate the fort and join him at Michilimackinac before he returned the island to the Americans. When Bulger left Prairie du Chien, he was to bring the detachment of Michigan Fencibles with him. Any who had been in the service of the United States were to be discharged at Prairie du Chien or Green Bay with thirty days' pay. Since the Mississippi Volunteers had been attached to British service at various places, Bulger was to discharge them where they entered service, also issuing thirty days' pay. All the men with the western Indian Department were to depart the prairie with Bulger. He was to bring the pay lists with him, but McDouall would not honor any officer or interpreter whose appointment had not been approved and certified by Bulger. McDouall would be sending provisions to help Bulger and the men on their journey to Michilimackinac.[4]

In regard to the Indians, Bulger was to tell them that with the end of the war, the American fleet would no longer hinder the movement of British gifts and goods for the tribes. The British would now be able to "attend to their wants, without interruption, & numerous traders will again be amongst them." McDouall also directed Bulger to convey another message to the Indians, one that demonstrated the weakness and vanity of which Dickson had accused him. The war was lost; McDouall needed someone to blame, so he blamed the people who would lose the most. Bulger was to tell the tribes

> [t]hat the King their Great Father, would, pursuant to his promises, have continued the war, and recovered the lands which the Americans had deprived them of, but that his red children were disunited, & did not act in concert against the common enemy that the very tribes who were most interested and had lost most, had made peace with the Big Knives, & had agreed to take up the hatchet against those who remained faithful to us.[5]

Though he had given Bulger detailed orders in what to do now that there was to be peace between the United States and Great Britain, his terse directions belied McDouall's feelings. In a personal note to Bulger, McDouall expressed his bitterness. He then told Bulger as to why he had not agreed to turn Mackinac Island over to the Americans on May 20. He wished to retain Michilimackinac "until all the Traders for the Mississippi have passed on, as I have my doubts, if the American would permit a grain of Powder to go to the Western Indians." By July 10, the date McDouall had set, the annual spring fleet of canoes from Montreal, filled with trade goods, would have reached the upper Mississippi.[6]

For more than two weeks, McDouall quibbled about what the peace meant, complaining that Drummond had not communicated with him directly. In Prairie du Chien, however, there was no uncertainty. Dickson and Graham accepted the dispatches from Colonel Russell and Governor Clark at face value. Dickson had already made plans and on April 27 addressed the Sac gathered at the prairie. Bulger was not present when Dickson talked with the Indians, but someone reported all to Bulger, adding fuel to the fire. Taking the informer's interpretation of Dickson's words to be true, Bulger again reprimanded Dickson, calling the manner in which he addressed the tribe and his language "reprehensible and more calculated to increase than lessen the suspicion which they naturally entertained of the views of the Government towards them." Bulger insisted Dickson's address had a "tendency to distroy my authority in the Country." He wished to censure Dickson publicly but instead pledged to bring the matter before His Excellency the governor in chief.[7]

The following day, on April 28, Dickson left Prairie du Chien for Mack-inac. His friends in the Indian Department, Duncan Graham, Michel Bris-bois Jr., and Joseph Renville, gave him a rousing send-off in which many toasts were drunk. Afterward, Graham and the others stopped at Captain Anderson's quarters. After a dispiriting winter, Bulger's final confronta-tion with Dickson, and the consumption of too much alcohol, Graham unloaded the thoughts he had been harboring for some time. Graham inquired of Anderson as to where he could find Bulger, as he wanted to "tell him my sentiments on what passed." He told Anderson that Dickson had left disgraced from the unjust manner in which Bulger acted the day previous. What had passed personally between Dickson and Bulger, Gra-ham knew nothing about, but Graham informed Anderson that Bulger had acted upon the information he had gotten "from a damned murderer and a noted thief, he did not think it worth his while to send for me, and ask me who was present when Mr. Dickson spoke to the Saulks." Graham stated he would make a written report that "would go before the British Parliament, and Captain Bulger, you may depend upon it, will be brought to an account for it."[8]

Before Graham could write his report, however, Anderson penned his own report and submitted it to Captain Bulger. Receiving the report, Bulger ordered that Captain Graham be placed in close arrest for language "tending to excite discontent and dissatisfaction against the commanding officer of Fort McKay, also calculated to create much mischief amongst the Indians." Bulger then wrote a report of the incident and sent it to McDouall, attributing Graham's actions to "Mr. Dickson's instigations," further proof "of his intriguing dangerous disposition." Graham refused to apologize for his conduct; per Bulger's orders he was escorted under guard to Michilimackinac.[9]

At the island, McDouall began to parse the terms of the Treaty of Ghent. He did not doubt the terms regarding the Indians, but upon close consider-ation he saw a glaring inconsistency between the treaty and Drummond's orders regarding the handing over of Fort McKay to the Americans. In McDouall's interpretation, the "literal meaning & spirit of the Treaty as understood by both Governments is, that the Indian country, shall be mu-tually evacuated by both parties" (original emphasis). McDouall therefore issued new orders pertaining to Fort McKay, writing to Bulger:

You will take immediate steps for distroying the Fort, and withdrawing the Garrison, taking care that the Guns, Gun-carriages & ord[n]
ance stores taken with the place, be correctly restored to the American Government by the best & most convenient mode: either by
sending them down the Mississippi, or if that is not practicable, by
bringing them to be given up at this Garrison, acquainting the officer
commanding at St. Louis of the arrangement made.[10]

In his letter of May 5, McDouall impressed upon Bulger the importance
of maintaining harmony among all involved in the transfer of the prairie to
the Americans. He cited three different scenarios that could occur, in two
of which Bulger was to "[destroy] and evacuate the Fort as before directed."
As to the three-pound cannon Sergeant Keating had manned to bombard
Fort Shelby and the *Governor Clark*, this had been a present to the Sioux
and was to be left with them. Though McDouall had ordered the return
of Dickson to Michilimackinac, McDouall told Bulger, "Mr. Dickson will
of course render you every assistance in carrying your arrangements into
execution."[11]

Although razing the fort and removing the troops from the garrison
required planning, the bigger undertaking was informing the Indians of
the Mississippi of the declaration of peace. As word of the peace agreement
spread, Indians began to arrive at Prairie du Chien, including the head
chiefs of the neighboring tribes. When they learned of the article in the
treaty that pertained to the Indians, many of the chiefs angrily expressed
their determination not to abide by the treaty.

The Treaty of Ghent was composed of eleven articles; Article 9 pertained to hostilities with the tribes or nations of Indians. Pushed by the
American commissioners and with a desire for peace, the British commissioners agreed to return to the status quo prior to the war and the mutual
restoration of all forts. They abandoned the demands they had made the
previous summer that the tribes retain the lands they held as of 1811. In
Article 9, the United States agreed to end all hostilities with the tribes or
nations with whom they had been at war and

to restore to such Tribes or Nations respectively all the possessions,
rights, and privileges which they may have entitled to in one thou-

sand eight hundredand eleven previous to such hostilities. Provided always that such Tribes or Nations shall agree to desist from all hostilities against the United States of America, their citizens, and Subjects upon Ratification of the present Treaty.[12]

McDouall expressed disgust with this article, writing Bulger, "Our negotiators, as usual, have been egregiously duped: as usual they have shown themselves profoundly ignorant of the concerns of this part of the Empire." Though "penetrated with grief" at returning Mackinac Island and "mortified" at the loss of Fort McKay to the Americans, "when the Treaty itself specifies that the Indians are to be on the same footing as before the war," he ordered Bulger to make sure the Indians accepted the treaty and did not attack any Americans. So Bulger spent part of each day in the council house, accompanied by an interpreter for each tribe, holding conferences with the chiefs and principal men of each tribe. He was able to convince some of the chiefs to view the treaty "in a more favorable light." Some tribes continued to oppose the treaty. Finally, on May 20, Bulger received an official dispatch from British headquarters announcing the peace. Included were instructions on how Bulger was to officially announce the declaration of peace to "the Indians of the Mississippi."[13]

The war belt that Bulger had requested of Dickson represented the uniting of the western Indian nations with the king of Great Britain to attack the Americans. On the belt were woven a chain of figures hand-in-hand and a "castle"—a figure for each Indian nation and their English Father, with the castle being St. Louis. The belt had been woven using white and purple-black wampum, or shell beads. The white beads had been tinted red, the color of war. With Dickson gone and the belt finally in Bulger's possession, Bulger ordered the red be removed. The beads again white, Bulger then ordered that they be dyed blue. The belt now became a symbol of peace. A pipe was prepared and decorated in the Indian fashion and a speech written and addressed, "To the brave and faithful—the Chiefs and warriors of the nations of the Mississippi from their Great Father the King of England, through the Great Chief representing His Majesty at Quebec."[14]

Wishing to make the announcement of peace before more Indians arrived at the prairie, Bulger worked quickly. Members of the Indian Department arranged the council house, which stood not far from the fort, for the ceremony, which would take place on May 22. At one end of the building, under the smoke hole, a platform was erected. On this, the men placed a table covered with a blue cloth, a chair for the commander, and a flagstaff that passed through the smoke hole. Fearing that once the Indians heard of the peace, there might be some "treachery," Bulger ordered the troops to stay under arms within the fort and with the gate closed. Only Bulger; Anderson, now the acting head of the Indian Department; and a few other officers would attend the ceremony. When the men arrived at the council house, the grounds were filled with Indians. Entering the council house, Bulger found about seventy chiefs and principal warriors seated within the building, forming three sides of a square. The interpreter for each nation sat in front of the chiefs of their respective tribe. Bulger seated himself, surrounded by his staff; a gun was fired from the fort, and the council began. The principal interpreter stepped into the center of the square carrying the great belt of wampum used in 1813 to summon the tribes of the Mississippi to join the British. He laid it on the ground for all to see, now with blue tinted beads representing peace. The blue was to assure the tribes that they could place confidence in what Bulger would say to them "in the name of the king their great father."[15]

Bulger directed Anderson to make known to the tribes that peace had been declared between Great Britain and the United States, in which they were all included. All the terms of the treaty were presented to the tribes. When Anderson read the ninth article, Bulger added a bit of elucidation reflective of the loathing he held for Dickson. Anderson was to explain that the article

> secured them in the rights to which they were entitled before the
> war, and Great Britain became the guarantor of those rights; but the
> lands that had been promised to them by their Father the "Red Head"
> in the name of the British government, the Americans had refused
> to give up.

As each paragraph was read, the interpreters immediately translated Anderson's words. When the reading was complete, each chief stood up and offered a response. When it was Black Hawk's turn to speak, he declared he would follow the counsel and "endeavour to cultivate peace; but that he could not answer for his people, if any new act of aggression should be committed against them." Other chiefs echoed Black Hawk's sentiments. Joseph Renville then brought forward the pipe and presented it to Bulger. He smoked it, then passed it to the nearest chief. Renville then presented it in succession to the other chiefs and warriors in council. The ceremony lasted five hours, ending with a salute of nineteen guns fired from the fort, thus announcing the end of the war on the Mississippi. Messengers were sent to the principal Indian villages throughout the Northwest to disseminate news of the peace.[16]

Formalities with His Majesty's allies concluded, Bulger finally sent a message to William Clark acknowledging reception of his letter and the meeting with Colonel Russell. He told Clark that he proposed to evacuate Fort McKay on May 24, taking with him to Mackinac the guns captured in July 1814. At Mackinac, the arms would be delivered to the Americans when they arrived at that post. He told Clark that he had chosen this option, for he feared that were both British and United States troops together at Fort McKay it might cause "a fresh rupture with the Indians, which I presume it is the wish and desire of both Governments to avoid."[17]

Bulger feared that if he and the troops stayed any longer, the Indians who had come to the council would assemble and attack the men. So as he had written to Clark, he withdrew from Fort McKay on the twenty-fourth, taking anything that could be removed. On the way, he met bateaux filled with Indian presents that McDouall had dispatched to Prairie du Chien. Bulger ordered the boats to continue on to the prairie where the items were distributed. Bulger felt that he had left the Indians on the Mississippi "above want; their situation, in comparison with former years, is comfortable." He praised the Fencibles and volunteers who had journeyed with him, the "cordial support which I have received from Captain Anderson," and the good conduct of Lieutenant Keating. Bulger ended his report with these few words: "The Fort has been destroyed."[18]

The British were gone from Prairie du Chien, having stripped the fort of all they could carry before destroying it. They passed through La Baye on the way to Mackinac Island, withdrawing any stores that had been part of the Indian Department. They retired to Mackinac Island and would remain there until July 18 when troops of the Second Regiment of US Riflemen under the command of Colonel Anthony Butler arrived. With Mackinac

Island in American hands, the British forces under McDouall, members of the Indian Department, and others traveled to Drummond Island to establish a garrison so that Great Britain could maintain a presence at the Straits of Mackinac. From this place, McDouall hoped to convince the Chippewa and Ottawa to carry on their alliance with Britain.

The British left behind the American Indian tribes who had given the British strength in the west and instilled fear in the Americans living in Illinois and St. Louis. The British also left behind the inhabitants of La Baye and Prairie du Chien, who had given all that they could of their crops to keep the garrisons at Michilimackinac and Fort McKay from starvation; there had been very little seed to plant the spring of 1815. Despite the departure of the British military, General Clark and the Americans still regarded Prairie du Chien as a British stronghold, and La Baye and the prairie as places of prime importance for control of the fur trade and dealings with the American Indians. As summer approached, all the residents of the region west of Lake Michigan and the upper Mississippi questioned what would happen to them.

This painting, commissioned by Captain Andrew Bulger and painted by Peter Rindisbacher in 1823, shows Bulger's leave-taking of his Indian allies as he departs Fort McKay.
WHI 42292; ORIGINAL HOUSED AT THE AMON CARTER MUSEUM OF AMERICAN ART

Indeed, even though the British officers and soldiers were actively leaving the forts, McDouall was thinking of the future. Previous to the peace, McDouall had ordered provisions and gifts for the Indians in anticipation of a continued conflict. Now he laid a strategy to ensure that the British traders would be able to maintain their stronghold in the region. He had changed the date for the exchange of Mackinac Island for Amherstburg from May 20 to mid-July. He had retained the island "until all the Traders for the Mississippi have passed on." He had ensured that the goods ordered for the Indians would be distributed to the tribes. By delaying the date, the Indians would be well supplied, and the traders would not have to pay import taxes on the goods.[19]

—⊣⊢—

The Treaty of Ghent had dealt with the many issues that had caused the United States to declare war on Great Britain, in particular the boundary between the United States and Canada and the nations of Indians involved in the hostilities. Of all the articles in the treaty, Article 9 was of the most concern to the US secretary of war, James Monroe, in particular the agreement that "hostilities are to cease with both Indians and their allies." In order for this to be effected, the United States needed to negotiate a new treaty of peace with each Indian nation. To this end, Clark, Edwards, and Chouteau had been given "full power to conclude a treaty with all those tribes." These commissioners were to invite the tribes to send a deputation of chiefs to convene "at such place or places, as you may appoint," the purpose of which was to conclude a "treaty of Peace and amity between the United States and all those Tribes." No other topics, such as acquisition of lands, were to be discussed. The treaty to be signed by each individual tribe was to be confined "to the sole object of peace."[20]

The commissioners needed to act quickly. Before the dispatch announcing peace had reached Prairie du Chien, bands of Sac from the Rock River had roamed down the Mississippi River and attacked settlements in Illinois and Missouri territories. Then on May 24, two days after he sat in conference with Bulger, Black Hawk led a band of fifty warriors in an attack on a company of rangers. When the American soldiers counterattacked, the Indians barricaded themselves in a sinkhole, from which the rangers could not displace them. Constrained by the terms of the treaty from responding, Clark wrote to Secretary Monroe for direction, saying, "I am under some apprehension that it will be necessary to cut off the Rocky River Tribes before we shall be at peace."[21]

Under pressure from the St. Louis press to take action against the Sac, the commissioners selected Portage des Sioux as the site for the gathering of tribes. The portage was a vast alluvial prairie at the confluence of the Mississippi and Missouri Rivers. It had the advantages of being accessible to the tribes coming down both rivers, was far from St. Louis, and could be easily defended if all did not go well. The commissioners dispatched invitations to thirty-seven tribes to gather at Portage des Sioux on July 6. Manuel Lisa, US Indian agent for the tribes located above the mouth of the Kansas River, was to inform and bring the Missouri River tribes to the portage, and Thomas Forsyth, American agent to the Sac and Fox, was responsible for notifying all of the tribes as far north as the Sioux and Menominee along Green Bay. Forsyth employed Petchaho, a Potawatomi chief, to deliver Clark's letter to his tribe, and then asked his assistance to notify other tribes. Petchaho said he would use Potawatomi and Kickapoo familial connections to reach the Winnebago, Chippewa, Menominee, and Ottawa. By some means, the message for the Menominee came into the possession of Pierre Grignon. He then gave the letter to Jacques Porlier to give to Louis Grignon. Pierre requested that Louis "try and make tomas [Tomah] do his duty[;] they say he wishes to give a favorable reply to the Americans. Tell him to take care."[22]

The messengers sent up the Mississippi to invite the Sioux bands to the treaty gathering met opposition from the Sac and Fox at the Rock River. One messenger was killed and others turned back. The *Missouri Gazette* reported this was the work of Captain Duncan Graham, "deputy scalping master general," because he had provided the Sac with gunpowder and "twenty fusees as a reward for their services in butchering helpless women and children on the frontiers." George Kennerly, aide to William Clark, finally volunteered to take invitations to the tribes at Prairie du Chien and above by traveling up the Missouri River and then eastward over present-day Iowa.[23]

By July 6, almost all of the tribes that had received invitations had arrived at Portage des Sioux. A few Sac and Fox were present, but the two Sac chiefs, Keokuk and Black Hawk, did not attend. Clark opened the council on July 10 with American military pageantry. The US Regulars had lined up their one hundred tents in meticulously straight rows, the gunboats *Governor Clark* and *Admiral Perry* patrolled the Mississippi, and drums rolled to announce the opening of speeches. Clark stood beneath a brush arbor and addressed each tribe individually, detailing with each the conduct of the nation during the war with the British. He informed them that their "Great Father in Washington" wished "to bury the tomahawk and forget their past transactions."[24]

Lastly, he addressed the Sac and Fox chiefs. Standing before them, he told them he did not wish to speak with them, telling them he must see La Moite, the head Sac chief, or Black Hawk. He told them to tell La Moite and Black Hawk that they were to appear before him in thirty days. If they did not come to the portage, Clark said he would ascend the river and find them. To guarantee that La Moite and Black Hawk would heed his words, he told the chiefs present that they would be held until his summons was obeyed. If La Moite and Black Hawk did not come, "blood would be spilt for their disobedience." This excited the traditional enemies of the Sac and Fox, who yelled "for Joy" at each sentence. The next morning the Sac chiefs had disappeared from the portage.[25]

After speeches by several chiefs, negotiations with each individual tribe began. By July 22, chiefs representing seven tribes had signed a treaty with the United States. The treaties, which would be ratified in December, were brief and to the point. "The parties being desirous of peace and friendship between the United States and said tribe" agreed to three articles:

Every injury or act of hostility . . . mutually forgiven and forgot.

There shall be perpetual peace and friendship between the United States of America and all the individuals composing the tribe.

The undersigned chiefs and warriors, for themselves and their tribes, do hereby acknowledge themselves and their tribes to be under the protection of the United States, and no other power, nation, or sovereign.

After the first set of tribes signed, Clark adjourned the council to await the deadline to see if the Sac and Fox arrived. He was also hoping to learn that Kennerly had been able to bring in more tribes from the north. Clark remained convinced that the pro-British bands on the upper Mississippi would be brought to agreement only "at the point of a bayonet." By the end of September, thirteen separate treaties had been signed. But the southwestern Chippewa, Menominee, and Winnebago had not sent a single representative to the council. The Sac of the Rock River, now called the "British Band," failed to appear, even with the threat of future war.[26]

Instead of attending the council, Black Hawk and La Moite had gone to Prairie du Chien with members of Black Hawk's band. Having heard of the attacks on Americans in Illinois and Missouri, McDouall wanted to ensure that all the former Indian allies were aware that peace had been concluded between the United States and Great Britain. McDouall ordered Anderson to return to Prairie du Chien with three bateaux of goods for distribution to the tribes. He wrote a speech for Anderson to deliver. By August 3, Anderson was at the prairie. Speaking in McDouall's stead, Anderson stated that McDouall had purchased gifts for the tribes as a token of gratitude for having listened to him and to help them pass the winter. He repeated what they had heard before: "Your Great Father the King, has made Peace with the Big Knives, and that all his Red children are included in it." He commanded that they bury the tomahawk and live in harmony with the Americans. He recommended that they treat the traders well so that they would return to the Indian villages and restrain the young men from killing the cattle and destroying the grain of the inhabitants. They were to use the arms and ammunition he gave them for the support of their families in winter. He concluded by inviting all to come to Drummond Island once a year "that you may receive that bounty."[27]

La Moite responded to Anderson, saying, "The Chiefs Warriors and young men you see hereabouts are all of the same opinion, they love their English Father," and thanked him for what they had heard and received. In the evening, over supper at Thomas Anderson's home, La Moite asked to speak in private to Anderson, letting him know he could repeat what he would tell him to "Our Father at Michilimackinac." He then told Anderson in detail how Clark had treated the Sac chiefs, threatening to kill them if La Moite and Black Hawk did not come to sign the treaty. La Moite also informed Anderson of what Clark had told the Kickapoo:

You must never expect to see your English Father again, you have
rendered yourself miserable by following his advice by going to
war with us. We are going to build Forts on the Mississippi, we have
driven your English Father from thence, and Michilimackinac, you
are miserable, you will not have an English Trader amongst you;
*How can they come?*

La Moite continued, asking, "Why do not the Big Knives shut their bad
mouths and not insult us?" He thanked Anderson for the words and gifts,
and then concluded with his thoughts on the Americans. He said if they
came up the river as traders and treated the Sac well, they would be happy
to see them, but the soldiers could not come higher than Fort Madison.
The Sac would listen to the British, but added, "We are not women,—we
will not commence quarreling with them, but if they begin to molest us in
the least, we fear them not and will defend ourselves like men."[28]

In the council, Black Hawk also addressed Anderson, saying, "I am one
of those very few Indians, who speak my sentiments openly and without reserve—do not therefore be angry at what I am going to say." He recounted
all the promises the British had made to the Sac to get them to make war on
the Americans, but the promises were not kept. Now the Americans "are
Masters of us and our Lands," but as asked, the Sac would remain quiet.
He hoped that he would "not be obliged to dig up my Hatchet[;] I know
these Big Knives have sweet tongues and fear they had cheated us all."[29]

The thirty days Clark had allowed for the Sac chiefs to appear at Portage
des Sioux had long since passed. They understood that the Americans now
looked upon them as enemies and asked Anderson for advice as to what
they should do. Anderson replied that he did not think anything would
happen. As La Moite had told Anderson, the Sac chiefs at Portage des Sioux
had voiced their unhappiness with Clark to Nicolas Boilvin. Boilvin told
them what Clark had said was "not the words of the *Great American Chief,*
he had made that bad news himself" (original emphasis). In other words,
their quarrel was with Clark, not the United States. Boilvin had spent the
winter in Washington and knew "it was not the wish of the Great American
Chief at that place to hurt any of the Indians." Anderson advised the Sac to
wait for Boilvin, who was expected to arrive soon at Prairie du Chien, and
when he came, to be friendly and present him with the "pipe of peace." To

this they would not agree, but stated if Boilvin would give them a pipe of peace, they would smoke it.[30]

At the end of the meeting, Black Hawk thanked Anderson for the goods, "which will save our families from perishing in the winter." He promised that "next Canoeing season" he would see his "Father":

> It is a long way to go every year for our supplies, but you say every-
> thing is arranged for our good, and next hot season at least one hun-
> dred of my Warriors will go and see you. . . . When I look down this
> River some bad blood that remains in my heart jumps to my throat,
> and if it were not for your councils, I would free myself of it.

The Sac then departed for the Rock River.[31]

Nicolas Boilvin had wanted to return to Prairie du Chien as soon as peace had been declared. He felt disgust with Clark's action toward the Sac at the Portage des Sioux and laid the blame for some of the attacks by the Sac with the "administration at St. Louis," denouncing Clark as a war-monger. He told the secretary of state that all would have gone smoothly at the council had he been sent to announce the treaty to the chiefs. He was delighted to be reappointed Indian agent at the prairie, stating, "I go as a simple person in order not to lose the influence which I have always had with the tribes."[32]

In mid-August, Boilvin and an interpreter arrived at the Rock River to talk with the Sac. For two and a half days they sat in council. The chiefs expressed fear of an American trick. Boilvin stated they would be pardoned if they remained at peace and sent a delegation to the Portage des Sioux. The chiefs agreed, telling Boilvin to continue on to Prairie du Chien, where the Fox, Sioux, Menominee, and Winnebago awaited him. Boilvin and his family, who had made the journey with him, arrived at Prairie du Chien the first of September to find what remained of their house and belong-ings. Going back on their word, the Sac did not send representatives to the portage. Not until May 13, 1816, would the chiefs of the Sac of the Rock River sign the treaty with Commissioners Clark, Edwards, and Chouteau.[33]

At Prairie du Chien, Boilvin did all he could to persuade the northern tribes to agree to peace. In September, he met in council with six thousand Indians, from which he sent the secretary of war five pipes given by the tribes as symbols of peace. He had come to the prairie on his own, with no military support and no provisions for the Indians. In the packet of pipes sent to Washington, Boilvin enclosed a letter telling the secretary that he was "now here at the Mercy of these Indians, without provisions when they ought to have been sent from St. Louis, it is lucky for me that their Former Confidence in me Still exists." Saying he would meet with about ten thousand more Indians, he questioned how he could keep them allied to the United States when he had nothing to give them. He told the secretary that "a Number of them will proceed to Fort Drummon[d] on Lake Huron to receive a Quantity of Goods from the British Government." In October and again in January 1816, Boilvin lamented the trade that continued between the British and the Indians. He accused the traders of urging the Indians "to hold themselves in instant readiness for another war."[34]

—ɪɪ—

As the United States tried to establish peace with the tribes of the western Indians, the inhabitants of La Baye and Prairie du Chien attempted to re-establish the pattern of their lives. Over the summer and fall of 1815 they attempted to plant crops to restock their granaries and, for those who had been part of the British fur trade, revitalize their commerce with the Indians. Through McDouall's careful maneuvering, the British had given the tribes arms, ammunition, fishhooks, and spears. All on the prairie hoped the trade that season would be good.

Indeed, many of the traders at Prairie du Chien and La Baye were able to pick up their trade with little trouble. John Lawe, Jacques Porlier, and Pierre Grignon returned to the fur trade, which none had completely put aside when accepting a commission. The war had never stopped James Aird from trading on the upper Mississippi, and when he received a good supply of goods for the winter of 1814–1815, Dickson thought he would "make out well." Joseph Rolette had competed with John Lawe on the Trempealeau River in the winter of 1812–1813, and it can be assumed that Rolette traded during the following winter.[35]

After his confrontation with Captain Bulger, Duncan Graham left the Indian Department and returned to the fur trade. He set up a post on a peninsula that jutted into Devil's Lake in what is now Minnesota. He also assisted the colonies along the Red River, helping to negotiate a truce and trade agreement between the Red River Colony and the North West Company.[36]

Francis Michael Dease remained at Prairie du Chien, where he maintained a local militia. The prairie was without any military protection, so he drilled the men to keep them prepared in case of attack by Indians upset with the peace. He had left the prairie by 1816 and traveled to the Red River, becoming a constable at the Selkirk Settlement on the Red River.[37]

Unlike the other major traders at Prairie du Chien, Robert Dickson had not been able to continue any trading activities on the Mississippi or St. Peter's River. His responsibilities as agent and superintendent had required all of his energy and time. After the declaration of peace, a hearing was conducted in Quebec regarding Lieutenant Colonel Robert McDouall's charges against Dickson. Dickson was cleared of charges and rewarded for his services with the title of lieutenant colonel. He retired from the Indian Department with a pension. Dickson applied in June 1816 for the vacant position of superintendent of the Indian Department at Amherstburg. He did not receive the appointment, so he went into the Northwest and resumed trading. He became the leader of a group of traders that included Duncan Graham, Joseph Renville, Amable Grignon, Charles Brisbois, and Henry Munro Fisher.[38]

Others who had resided at the prairie or at La Baye chose to remain with the British. Thomas G. Anderson and Joseph Renville both left Prairie du Chien and continued to work for the British Indian Department. McDouall appointed Anderson a captain in the Indian Department. John Askin Jr. had also remained with the Indian Department and moved the Indian Department store to Drummond Island. When Anderson returned from Prairie du Chien in September, Askin asked Anderson to take charge of the store at Drummond Island. When the British moved their post to Penetanguishene, Anderson followed. Anderson would go on to be stationed at Coldwater and Manitoulin Island. In 1845, he succeeded Colonel S. P. Jarvis as superintendent of Indian affairs for west Canada.[39]

The British respected the influence Joseph Renville had among the Sioux and retained him as an interpreter. While in their employ, Renville also traded with the Hudson's Bay Company, residing in the winter with his family among the Dakota. Each summer he visited the British settlements on the Red River to receive presents to be distributed to the Indians.[40]

Lewis Cass, governor of Michigan Territory, was aware of the trading activities of these men and other "British traders" within what was now defined as part of the United States. Like Boilvin, he believed that the privilege these men enjoyed to carry on "a lucrative commerce" with

This map from the 1814 American *Pocket Atlas* depicts the Northwest Territory according to its boundaries at the conclusion of the War of 1812. COURTESY OF MARY ELISE ANTOINE

the Indians was the reason for all the difficulties the United States experienced in establishing relations with the tribes. Even though the war had ended, he believed that the British Indian Department would continue supporting the tribes "but with a renewed activity and increased exertion." The presents and invitation McDouall had extended to the Sac to visit the British each year at Drummond Island, which he also extended to the Fox and Kickapoo, put truth to Cass's supposition. Having learned that "a large quantity of goods have arrived at Malden to be distributed as presents and the Agents and subordinate officers are more numberous that at any former period," Cass told the secretary of war that soon the Indian country would be filled "with agents and Interpreters and traders which at all former periods kept the North Western frontiers in a state of feverish alarm."[41]

Cass further informed the secretary of the "three great channels of communication" by which British traders could bring goods into American territory: from Chicago down the Illinois River, from Green Bay up the Fox River and down the Wisconsin River, and via a small river which entered Lake Superior near Grand Portage. By these means British trade goods could enter the Mississippi and Missouri country. Cass estimated that no more than one-third of the people who traded in this country paid duties, and he suggested that military posts be established at Green Bay, Prairie du Chien, and Chicago. These would close the means by which unlicensed traders could bring goods into the country. The only practical route besides these led from Lake Superior to the small lakes at the head of the Mississippi River, so, Cass argued, a post should also be opened at the Grand Portage. The posts in place, the British traders could be admitted and duties collected "without very serious inconvenience."[42]

A. J. Dallas, acting secretary of war, found that the Indians as well as the British traders were a "menace" and "required immediate attention." To restore harmony, preserve peace, and defeat "the arts employed by intrusive traders to generate Indian hostilities," he recommended the immediate establishment of an Indian agency on the Fox River, preferably Green Bay. The agent would maintain "an armoury proper for the accommodation of the Indians," at which two companies of United States troops would be stationed. In addition, a fur factory would be opened, supplied with merchandise for the Indians that would be distributed "from time to time."

He recommended that Charles Jouett, a former military agent at Chicago, be appointed agent. President Madison approved this on June 20, 1815.[43]

In Missouri, Clark attempted to maintain peace while land-hungry citizens of the territory pushed onto Indian lands. As the complaints from the tribes became more numerous, he finally had to announce that the intrusion of "white persons" onto Indian lands would no longer be permitted and threatened to use the militia to evict trespassers. Across the Mississippi, Clark's edict enraged Governor Edwards, who wrote to Secretary of State James Monroe voicing his displeasure. He told Monroe that there was one description of intruders who should be entitled to no favors and against whom

> the most rigid execution of the proclamation [is] in my opinion rec-
> ommended. I mean those British subjects who have settled them-
> selves at the village of La Bay . . . and at the village of Prairie du Chien
> on the Mississippi. At both of which places, those intruders are not
> only engaged extensively in agriculture, but constantly carry on such
> an intercourse with the Indians, as is prohibited to our best citizens.

To allow them to reside in US territory would mean that "a set of un-principled British spies, ever ready to communicate the measures of our gov't" lived on land forbidden to American citizens. The produce from their farms had enabled the British to rally a large number of Indians against the United States. He suggested that the residents of the two communities be removed from the settlements and the land given to "good American citizens," who could support the garrisons, the trade, and the Indians.[44]

The Treaty of Ghent ended armed combat between the governments of Great Britain and the United States; peace had been proclaimed. The treaty, however, did not end hostilities on the upper Mississippi frontier.

# Conclusion

At the close of the War of 1812, of utmost concern to the men in positions of authority within the United States government were implementing the means to exert dominance in relations with the western Indians and control of the fur trade. The American agents of government also continued to see the inhabitants of Prairie du Chien and La Baye as intruders without claim to the homes and settlements they inhabited. William Woodbridge, acting governor of Michigan Territory, wrote Alexander Dallas, the acting secretary of war, in May of 1814, stating his view that strong force was needed to control the Indian populations:

> I know of nothing that will check the murderous temper among the Indians, unless it be an active, exterminating war on our part—or the location of a large military force—at this place [Detroit]—at Michilimackinac—at Green Bay & at Chicago. . . . An imposing military force properly located may probably save the sacrifice of many lives.[1]

Once Lewis Cass was appointed governor of Michigan Territory, he expressed a similar opinion in regard to the continuance of British traders in the region, recommending the establishment of military posts as a means of blocking the routes by which British traders could continue to bring goods into the Mississippi and Missouri regions.[2]

Even before these letters were written, the War Department had adopted plans to create military posts and fur factories that would impede the British traders' use of the Fox, Wisconsin, and Mississippi Rivers from Michilimackinac to the Falls of St. Anthony and to reestablish posts at the foot of Lake Michigan and on the Mississippi below Prairie du Chien.

Dallas also recommended that an Indian agency be immediately estab-lished on the Fox River in the neighborhood of Green Bay "for restoring harmony, preserving peace, and defeating the arts employed by intrusive traders to generate Indian hostilities."[3]

To further frustrate any attempt by the British to continue trade in the northern regions of the Northwest Territory, on April 26, 1816, the United States Congress passed a supplement to the 1802 act regulating trade and commerce among the Indians. The supplement stated, "Licenses to trade with the Indians within the territorial limits of the United States shall not be granted to any but citizens of the United States." Goods or pelts carried by a foreigner would be confiscated, foreigners traveling without a passport within the territory would be seized, fined, or imprisoned de-pending on the severity of the offense, and military force would be used to enforce the act.[4]

The act had been in effect for less than two months when the Indian agent at Mackinac seized "twelve or fifteen thousand dollars" worth of furs that had come from the upper Mississippi and were being transported to Drummond Island by men in the employ of Louis Grignon. More bales of fur remained at La Baye, so Pierre Rocheblave, agent for the Southwest Fur Company, counseled both Grignon and Jacques Porlier to come to Michilimackinac with their packs at once "and run the risk of a lawsuit, rather than run the risk of a seizure at your place." He also recommended that both men put any merchandise they had "in a place of safety for fear of a visit."[5]

With that number of pelts having been carried on the Fox-Wisconsin waterway from the upper Mississippi, it is obvious that Prairie du Chien and La Baye were still under the control of men with British trading li-censes. Likewise, James Aird and John Lawe were transporting furs to the new British post on Drummond Island. The United States needed to gain control of the Indian country. That control arrived at Prairie du Chien in the summer of 1816 in the form of US military forces.

In the fall of 1815, part of the Eighth US Infantry was sent up the Mis-sissippi River from St. Louis, going into winter quarters on the Illinois side of the river. In April 1816, Brevet Brigadier General Thomas A. Smith arrived at the camp, Cantonment Davis. He took over the expedition, and the force then proceeded up the river, setting up camp on a large island in the Mississippi River above the mouth of the Rock River. South of the island, along the Rock River, stood Saukenuk, the village where Black Hawk had been born. The island, which the Sac had used as a garden, had been acquired by the United States as part of the 1804 treaty with the Sac. Here, Smith spent a month overseeing the work necessary for the construction of a fort on the island, which would be named in honor of former secretary of war John Armstrong. This fort was to be a protection against the Sac and Fox, who were still considered to be friendly to the British, and was to keep open the lines of communication between St. Louis, Prairie du Chien, and points farther north. Then, with troops of the Rifle Regiment, Smith continued up the Mississippi to begin the erection of a post at Prairie du Chien.

John W. Johnson, a trader working for the United States who had been the factor at Fort Madison before the war, had been appointed the United States fur factor for Prairie du Chien in 1815, arriving at the prairie in March 1816. He had entered into an agreement with Francois Bouthellier, now an agent for John Jacob Astor's Southwest Fur Company, to rent the buildings occupied by Bouthellier for twenty-seven dollars a month. These were the same buildings that the Michilimackinac Company used and that Clark had confiscated for use by US forces the summer of 1814. Johnson easily adapted the buildings for the purposes of the US fur factory and stored the trade goods he had brought with him. Bouthellier departed the prairie for Mackinac Island.[6]

When General Smith arrived on June 20, Major Richard Graham, Indian agent for the Illinois Territory, accompanied him and the troops. The following day Smith and Graham began to assert their authority on the prairie. They required all traders to show their licenses, seizing the goods of those who could not comply. The troops took possession of some houses that Smith had designated as necessary for public purposes. Smith approved Johnson's actions in situating himself and the factory in appropriate buildings, but he told Johnson that he should no longer pay rent for the buildings and took possession of the buildings "for the use of the United States." Johnson immediately wrote to Bouthellier telling him the news: "Thus you find how things are changed."[7]

Smith justified his actions in taking command of the homes along the waterfront in the Main Village and the Southwest Fur Company buildings because he felt the inhabitants of the prairie were "intruders." He stated:

The only claim they had to the soil was the permission of the Indians to reside there for the purpose of trade. These persons having, in violation of the laws, taken possession of public lands, [are] subject to fine and imprisonment.[8]

Smith could not imprison all the inhabitants, but he did bring charges with him from St. Louis against one of the residents of Prairie du Chien. Johnson wrote to Bouthellier that Michel Brisbois had been arrested and would be sent to St. Louis for trial. Johnson speculated, "Perhaps others here will accompany him."[9] Brisbois was accused of being involved in "treasonable practices" during the late war. Brisbois had held an American commission as a lieutenant of the militia in Illinois Territory. Robert Dickson and Henry Munro Fisher had also held commissions in the Illinois Territory. But they had left Prairie du Chien; only Michel Brisbois remained to be prosecuted.

Brisbois was kept in confinement for several days and then taken to St. Louis under the guard of Philip Fouke, marshal of the Illinois Territory. Smith refused the request of Madame Brisbois to give her husband a packet of beaver so he could raise money to pay his expenses once he reached his destination. The guard bundled him on a boat and took him to St. Louis. Once there, he was left at the levee. Brisbois located friends in the city who assisted him in returning to the prairie. In the meantime, Colonel Hamilton, who was supervising the construction of the new American fort, ordered Madame Brisbois, pregnant with her eighth child, and her family, which included Fisher's two children, out of their home. The military took possession of it. The flour that had been brought for the soldiers had become damp on the journey up the river; the flour was spread out to dry on the floors of the Brisbois house. Requiring the means to bake bread, the military also took possession of the Brisbois bake house, behind which was stacked about two hundred cord of dry wood. The commissary now had the means and supplies to bake daily rations.

Colonel Smith had selected the site of Fort Shelby/Fort McKay, the most prominent spot in the Main Village, as the location for a post that would have the potential to house six companies of soldiers. A post of this size required more land than had Shelby/McKay, and on the property

The main village of Prairie du Chien, drawn by Lt. Seth Eastman in 1829, depicts the village as it would have looked after the construction of Fort Crawford in 1816. COURTESY OF THE PEABODY MUSEUM OF ARCHAEOLOGY AND ETHNOLOGY, HARVARD UNIVERSITY, PM# 41-72-10/80 (DIGITAL FILE# 60742106).

Smith desired was the "ancient burying ground of the Prairie." Again asserting his authority, Smith ordered the residents to dig up their dead and bury them elsewhere. Smith would have gone even further had he been able. If he had had his way, he "would have destroyed the settlement, and delivered the male part of the inhabitants to the civil authority to be prosecuted for intrusion." When Smith left Prairie du Chien in July, turning over command to Captain Willoughby Morgan, he granted Morgan "authority to carry this view of the subject into effect whenever he should deem it expedient."[10]

At the eastern end of the Fox-Wisconsin waterway, United States forces were on the way to institute US authority at La Baye. Two companies of infantry and one company of artillery under the command of Colonel John Miller dropped anchor in Green Bay on July 29, 1816. The force, piloted by Augustin Grignon, had sailed from Mackinac to build a fort at La Baye and landed without opposition. Accompanying this force were two companies of riflemen and two companies of infantry commanded by Brevet Lieutenant Colonel Talbot Chambers "as a precaution against any opposition

from the Indians." Chambers had arrived at La Baye from a command at
Mackinac where he had displayed "exertions to arrest [British traders]
unremitting," promising that none would "be able to escape."[11]

The site where the old French fort once stood was selected as the location of the American post. A half mile below the fort setting, Chambers
found "a Mongrel French settlement that extends about five miles on both
sides of the river and is occupied by about forty families, many of whom
are reduced to the most distressing want." But the impoverished settlement of La Baye, set distant from where Chambers would oversee the post
construction, was of little interest to Chambers. Rather, once Chambers
determined the residents were in acceptance of the peace, Chambers had
little to do with them. Some of the residents of La Baye saw the American
presence as an opportunity. Louis Grignon secured the contract to supply
timber for the construction of the new garrison, named Fort Howard in
honor of General Benjamin Howard. Charles Jouett had been appointed
Indian agent for the Green Bay area, and John Lawe supplied goods to the
American agency.[12]

In Prairie du Chien, Major Hamilton continued to oversee the construction of the fort that had been named Fort Crawford in honor of the
present secretary of war, William H. Crawford. In the fall, the prairie had
a visitor: Major Zachary Taylor. With Taylor were Captain Gary and Lieutenant Hopkins. They inspected Fort Crawford but were bound for Green
Bay. Taylor was to take command of Fort Howard in the spring of 1817 and
wished to see where he would be stationed. Robert Dickson was at Prairie
du Chien, and as a sign of courtesy, he offered to escort the officers to La
Baye.[13]

Major Taylor returned to Green Bay with his family in April and proceeded to take command of Fort Howard. Colonel Chambers transferred to
Prairie du Chien. Like Smith, Chambers treated the inhabitants as intruders. Assessing the position of Fort Crawford, Chambers was not pleased
with the line of sight from the fort to the river. He therefore ordered that
the houses in front of and around the fort be removed to the lower end of
the Main Village. One of the houses had been the home of Robert Dickson
and his family.

James Lockwood, an American, had arrived on the prairie as a clerk
to the American Fur Company when Smith commanded Fort Crawford.

He recalled that

> the officers of the army treated the inhabitants as a conquered peo-
> ple, and the commandants assumed all the authority of governors
> of a conquered country, arraigning and trying citizens by courts-
> martial, and sentencing them to ignominious punishments. Cham-
> bers banished Joseph Rolette to an island, about seven miles north
> of the prairie, where he was obliged to spend the winter.[14]

John Shaw, an American who came to Prairie du Chien to build a grist-
mill, was similarly disgusted by Chambers's behavior. He said Chambers
"loved to make a display, was fond of drinking freely, naturally tyrannical
and over-bearing—and, when intoxicated was desperate and dangerous."
Once, when drunk, Chambers chased a young woman into the home of
Jacques Menard. Menard reproached him, so Chambers ordered a file of
soldiers to tie him up, strip off his shirt, and give him twenty-five lashes
with a cat-o'-nine-tails. Nicolas Boilvin's son pleaded on Menard's behalf,
and after two or three blows, Chambers ordered Menard released.

To both longtime inhabitants and those newly arrived, it was clear
that Prairie du Chien was now under strict United States occupation. So
too was the rest of the upper Mississippi territory. By the end of 1816, the
residents of Prairie du Chien and La Baye, by this time called Green Bay,
had accepted the fortifications within their communities. John Jacob Astor
and the American Fur Company quickly moved into the vacuum caused
by the requirement that trading licenses could be issued only to American
citizens and worked to monopolize the trade. Michilimackinac became
the headquarters of the company and Ramsey Crooks and Robert Stuart
served as its agents. For the next few years they made arrangements with
the Grignons, John Lawe, and Jacques Porlier in Green Bay. Crooks had to
acknowledge the power of Joseph Rolette at Prairie du Chien and allowed
him independence as he traded. Those who had known only the fur trade
as either trader, clerk, or voyageur could continue what they knew, but
now only under employment with the American Fur Company. No longer
could the residents trade on their own. As Boilvin reported:

> The citizens of this place [have] no other way of supporting their

families but by trading and now they are not permitted, for as soon as an agent attempts to grant them a license, the Indian Factor reports them officially as disaffected persons to the government, and consequently the agent is not justified in giving the citizen permission.[15]

Some at Prairie du Chien accepted employment with the American Fur Company, while others began to migrate further north.

During this period, the residents of the villages at Prairie du Chien began to question their future security. It may be that Colonel Smith had demanded proof that the people who lived on their lots had title to their land and homes. In any case, in 1816, fifty-four residents of Prairie du Chien petitioned the United States Congress to grant them legal title to their houses and land. In the petition they claimed that they and their ancestors had lived on the prairie without any formal documentation. In submissive language, they assured the Congress of their loyalty to the United States and were hopeful that the request would be kindly received.

> Your petitioners respectfully suggest that it would ill comport with the magnanimous policy which the government of the Republic has constantly displayed towards the rest of her adopted citizens, to take advantage of the circumstances of your petitioners and expel them from their homes, because of their remoteness and seclusion from the world, their ignorance of tenures, and their confidence in the government, had prevented them from being supplied with bits of parchment to protect themselves in the possession of their ancestors.

They concluded with the prayer that the "present inhabitants of the village of Prairie du Chien may be confirmed in their possessions of village lots and lands."[16]

Congress took the petition under consideration. But Prairie du Chien was not the only community where the residents had tenuous title to the land they occupied. On May 11, 1820, Congress passed "An Act to revive the powers of the commissioners for ascertaining and deciding on claims to land in the district of Detroit, and for settling claims to land at Green bay and Prairie des Chiens, in the Territory of Michigan." Isaac Lee was appointed the agent to ascertain the titles and claims. In August 1820 he traveled to Green Bay. Arriving there, he found "that the principle land claimants were absent." He gave personal notice at each house of his business and then continued on to Prairie du Chien.[17]

On October 2, 1820, Lee arrived at the prairie. He immediately visited each house, telling the residents he was going to collect testimony from each claimant as to the land being claimed and the size of each claim. For each claim, he interviewed the claimant. That person had to present at least two witnesses who could swear to the validity of the claim. By October 24, Lee had completed the interviews, recorded each claim and testimony, and drawn a rough map of the prairie and the location of the claims. He then returned to Green Bay. When he arrived on November 16, 1820, winter had already set in. Lee stayed in the community until the waters opened. During that time, he heard claims and took testimony as he had done at Prairie du Chien. In the spring of 1821, Lee presented his report to the commissioners at Detroit. The report for each community began with a history as best remembered by the oldest residents. Then followed the claims and testimony. The commissioners then issued their report. As Lee was unable to locate "no one perfect title, founded upon French or British grant, legally authenticated," the commissioners decided that for an individual to receive confirmation of land title, there must be proof "of continued possession since 1796."[18] Some residents at Green Bay and Prairie du Chien had not occupied the land upon which they lived for that long a period nor could they prove continuous occupation of the lot since 1796. So, for a few farm lots at La Baye and a few village and farm lots at Prairie du Chien, title was not granted. Most residents, however, continued to reside in the communities and in time gained title or moved northward.

Despite the eventual recognition of legal titles for many of the inhabitants of Prairie du Chien and Green Bay, relations with the Indian nations did not improve as the War Department and the Indian agents had hoped. The tribes in the upper Mississippi valley did not accede to US rule as the residents of the prairie and Green Bay had. Boilvin had concluded his councils and wrote to the secretary of war in February 1817. Having been among the tribes of Michigan Territory and the upper Mississippi for forty years, Boilvin made an assessment: "They are ill disposed toward the United States government, according to the speeches, because of the change towards them every year."[19] He would maintain an open door to

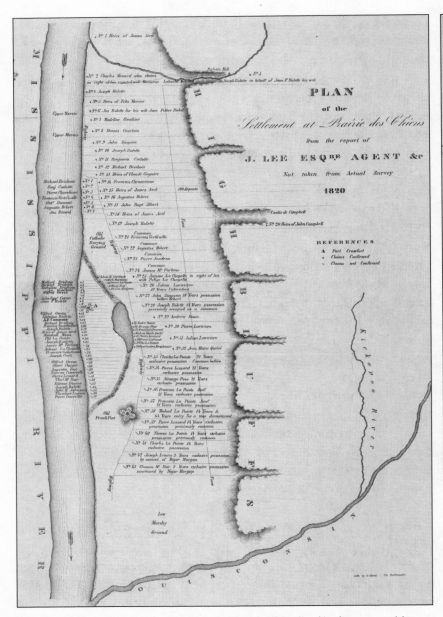

For many years, residents at Green Bay and Prairie du Chien lived in the communities without title to their land. In 1816, the residents of Prairie du Chien petitioned Congress to grant them title to their lots. The maps of Prairie du Chien (left) and Green Bay (right) show lot lines and names of the head of household, and were appended to surveyer Isaac Lee's report on the residents' land claims. WHI IMAGE ID 79654

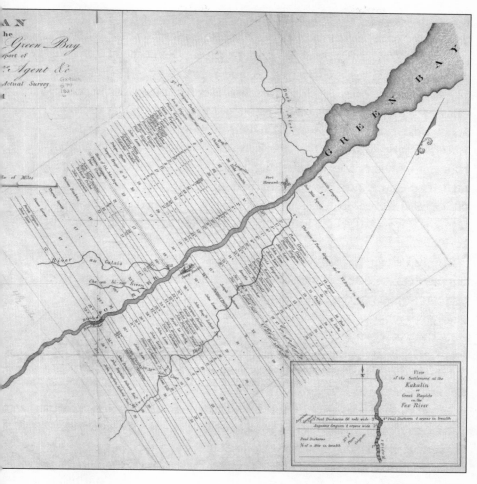

WHI IMAGE ID 39765

meet with the Indians and to advocate for supplies and fair treatment of the tribes, so there continued to be a constant flow of Indians in and out of Prairie du Chien.

In the meantime, though, Indian lands were diminishing. From 1816 to 1821, Governor Edwards in Illinois Territory and Governor Cass in Michigan Territory negotiated treaties. In the course of these treaties, the Sac and Fox affirmed acceptance of earlier treaties, the Kickapoo were removed from Illinois, and the Chippewa ceded land. In 1821, negotiations began for the Oneida to acquire Menominee and Winnebago lands along the Fox River. Soon after the end of the war, men from Missouri and Illinois moved onto Sac land at the Fever River to mine lead and eventually push northward onto Winnebago land. As tribes were pushed north and westward under pressure from treaties and encroaching settlers, friction arose among the tribes. Intertribal warfare recurred among the Sioux and Chippewa, endangering peace in the upper Mississippi and between the Sioux and the Sac. Rumors reached Boilvin of a plot among the Winnebago and other tribes to destroy the American forts, and in 1820 the Winnebago killed two soldiers at Fort Armstrong. In response, the United States extended its control into the upper Mississippi. In 1820, construction began on Fort Saint Anthony, located on the land Zebulon Pike had obtained from the Dakota Sioux in 1805. Upon its completion, the post was renamed Fort Snelling.

With the tribes greatly affected by the unrest, Lawrence Taliaferro, Indian agent at Fort Snelling, advocated a gathering of all the tribes. The secretary of war agreed and appointed William Clark and Lewis Cass peace commissioners and Prairie du Chien as the site for the council. The stated goal of the council was to promote peace among the tribes by fixing boundaries between them. Clark sent letters to all the Indian agents telling them to announce the council and invite all tribes to come. The Great Council began on August 5, 1825. To this gathering came the chiefs, principal men, and warriors of each tribe, and with them traveled their families. Taliaferro arrived with almost 400 Dakota and Chippewa. Governor Lewis Cass and Henry Schoolcraft brought 150 Chippewa and the leaders of the western Ottawa. Nicolas Boilvin gathered the Winnebago, Menominee, and their allies. William Clark arrived with the Ioway. Lastly, a flotilla of Sac and Fox led by Keokuk arrived after the council began. Notably, Black Hawk and his band did not attend the council.

Both banks of the Mississippi and islands in the river above and below Prairie du Chien were covered with buffalo-hide tents and woven grass and bark shelters. Estimating that the council would last fifteen days, the government had shipped food and supplies to feed two thousand Indians. In addition, the soldiers had erected a bower of trees and a raised platform near Fort Crawford for the use of the United States commissioners.

On the first day, General Clark addressed the assembly. He spoke of the United States' desire for peace "as brothers of one great family." He told all assembled:

Your great father has not sent us here to ask anything from you—we want nothing—not the smallest piece of Your Land—not a single article of your Property. . . .

[The Great Father] desires that his red children should bury the Tomahawk & he has sent us here to inform you what are his wishes. We therefore propose to you to make peace together & to agree upon fix'd boundaries, for your country, within which each tribe should hunt & over which others shall not pass without their consent.[20]

The next day, the chiefs expressed their thoughts, some favoring the establishment of boundaries between tribes, others feeling boundaries would cause more problems. From then until August 18, the commissioners and the chiefs negotiated the boundaries. After each discussion, a map was drawn to be reviewed the following day. But as Carramanee, a Winnebago chief, pointed out, the land he lived on "belongs as much to one as the other." He had "thought the Rivers were the common Property of all red skins & not used exclusively by any particular nation." Native

The 1825 Great Council and Treaty held at Prairie du Chien as drawn by James Otto Lewis. The meeting, meant to establish boundaries to prevent conflict between the tribes, also established the basis for future land treaties. These treaties led to the land cessions and eventual removal of tribes from their native land. WHI IMAGE ID 3142

people did not have the same concept of land ownership as the white man. Chambler, an Ottawa, concurred, saying, "I have never heard from my ancestors that any one had an exclusive right to the Soil."[21]

Under pressure from Clark and Cass, the chiefs set boundaries. August 19, 1825, the treaty of peace, embodying all the agreements as to boundaries between the tribes, was read and explained to all present. Then the commissioners and principal tribal delegates signed the document. A wampum belt was passed from hand to hand, and a pipe was smoked as a solemn promise of peace between all peoples represented at the Great Council and Treaty.

Peace lasted for only a few months. The push of white settlers and miners continued to cause tensions, especially among the tribes. With Prairie du Chien still seen as a gathering place for tribes, the community often witnessed and felt the effects of white incursions onto Indian lands. In spring of 1826, a Prairie du Chien family was killed while they worked in their sugar bush. Winnebago were accused; the tribe handed over some young men to Nicolas Boilvin and the commandant of Fort Crawford. Two men were found guilty; they were transported and imprisoned at Fort Snelling. Rumors were spread that the American soldiers had released the two Winnebago and they had been killed by Chippewa. The Winnebago designated Red Bird to seek retribution. In June 1827, he and others entered the Gagnier house at Prairie du Chien and killed two men. A few days later, Winnebago attacked a keelboat. Four-Legs, a chief of the eastern Winnebago, met in council at Butte des Morts with United States commissioners who demanded Red Bird's surrender. Worried that the Americans would not be satisfied even though Red Bird would have given himself up, Four-Legs and twenty other Winnebago traveled to Drummond Island. Four-Legs told the commander that he had not been to the island for four years, but he had to see the British, as "[t]he country I come from has been several years enveloped in a dense cloud." He explained that he had been bent down for two years by the Americans, and now he had heard from a Menominee "that we have but a short time to live, this friend told me that when the grass would get to a certain height we would be cut off by the Americans."[22] Though they were not killed as Four-Legs feared, in a series of treaties signed at Prairie du Chien beginning in 1829, the Winnebago relinquished all their land in Michigan Territory, and with the passage of the Indian Removal Act of 1830, relocation began to move the tribe west of the Mississippi River.

The Winnebago were not the only tribe who sent representatives to the British on Drummond Island in 1828. The western Indians sent a message through the Ottawa that "a certain nation of Whites wearing hats have destroyed its [their country's] appearance." The Ottawa asked Thomas Anderson, still an Indian agent on Drummond Island, what to do, for the Ottawa were "much afraid of the Big Knives." An Indian from Milwaukee visited Anderson two days later on July 8. He came with a message from the "Sauks, Kickapoos, Foxes, Mianmies [Menominee], Avoyais [Folles Avoines] as also all the Indians west of the Mississippi." Their message was that

> they are almost consumed by the Big Knives & ask us to become one with them, and be ready the moment we hear the sound of their war club, which will be a very short time, to raise ours at the very same moment and crush the Big Knives.[23]

Sympathetic to their distress, the British continued to give presents to the tribes who visited Drummond Island, but offered no military support. The uprising did not occur, but the United States did little to protect the Indians from encroaching Americans.

Though the Sac had continued to live on land east of the Mississippi River and along the Rock River after the 1804 treaty, by 1829 thousands of settlers and miners had swarmed into the Rock River region to farm or mine lead, without regard for treaties or the original inhabitants. Keokuk and other Sac leaders, who thought it was futile to resist overwhelming white military force, complied with an 1829 government order to move across the Mississippi in return for enough corn to get through the winter. With the Sac now thought to be infringing on Sioux lands, the Dakota fought to drive them off the lands the United States had awarded them.

In May 1830 the animosity reached Prairie du Chien. Dakota and Menominee warriors killed fifteen Fox men who were attending a conference at Prairie du Chien. In retaliation, the following July the Sac and Fox attacked a band of Menominee visiting the prairie. Twenty-five were killed, including women and children. The United States Army pursued the warriors only to learn that they had joined Black Hawk and his band. When the Sac refused to surrender those who attacked the Menominee, General Henry Atkinson was ordered to take six companies of infantry to the Rock River and demand the murderers.

The United States had failed to honor its promises to the Sac to give them corn in return for moving across the Mississippi. In need of food, a group of about twelve hundred Sac under the leadership of Black Hawk decided to cross to the Illinois side of the river in hope of re-occupying their homeland and harvesting their corn. Bolstered by a discussion with Napope, a spiritual leader of the Sac who had just returned from visiting the British at Malden, and White Cloud, called The Prophet, Black Hawk believed that his Winnebago neighbors would join his "British Band" in fighting the Americans if necessary, and in the event of full-scale war the British would also come to his aid. In the fighting that ensued, Black Hawk learned he stood alone in his opposition to the United States. In August 1832, after the massacre at the Bad Axe River, Black Hawk gave himself up but refused to surrender to Colonel Zachary Taylor, commander of Fort Crawford. Rather, he capitulated to Joseph Street, the Indian agent who had argued long and fruitlessly for the Winnebago.

With the end of the Black Hawk War, the United States accomplished what it had set out to do twenty years before: establish control of the region west of Lake Michigan and Prairie du Chien. Black Hawk was the last of the "British agents" William Clark had so disliked. Wisconsin Territory would be created in 1836. Agents for the United States would negotiate treaties with the tribes remaining in the territory and continue the treaty-making when Wisconsin became a state in 1848. As the Indian nation signed treaties, they lost their land. Instead of gathering at wintering posts to trade fur for goods, tribal members gathered at Indian agencies to collect annuity payments. By 1856, all of the tribes had been placed on reservations within the state or removed west of the Mississippi River.

By 1840, not only had the French and British Canadians disappeared from the fur trade and the Indian nations been confined to reservations, but the character of La Baye and Prairie du Chien had also changed. Many of the French-speaking men had taken their families and moved north and west with the trade. They had sold their long lots to speculators from the East who saw the value of the land platted into blocks and lots, ready to sell to settlers pushing ever westward. Farm lots became developments named Astor, Navarino, Lockwood's Addition, and Prairie du Chien Land Company No. 1.

—‖—

The Treaty of Ghent ending the War of 1812 contained nothing to suggest that the United States had achieved any of the aims for which the nation had gone to war with Great Britain. It did not address the Orders in Council, impressment of sailors into the British navy, or American shipping rights. Yet Americans saw the war as a victory. For the second time, the new nation had faced the most powerful nation in the world and triumphed. National self-confidence grew and encouraged expansionism. In the years before the war, the United States had begun to consider how to expand its territory. Native leaders emerged in response to the expansionism with a single concern: to protect their tribal lands. In the Northwest, Tecumseh attempted to create an Indian nation. The defeat at Tippecanoe made him and other Native leaders turn to their long-time trading partners, the British, to help the tribes keep American citizens and the United States government from seizing their land. The British were willing to continue to give the tribes the needed supplies and had never sought to drive them from their traditional lands. Therefore, once war began, most tribes allied themselves with Great Britain.

The death of Tecumseh at the Battle of the Thames and the terms of peace broke the power of the Indian nations. When the British military and members of the Indian Department withdrew into Canada, the American tribes lost their only ally to resist American expansionism. The establishment of US fur factories at traditional Native gathering sites used by the British traders and the issuance of trading licenses only to American citizens ended British trade south of the Great Lakes and affected the lives of many who had engaged in the trade. By 1830, the fur trade continued only through the monopoly of the American Fur Company. But as the Indians lost their lands through treaties with the United States, even John Jacob Astor foresaw the end of the trade. With the defeat of Black Hawk, the last vestige of opposition to American expansionism into the upper Mississippi ended. The way of life at Prairie du Chien, where Indians, French, and British had gathered in commerce and society, ceased to exist. The United

States gained political and economic control of "Indian Country," and Americans swarmed into the prairies and woodlands. For those caught in the crosshairs of expansionism, the end of the war was the beginning of the loss of their lands and livelihoods. But for Americans intent on acquiring lands in the Northwest, the War of 1812 truly was a victory.

# NOTES

## Introduction

1. William Clark to Secretary of War Armstrong, 2 February 1814, *The Territorial Papers of the United States*, ed. Clarence E. Carter, 28 vols. (Washington, DC: Government Printing Office, 1934–75), 14:738–740.

## Chapter 1: La Baye and Prairie du Chien: French Origins and Settlement

1. W. J. Eccles, *The Canadian Frontier, 1534–1760* (Albuquerque: University of New Mexico, 1983), 1–11.
2. Louise Phelps Kellogg, *French Regime in Wisconsin and the Northwest* (Madison: State Historical Society of Wisconsin, 1925), 159–172.
3. Eccles, *The Canadian Frontier*, 1–11.
4. Alice E. Smith, *The History of Wisconsin*, vol. 1 (Madison: State Historical Society of Wisconsin, 1985), 37–38.
5. Kenneth P. Bailey, ed. and trans., *Journal of Joseph Marin: French Colonial Explorer and Military Commander in the Wisconsin Country, August 7, 1753–June 20, 1754* (Irvine, CA: The Editor, 1975), 71.
6. David A. Armour, *Colonial Michilimackinac* (Mackinaw City, MI: Mackinac State Historic Parks, 2000), 52–68; Smith, *The History of Wisconsin*, 1:52–53; *American State Papers, Public Lands*, vol. 4, *Documents, Legislative and Executive of the Congress of the United States, from the First Session of the Fourteenth to the First Session of the Eighteenth Congress, Inclusive*, 34 vols. (Washington, DC: Gales and Seaton, 1834), 854.
7. *American State Papers, Public Lands*, 4:854, 856.
8. Jonathan Carver, "Travels Through the Interior Parts of North American in the Years 1766, 1767, and 1768," in *Wisconsin Historical Collections*, vol. 18 (Madison: State Historical Society of Wisconsin, 1908): 282–283.
9. Peter Pond, "Journal of Peter Pond," in *Wisconsin Historical Collections*, 18:339–341.
10. Kaskaskia Book of Records, C:56, microfilm, Illinois State Archives, Springfield, IL.

11. Robert C. Wiederaenders, *Jean-Baptiste Cardinal and the Affair of Gratiot's Boat: An Incident in the American Revolution* (Naperville, IL: Center for French Colonial Studies, 1999), 14–33; American State Papers, Public Lands, 4:866.
12. *American State Papers, Public Lands*, 4:851–852, 864, 866–867.
13. Ibid., 863–879.
14. Gary Clayton Anderson, *Kinsmen of Another Kind* (St. Paul: Minnesota Historical Society Press, 1997), 66–68.

### Chapter 2: British Trade in United States Territory

1. Robert S. Allen, *His Majesty's Indian Allies: British Indian Policy in the Defense of Canada, 1774–1815* (Toronto: Dundurn Press, 1992), 56.
2. Francis Paul Prucha, *The Sword of the Republic: The United States Army on the Frontier, 1783–1846* (Lincoln: University of Nebraska Press, 1986), 1–8.
3. Andrew L. Cayton, "The Northwest Ordinance from the Perspective of the Frontier," *The Northwest Ordinance 1787: A Bicentennial Handbook* (Indianapolis: Indiana Historical Society, 1987), 1–3.
4. Prucha, *The Sword of the Republic*, 20.
5. Francis Paul Prucha, ed., *Documents of United States Indian Policy* (Lincoln: University of Nebraska Press, 1990), 14–21.
6. Allen, *His Majesty's Indian Allies*, 84.
7. Francis Paul Prucha, *The Great Father: The United States Government and the American Indians* (Lincoln: University of Nebraska Press, 1986 ), 33–40.
8. For an analysis of United States treaties, see Francis Paul Prucha, *American Indian Treaties: The History of a Political Anomaly* (Berkeley: University of California Press, 1997).
9. Prucha, *The Great Father*, 19–22.
10. Landon Y. Jones, *William Clark and the Shaping of the West* (New York: Hill and Wang, 2004), 151; Prucha, *The Great Father*, 34–37.
11. Charles B. Lasselle, "The Old Indian Traders of Indiana," *The Indiana Magazine of History* 2, no. 1 (March 1906): 1–13; Prucha, *The Great Father*, 35–38.
12. *American State Papers, Public Lands*, vol. 4, *Documents, Legislative and Executive of the Congress of the United States, from the First Session of the Fourteenth to the First Session of the Eighteenth Congress, Inclusive*, 34 vols. (Washington, DC: Gales and Seaton, 1834), 867, 868, 874, 875.
13. George F. Robeson, "Fur Trade in Early Iowa," *The Palimpsest* 6, no. 1 (January 1925): 1–41.
14. Pierre LeBeau, et al., *Plumbing the Depths of the Upper Mississippi Valley* (St. Louis: Center for French Colonial Studies, 2008), 35.

15. Jacob Van de Zee, "Episodes in the Early History of the Des Moines Valley," *Iowa Journal of History and Politics* 14, no. 3 (July 1916): 332–333; *American State Papers: Public Lands*, 4:875.

16. Van de Zee, "Episodes in the Early History," 331–332.

17. Bruce E. Mahan, *Old Fort Crawford and the Frontier* (Iowa City: State Historical Society of Iowa, 1926), 14–15.

18. Marjorie Wilkins Campbell, "OGILVY, JOHN," in *Dictionary of Canadian Biography*, vol. 5, University of Toronto/Université Laval, 2003–, http://www.biographi.ca/en/bio/ogilvy_john_5E.html.

19. Sheldon J. Godfrey, "FRANKS, JACOB," in *Dictionary of Canadian Biography*, vol. 7, University of Toronto/Université Laval, 2003–, http://www.biographi.ca/en/bio/franks_jacob_7E.html.

20. Peter L. Scanlan, *Prairie du Chien: French, British, American* (Appleton, WI: The Banta Company, 1937), 86.

21. Robert M. Taylor Jr., ed., *The Northwest Ordinance, 1787: A Bicentennial Handbook* (Indianapolis: Indiana Historical Society, 1987), 31–77, 100–101.

22. Scanlan, *Prairie du Chien*, 166; William D. Platt, *A History of the National Guard in Indiana* (Indianapolis: W. D. Pratt, 1901), accessed online at www.archive .org/details/historyofnationa00inprat_13.

23. Augustin Grignon, "Seventy-two Years' Recollections of Wisconsin," in *Wisconsin Historical Collections*, vol. 3 (Madison: State Historical Society of Wisconsin, 1904): 246–250.

24. James L. Hansen, "The Campbell Family of Prairie du Chien" (unpublished manuscript, 1999); *American State Papers: Public Lands*, 4:873.

25. *American State Papers: Public Lands*, 4:868, 873; Myron Momryk, "TODD, ISAAC," in *Dictionary of Canadian Biography*, vol. 5, University of Toronto/Université Laval, 2003–, http://www.biographi.ca/en/bio/todd_isaac_5E.html; Sharon Halevi, ed., "The Memoirs of Elizabeth Fisher," in *The Other Daughters of the Revolution* (Albany: State University of New York Press, 2006), 73–114.

26. Louis A. Tohill, "Robert Dickson, the Fur Trade, and the Minnesota Boundary," *Minnesota Magazine of History* (December 1925): 330–342.

### Chapter 3: Zebulon Pike Explores the Upper Mississippi River

1. Zebulon Pike, *The Expeditions of Zebulon Montgomery Pike, to the headwaters of the Mississippi River, through Louisiana, and in New Spain during the years 1805-6-7*, ed. Eliot Coues, vol. 1, *Memoir of the Author: Mississippi Voyage* (New York: Dover, 1987), viii–ix (hereafter cited as The Expeditions); Jay H. Buckley, "Pike as a Forgotten and Misunderstood Explorer,"

in *Zebulon Pike, Thomas Jefferson, and the Opening of the American West* (Norman: University of Oklahoma Press, 2012), 21–29; James P. Ronda, "Pike and Empire," in *Zebulon Pike, Thomas Jefferson, and the Opening of the American West,* 65–66.

2. Pike, "Itinerary: St. Louis to St. Paul, August 9th–September 21st, 1805," in *The Expeditions,* 1–35, 225–226.

3. Pike, "Geography of the Mississippi," in *The Expeditions,* 303.

4. Pike, "Itinerary: St. Louis to St. Paul, September 5th–September 7th, 1805," 35–38.

5. Ibid., 39–40.

6. Pike, "Correspondence and Conferences," in *The Expeditions,* 223–224, 225.

7. Pike, "Itinerary: St. Louis to St. Paul," and "Correspondence and Conferences, Sept. 23rd, 1805," in *The Expeditions,* 42, 242.

8. Pike, "Itinerary: St. Louis to St. Paul," 66.

9. David A. Armour, "BLEAKLEY, JOSIAH," in *Dictionary of Canadian Biography,* vol. 6, University of Toronto/Université Laval, 2003–, http://www.biographi.ca/en/bio/bleakley_josiah_6E.html.

10. Pike, "Itinerary, Continued: St. Paul to Leech Lake, September 22d, 1805–January 31st, 1806," in *The Expeditions,* 82–88.

11. Pike, "Correspondence and Conferences," 231–241.

12. Pike, "Itinerary: St. Louis to St. Paul," 46–48; Pike, "Itinerary, Continued," 83–84; Pike, "Itinerary, Concluded: Leech Lake to St. Louis, February 1st–April 30th, 1806," in *The Expeditions,* 196; Pike, "Correspondence and Conferences," 231, 240; and Ronda, "Pike and Empire," 66–67.

13. F. Kent Reilly, "Displaying the Source of the Sacred: Shell Gorgets, Peace Medal, and the Assessing of Supernatural Power," in *Peace Medals: Negotiating Power in Early America* (Tulsa, OK: Gilcrease Museum, 2012), 9–17.

14. Pike, "Correspondence and Conferences," 241.

15. Pike, "The Mississippi Voyage. Chapter III. Itinerary, Concluded: Leech Lake to St. Louis, February 1st–April 30th, 1806," 152–156.

16. Pike, "Correspondence and Conferences," 247–250.

17. Ibid., 251–254; Ronda, "Pike and Empire," 67–69.

18. Pike, "Itinerary, Concluded," 173, 194, 201, 202, 204.

19. Ibid., 206–207; Pike, "Correspondence and Conferences," 263–264.

20. Pike, "Itinerary, Concluded," 209.

21. Pike, "Ethnography of the Mississippi," in *The Expeditions,* 352.

22. Pike, "Itinerary Concluded," 215; "Correspondence and Conferences," Pike to Wilkinson, April 18, 1806 and May 26, 1806, in *The Expeditions,* 215, 263, 270.

23. Pike to Wilkinson, 26 May 1806, in *The Expeditions*, 270–271.

24. Ibid.

25. Ibid.

26. Francis Paul Prucha, *Documents of United States Indian Policy* (Lincoln: University of Nebraska Press, 1990), 23.

### Chapter 4: United States Indian Agents at Prairie du Chien

1. Josiah Dunham to William Clark, 20 August 1807, in *The Territorial Papers of the United States*, ed. Clarence Edwin Carter, 28 vols. (Washington, DC: Government Printing Office, 1934–1975), 10:127–129.

2. Ibid.

3. Ibid.

4. Appointment of John Campbell as Indian Agent, 9 December 1807, *Territorial Papers*, 14:155.

5. James L. Hansen, "The Campbell Family of Prairie du Chien" (unpublished manuscript, 1999); "Sale of the Property of John Campbell, Esqr. Deceased," 5 January 1809, J. Campbell Estate Papers, 33(I) 3/217, 1814, Illinois Regional Archives Depository (IRAD) at Southern Illinois University, Carbondale, Illinois.

6. Ibid.

7. William Clark to Secretary of War, 18 August 1808, and Governor Lewis to Secretary of War, 20 August 1808, in Carter, *Territorial Papers*, 14:208, 213.

8. Capt. Peter Drummond to Capt. James Green, 29 June 1797, *Michigan Pioneer and Historical Collections*, vol. 20 (Lansing: Michigan Pioneer and Historical Society, 1886–1912), 518–519.

9. William H. Harrison to John Campbell, 10 February 1808, MO364, box 1, folder 14, William Henry Harrison Papers, Vincennes, Indiana Historical Society, Indianapolis, Indiana.

10. William Clark to Secretary of War, 28 September 1810, in Carter, *Territorial Papers*, 14:415; Capt. Lewis Howard to Secretary of War William Eustis, 1 October 1809, *Michigan Pioneer and Historical Collections*, 40:307–308.

11. Governor Lewis to Secretary of War, 20 August 1808, in Carter, *Territorial Papers*, 14:213.

12. Henry Dearborn to Nicolas Boilvin, 10 April 1806, in *Wisconsin Historical Collections*, vol. 19 (Madison: State Historical Society of Wisconsin, 1910): 314–316.

13. Peter L. Scanlan, "Nicolas Boilvin, Indian Agent," *Wisconsin Magazine of History* 27, no. 2 (December 1943): 145–146.

14. Robert Dickson to F. Bates, 1 April 1808, transcript, Mss D, box 9, folders

1–4, Peter L. Scanlan Papers, Wisconsin Historical Society, Platteville Area Research Center, Platteville, WI.

15. Governor Lewis to Nicolas Boilvin, 14 May 1808, in Carter, *Territorial Papers*, 14:216–219.

16. Ibid.

17. Ibid.

18. Henry Hastings Sibley, "Memoir of J. B. Faribault," *Collections of the Minnesota Historical Society*, vol. 3 (St. Paul: Minnesota Historical Society, 1880), 173; Milo M. Quaife, ed., *The John Askin Papers*, vol. 2 (Detroit: Detroit Library Commission, 1931), 608–609.

19. Resolution Relative to the Death of John Campbell, 27 August 1808, signed by Capt. Lewis Howard, *Michigan Pioneer and Historical Collections*, 40:261–262.

20. Lewis Howard, et al. to Henry Dearborn, 15 September 1808, *Michigan Pioneer and Historical Collections*, 40:262–267.

21. Ibid.

22. Governor Lewis to Secretary of War, 20 August 1808, in Carter, *Territorial Papers*, 14:213.

23. Thomas Auge, "The Life and Times of Julien Dubuque," *The Palimpsest* 57, no. 1 (January/February 1976): 2–13.

24. Ibid.

25. J. Dubuque to Abbot and Hoffman, 13 June 1809, Michigan Pioneer and Historical Collections, 40:284–286; William Clark to Secretary of War, 7 October 1808, transcript, Scanlan Papers; George Hoffman to Secretary of War, 20 July 1809, *Michigan Pioneer and Historical Collections*, 40:290–292.

26. Ibid.; Auge, "The Life and Times of Julien Dubuque."

27. Nicolas Boilvin to William Clark, 21 April 1809, in Carter, *Territorial Papers*, 14:272.

28. Nicolas Boilvin to Most Honored Madison, 28 July 1809, transcript, Scanlan Papers.

29. "Sale of the Property of John Campbell, Esqr. Deceased," 5 January 1809, J. Campbell Estate Papers.

30. Nicolas Boilvin to Secretary of War, 17 October 1809, in Carter, *Territorial Papers*, 14:330–332.

31. Nicolas Boilvin to Secretary of War, 27 January 1810, in Carter, *Territorial Papers*, 16:69–71.

32. Frederick Bates to Nicolas Boilvin, 2 November 1809, in *The Life and Papers of Frederick Bates*, vol. 2, ed. Thomas M. Marshall (St. Louis: Missouri Historical Society, 1926), 103–104.

33. Frederick Bates to Nicholas Boilvin, 4 November 1809, in Marshall, *The Life and Papers of Frederick Bates*, 106–107.
34. Nicolas Boilvin to William Eustis, 11 February 1811, transcript, Scanlan Papers.
35. Ibid.
36. Ibid.
37. Ibid.
38. Nicolas Boilvin to Secretary of War, 5 March 1811, transcript, Scanlan Papers.
39. Peter L. Scanlan, "Nicolas Boilvin, Indian Agent."
40. Nicolas Boilvin to Mr. Eustis, 11 March 1811, transcript, Scanlan Papers.
41. Secretary of War to Nicholas Boilvin, 14 March 1811, in Carter, *Territorial Papers*, 14:444–445.
42. Nicolas Boilvin to Secretary of War, 7 July 1811, in Carter, *Territorial Papers*, 16:168–169.

### Chapter 5: Tecumseh's Rebellion and the Declaration of War

1. John Askin Jr. to John Askin, 25 August 1811, in *The John Askin Papers*, vol. 2, ed. Milo M. Quaife (Detroit: Detroit Library Commission, 1931), 694.
2. Nicolas Boilvin to the Secretary of War, 13 December 1811, transcript, Mss D, Box 9, Folders 1–4, Peter L. Scanlan Papers, Wisconsin Historical Society, Platteville Area Research Center, Platteville, Wisconsin.
3. John Askin Jr. to John Askin, 25 August 1811, in Quaife, *The John Askin Papers*, 2:696.
4. Nicolas Boilvin to Secretary of War, 13 December 1811, transcript, Scanlan Papers.
5. Statement of Robert Dickson, 3 December 1812, in *Documents Relating to the Invasion of Canada and the Surrender of Detroit 1812*, ed. E. A. Cruikshank (Ottawa: Government Printing Bureau, 1912), 230–231.
6. John Askin Jr. to John Askin, 25 August 1811, in Quaife, *The John Askin Papers*, 2:694.
7. Nicolas Boilvin to Secretary of War, 13 December 1811, transcript, Scanlan Papers.
8. Ernest Alexander Cruikshank, "Robert Dickson, The Indian Trader," in *Wisconsin Historical Collections*, vol. 12 (Madison: State Historical Society of Wisconsin, 1892), 138–139; Account of Sundries del'd by Robert Dickson & Co., 20 July 1812, in *Michigan Pioneer and Historical Collections*, (Lansing: Michigan Pioneer and Historical Society, 1886–1912), 15:91.
9. Robert S. Allen, *His Majesty's Indian Allies: British Indian Policy in the Defense of Canada, 1774–1815* (Toronto: Dundurn Press, 1993), 113–114, 116–117.

10. R. David Edmunds, *The Shawnee Prophet* (Lincoln: University of Nebraska Press, 1985), 78; Donald Jackson, ed., *Black Hawk: An Autobiography* (Urbana: University of Illinois Press, Prairie State Books, 1990), 38–39, 110–112.

11. Nicolas Boilvin to the Governor of Louisiana Territory, 5 January 1812, in *The Territorial Papers of the United States*, ed. Clarence Edwin Carter, 28 vols. (Washington, DC: Government Printing Office, 1934–1975), 16:186–187.

12. Ibid., 186–188; Nicolas Boilvin to Secretary of War, 7 January 1812, and Nicolas Boilvin to Secretary of War, 12 June 1812, transcripts, Scanlan Papers.

13. Ibid.

14. Nicolas Boilvin to Secretary of War, 12 June 1812, Scanlan Papers.

15. William Clark to Secretary of War, 13 February 1812, in Carter, *Territorial Papers*, 14:518–520.

16. Arch C. Johnson, "The Enigma of the New Madrid Earthquakes of 1811–1812," *Annual Review of Earth and Planetary Sciences* 24 (1996): 339–384, http://gec.cr.usgs.gov/pdf/AnnualReviewofEarthandPlanetary-Sciences199%20Johnston.pdf.

17. Nicolas Boilvin to Secretary of War, 12 June 1812, transcript, Scanlan Papers.

18. Nicolas Boilvin to Secretary of War, 14 June 1812, transcript, Scanlan Papers.

19. Statement of Robert Dickson, 3 December 1812, in Cruikshank, *Documents*, 230–231.

20. Nicolas Boilvin to Secretary of War, 14 June 1812 and 12 July 1812, transcripts, Scanlan Papers.

21. From James Madison to the Delegations of Several Indian Nations, [ca. 22 August] 1812, Founders Online, National Archives, Washington, DC, http://founders.archive.gov/documents/Madison/03-05-02-0137, from *The Papers of James Madison*, Presidential Series, vol. 5, *10 July 1812–7 February 1813*, eds. J. C. A. Stagg et al, (Charlottesville: University of Virginia Press, 2004), 175–178.

22. Ibid.

23. Nicolas Boilvin to Secretary of War, 19 September 1812, transcript, Scanlan Papers.

### Chapter 6: Robert Dickson and "His Majesty's Faithful Indian Allies"

1. "Extracts from an American Newspaper, August and September, 1812: Statement of Robert Dickson," 3 December 1812, in *Documents Relating to*

*the Invasion of Canada and Surrender of Detroit 1812*, ed. E. A. Cruikshank (Ottawa: Government Printing Bureau, 1913), 105–106, 230–231.

2. J. B. Glegg to Robert Dickson, 27 February 1812, in Cruikshank, Documents, 17–18.

3. Robert Dickson to J. B. Glegg, 18 June 1812, in Cruikshank, *Documents*, 31–32.

4. E. A. Cruikshank, "Robert Dickson, the Indian Trader," in *Wisconsin Historical Collections*, vol. 12 (Madison: State Historical Society of Wisconsin, 1892), 139–141.

5. Captain Roberts to Mr. Robert Dickson, 10 July 1812, and Observations by Toussaint Pothier, in Cruikshank, *Documents*, 52 and 214–217.

6. Captain Roberts to Major General Brock, 12 July 1812, in Cruikshank, *Documents*, 54.

7. Ibid.; Robert Dickson to Major-General Brock, 13 July 1812, in Cruikshank, *Documents*, 56.

8. Observations by Toussaint Pothier, in Cruikshank, *Documents*, 214–217.

9. Captain Roberts to Major General Brock, 17 July 1814, in *Michigan Pioneer and Historical Collections*, vol. 15 (Lansing: Michigan Pioneer and Historical Society, 1886–1912) 108–110.

10. Major General Brock to Sir George Prevost, 26 July 1812, in Cruikshank, *Documents*, 90–93.

11. Captain Roberts to Major Glegg, 28 July 1812, in Cruikshank, *Documents*, 100–103.

12. Statement of Robert Dickson, 3 December 1812, in Cruikshank, *Documents*, 230–231.

13. Robert Dickson to James Franks, 8 September 1812, in *Wisconsin Historical Collections*, 10:96–98; Robert Dickson to Jacob Franks, 2 October 1812, in *Wisconsin Historical Collections*, 11:271–272.

14. Ibid.

15. Colonel Proctor to Major General Sheaffe, 30 October 1812, in *Michigan Pioneer and Historical Collections*, 15:174–175.

16. Captain Glegg to Colonel Edward Baynes, 11 November 1812, in Cruikshank, *Documents*, 227–229.

17. Robert Dickson to The Commander in Chief, 23 December 1812, in *Michigan Pioneer and Historical Collections*, 15:208–209.

18. Secretary Freer to Major General de Rottenburg, 2 January 1813, in *Michigan Pioneer and Historical Collections*, 15:210–211.

19. Military Secretary's Office to Major General Sheaffe, 14 January 1813, in *Michigan Pioneer and Historical Collections*, 15:217–218.

20. Ibid.

21. Instructions for Robt Dickson Esqr from George Prevost, 14 January 1813, in *Michigan Pioneer and Historical Collections*, 15:219–221; Cruikshank, "Robert Dickson," 142–143; Robert S. Allen, *His Majesty's Indian Allies: British Indian Policy in the Defense of Canada, 1774–1815* (Toronto: Dundurn, 1993), 140–141.

22. Instructions for Robt Dickson Esqr from George Prevost, 14 January 1813, 142–143; Allen, *His Majesty's Indian Allies*, 140–141.

23. Ibid.

24. Speech of Robert Dickson Esquire to Indian tribes, 18 January 1813, in Allen, *His Majesty's Indian Allies*, 223–224.

25. Carolyn Gilman, "Grand Portage Ojibway Give British Medals to Historical Society," *Minnesota History* 47 (Spring 1980): 26–32.

26. Robert Dickson to unaddressed, 15 February 1813, in *Michigan Pioneer and Historical Collections*, 15:250.

27. Robert Dickson to Noah Freer, 16 March 1813, in *Michigan Pioneer and Historical Collections*, 15:258–259.

28. Nicolas Boilvin to William Clark, 23 January 1813, and Joseph Roc to Nicolas Boilvin, 12 March 1813, transcript in Peter L. Scanlan Papers, Mss D, box 9, folders 1–4, Peter L. Scanlan Papers, Wisconsin Historical Society, Platteville Area Research Center, Platteville, Wisconsin; Testimony of Joseph Rolette in proceedings of Court of Inquiry at Prairie du Chien, January 1815, in *Michigan Pioneer and Historical Collections*, 16:25–26.

29. Joseph Roc to Nicolas Boilvin, 12 March 1813, Scanlan Papers; Testimony of Joseph Rolette in proceedings of Court of Inquiry at Prairie du Chien, January 1815, in *Michigan Pioneer and Historical Collections*, 16:23, 25–26.

30. Residents of Prairie du Chien to Captain Charles Roberts, 5 February 1813, in *Michigan Pioneer and Historical Collections*, 15:245–246.

31. La Feuille to Captain Roberts, 5 February 1813, in *Michigan Pioneer and Historical Collections*, 15:244–245.

32. Residents of la Baye to Captain Charles Roberts, undated, in *Michigan Pioneer and Historical Collections*, 15:246–247.

33. Joseph Roc to Nicolas Boilvin, 12 March 1813, Scanlan Papers; Proceedings of the Court of Inquiry at Prairie du Chien, January 1815, in *Michigan Pioneer and Historical Collections*, 16:18.

34. Nicolas Boilvin to William Clark, 23 January 1813, and Nicolas Boilvin to Secretary Eustis, 6 February 1813 and February 11, 1813, Scanlan Papers.

35. Frederick Bates to General Howard, 27 February 1813, in Carter, *Territorial Papers*, 14:638–639.

36. Nicolas Boilvin to Secretary Eustis, 11 February 1813, Scanlan Papers.

## Chapter 7: Dickson Unites the Tribes

1. Nicolas Boilvin to William Clark, 27 February 1813, transcript, Platteville Manuscripts V, vol. 3, Prairie du Chien Papers, Platteville Area Research Center, Platteville, Wisconsin.

2. Robert Dickson to unknown, 22 March 1813, in *Michigan Pioneer and Historical Collections* (Lansing: Michigan Pioneer and Historical Society, 1886–1912), 15:262.

3. Donald Jackson, ed., *Black Hawk: An Autobiography* (Urbana: University of Illinois Press, 1955), 65–66.

4. Report of Maurice Blondeau in council with the Sac and Fox at the Des Moines River, no date, in Prairie du Chien Papers.

5. Major General Sheaffe to Sir George Prevost, 5 April 1813, and Aide-de-camp Boucherville to Sir George Prevost, 13 June 1813, in *Michigan Pioneer and Historical Collections*, 15:271, 315–316.

6. Testimony in the Court of Inquiry at Prairie du Chien, January 1815, in *Michigan Pioneer and Historical Collections*, 16:4–11.

7. Ibid., 16:5–7.

8. Ibid., 16:5, 15.

9. Dickson Papers, Public Archives of Manitoba, Winnipeg, Manitoba.

10. Peter Douglas Elias, *The Dakota of the Canadian Northwest: Lessons for Survival* (Regina, Saskatchewan: University of Regina Press, 2002), 8–9.

11. General Proctor to Major General Sheaffe, 17 April 1813; Aide-de-camp Boucherville to Sir George Prevost, 13 June 1813; Captain Charles Roberts to Secretary Freer, 23 June 1813; and Robert Dickson to unknown, 21 June 1813, in *Michigan Pioneer and Historical Collections*, 15:273–274, 317–318, and 321–323.

12. Robert Dickson to Secretary Freer, 23 June 1813, in *Michigan Pioneer and Historical Collections*, 15:321–322; Madeline Askin to Madame Askin, 23 June 1813, in *The John Askin Papers*, vol. 2, ed. Milo M. Quaife (Detroit: Detroit Library Commission, 1931), 761–762.

13. Brig. General Proctor to Sir George Prevost, 9 August 1813, in *Michigan Pioneer and Historical Collections*, 15:347–348.

14. Court of Inquiry at Prairie du Chien, January 1813, in *Michigan Pioneer and Historical Collections*, 16:4, 16.

15. Jackson, *Black Hawk*, 67–68.

16. Unaddressed document, Montreal, 31 August 1813, in *Michigan Pioneer and Historical Collections*, 15:368–369.

17. Robert Dickson to John Lawe, 31 August 1813, in *Wisconsin Historical Collections*, 11:273; R. H. Sheaffe to unaddressed, 11 September 1813, in *Michigan Pioneer and Historical Collections*, 15:376–377.

18. Lt. Grignon to Robert Dickson, 18 September 1813 and 5 October 1813, in *Wisconsin Historical Collections*, 11:274–276. Captain Bullock to Major General Proctor, 25 September 1813, in *Michigan Pioneer and Historical Collections*, 15:391–393.

19. Captain Bullock to Major General Proctor, 25 September 1813.

20. Ibid.

21. Robert Dickson to Secretary Freer, 29 September 1813, in *Michigan Pioneer and Historical Collections*, 15:396–397.

22. Captain Bullock to Colonel Baynes, 21 October 1813, in *Michigan Pioneer and Historical Collections*, 15:421–422.

23. Robert Dickson to Secretary Noah Freer, 23 October 1813, in *Michigan Pioneer and Historical Collections*, 15:423–433.

24. Ibid.; Captain Bullock to Secretary Freer, 23 October 1813, and Captain Bullock to Colonel Baynes, 23 October 1813, in *Michigan Pioneer and Historical Collections*, 15:422–425.

25. Captain Bullock to Colonel Baynes, 23 October 1813, in *Michigan Pioneer and Historical Collections*, 15:422.

26. Robert Dickson to Grignon and Lawe, 13 November 1813, and Robert Dickson to Lt. John Lawe, 19 December 1813, in *Wisconsin Historical Collections*, 11:276, 279–281.

27. Robert Dickson to John Lawe, 5 December 1813 and 19 December 1813, in *Wisconsin Historical Collections*, 11:278–281.

28. Robert Dickson to John Lawe, 14 November 1813, in *Wisconsin Historical Collections*, 10:98–99.

29. Robert Dickson to John Lawe, 25 December 1813, in *Wisconsin Historical Collections*, 11:282.

30. Robert Dickson to John Lawe, 25 December 1813, and Louis Grignon to John Askin, 10 January 1814, in *Wisconsin Historical Collections*, 11:282–283; John Askin Jr. to Louis Grignon, 28 January 1814, in *Wisconsin Historical Collections*, 10:100–101.

31. Robert Dickson to John Lawe, 23 January 1814, in *Wisconsin Historical Collections*, 11:285–287.

32. Nicolas Boilvin to Secretary of War, 5 December 1813, in Prairie du Chien Papers.

33. Nicolas Boilvin to President James Madison, 10 December 1813, transcript, Peter L. Scanlan Papers, Platteville Area Research Center, Platteville, WI; Robert Dickson to John Lawe, 4 February 1814, in *Wisconsin Historical Collections*, 11:289–292.

34. Robert Dickson to John Lawe, 11 February 1813, 27 February 1813, and 2 March 1813, in *Wisconsin Historical Collections*, 10:102–104, 105, 108–111.

35. Lt. General Gordon Drummond to Secretary Freer, 5 February 1814, and Lt. General Drummond to Secretary Freer, 16 February 1814, in *Michigan Pioneer and Historical Collections*, 15:487, 491–492.

36. Robert Dickson to John Lawe, 14 February 1814, *26 February 1814, and 31 March 1814, in* Wisconsin Historical Collections, 11: 293–295, 300–302.

37. Testimony in a Court of Inquiry at Prairie du Chien, January 1813, in *Michigan Pioneer and Historical Collections*, 16:7, 11.

38. Sir George Prevost to Earl Bathurst, Secretary of State for War and the Colonies, 8 February 1814, in *Michigan Pioneer and Historical Collections*, 25:573–574.

39. Robert S. Allen, *His Majesty's Indian Allies: British Policy in the Defense of Canada, 1774–1815* (Toronto: Dundurn Press, 1992), 156.

40. Lt. Colonel McDouall to Lt. General Drummond, 26 May 1814, in *Michigan Pioneer and Historical Collections*, 15:564–565.

41. "Speech of the Sioux Chief named The Leaf Indian name Wabasha," in *Michigan Pioneer and Historical Collections*, 15:558–559.

42. "Speech of the Little Crow, a Sioux Chief, Indian named Chatewaco-namini," in *Michigan Pioneer and Historical Collections*, 15:559–560.

43. "Speech of Lassaminie a Chief of the Winibagoes [sic]," in *Michigan* Pioneer *and Historical Collections*, 15:560–561.

44. Speech delivered by Lt. Colonel McDouall at Michilimackinac, 5 June 1814, in *Michigan Pioneer and Historical Collections*, 15:581–584.

45. Robert Dickson to Secretary Freer, 18 June 1814, in *Michigan Pioneer and Historical Collections*, 15:593–594.

### Chapter 8: William Clark's Expedition to Prairie du Chien

1. Bruce E. Mahan, *Old Fort Crawford and the Frontier* (Iowa City: The State Historical Society of Iowa, 1926), 52.

2. William Wood, ed., *Selected British Documents of the Canadian War of 1812*, 17 vols. (Toronto: The Champlain Society, 1920–1923), 1:425.

3. Landon Y. Jones, *William Clark and the Shaping of the West* (New York: Hill and Wang, 2004), 209; Governor Howard to Secretary of War Eustis, 24 October 1812, in *The Territorial Papers of the United States*, ed. Clarence Edwin Carter, 28 vols. (Washington, DC: Government Printing Office, 1934–1975), 14:602–603.

4. Jones, *William Clark*, 212.

5. Ibid., 214.

6. William Clark to Secretary Armstrong, 12 September 1813, in Carter, *Territorial Papers*, 14:697–698.

7. Ibid.

8. Jones, *William Clark*, 215.

9. Dickson to Lt. John Lawe, 31 August 1813, 5 December 1813, and 4 February 1814, "Dickson and Grignon Papers, 1812–1815," in *Wisconsin Historical Collections*, vol. 11 (1883): 273, 291.

10. *Missouri Gazette* (St. Louis), 8 May 1813.

11. William Clark to Secretary Armstrong, 2 February 1814, in Carter, *Territorial Papers*, 14:738–739.

12. Ibid.

13. Ibid.

14. Ibid.

15. Secretary Armstrong to Edward Hempstead, 23 March 1814, in Carter, *Territorial Papers*, 14:746.

16. William Clark to Secretary Armstrong, 28 March 1814, in Carter, *Territorial Papers*, 14:746–747.

17. Ibid.

18. Ibid.

19. Ibid.

20. Secretary Armstrong to William Clark, 30 April 1814, in Carter, *Territorial Papers*, 14:762.

21. Gillum Ferguson, *Illinois in the War of 1812* (Urbana: University of Illinois Press, 2012), 152–153.

22. Jones, *William Clark*, 218.

23. Ferguson, *Illinois in the War of 1812*, 153; "Report of Lt. Joseph Perkins," August 1814, in Carter, *Territorial Papers*, 14:784–787.

24. "Report of Lt. Joseph Perkins," August 1814, In Carter, *Territorial Papers*, 14:784–787.

25. William Clark to Secretary Armstrong, 4 May 1814, in Carter, *Territorial Papers*, 14:762–763.

26. William Clark to General Howard, 5 May 1814, in Carter, *Territorial Papers*, 16:424.

27. General Howard to Secretary Armstrong, 15 May 1814, in Carter, *Territorial Papers*, 16:422–423.

28. William Clark to Secretary Armstrong, 5 June 1814, in Carter, *Territorial Papers*, 14:768–769; Donald Jackson, ed., *Black Hawk: An Autobiography* (Urbana: University of Illinois Press, 1990), 77.

29. William Clark to Secretary Armstrong, 5 June 1814.

30. Ibid.; *American State Papers, Public Lands*, vol. 4, Documents, *Legislative and Executive of the Congress of the United States, from the First Session of the Fourteenth to the First Session of the Eighteenth Congress*, Inclusive, 34 vols.

(Washington, DC: Gales and Seaton, 1834), 873–874; "Report of Lt. Joseph Perkins," August 1814, in Carter, *Territorial Papers*, 14:784–787.

31. William Clark to Secretary Armstrong, 5 June 1814 and 28 June 1814, *Territorial Papers*, 14:767–768, 775–777.

32. "Report of Lt. Joseph Perkins," August 1814, L. Homfray Irving, *Officers of the British Forces in Canada during the War of 1812* (Toronto: Canadian Military Institute, 1908), 218.

33. "Prairie du Chien Documents, 1814–15," in *Wisconsin Historical Collections*, vol. 9 (Madison: State Historical Society of Wisconsin, 1882), 262–266; Irving, *Officers of the British Forces*, 210–212.

34. "Report of Lt. Joseph Perkins," August 1814; *American State Papers, Public Lands*, 4:873–875.

35. "Report of Lt. Joseph Perkins," August 1814; *Missouri Gazette* (St. Louis), June 1814; Thomas G. Anderson, "Personal Experiences in the Northwest Fur Trade—British Capture of Prairie du Chien, 1814," in *Wisconsin Historical Collections*, 9:195.

36. General Howard to Secretary Armstrong, 20 June 1814, in Carter, *Territorial Papers*, 14:772–773.

37. Nicolas Boilvin to Secretary Armstrong, 9 September 1814, transcript, Scanlan Papers.

38. Ibid.

39. "Letter-Book of Thomas Forsyth, 1814–1818," in *Wisconsin Historical Collections*, 11:321, 324.

40. "Colonel M'Douall to General Drummond," 16 July 1814, in *Wisconsin Historical Collections*, 11:260–263, 324–325; "Drummond to Prevost," 11 August, 1814, in *Wisconsin Historical Collections*, 12:117; William Clark to Secretary Armstrong, 28 June 1814, in Carter, *Territorial Papers*, 14:775–776.

41. William Clark to Secretary Armstrong, 5 June 1814 and 28 June 1814, in Carter, *Territorial Papers*, 14:768–769, 775–776; "Report of Lt. Joseph Perkins," August 1814.

42. *Missouri Gazette* (St. Louis), 18 July 1814; *Niles' Weekly Register* (Baltimore), 20 August 1814.

43. William Clark to Secretary Armstrong, 28 June 1814, in Carter, *Territorial Papers*, 14:775–776; Benjamin Howard to Secretary Armstrong, 15 July 1814, in Carter, *Territorial Papers*, 16:444–446.

44. William Clark to Secretary Armstrong, 28 June 1814, in Carter, *Territorial Papers*, 14:775–776.

45. Ibid.; Report of Major Campbell, 24 July 1814, in Carter, *Territorial Papers*,

17:5–6; Ninian Edwards to Secretary Armstrong, 24 July 1814, in Carter, *Territorial Papers*, 16:451.

46. Report of Major Campbell, 24 July 1814.

47. Lt. John Campbell to Secretary Armstrong, 25 July 1814, in Carter, *Territorial Papers*, 14:784–787; Jackson, *Black Hawk*, 77–78.

### Chapter 9: The Battle for Prairie du Chien

1. Speech delivered by Lt. Colonel McDouall to the Indian Chiefs and Warriors at Michilimackinac, 5 June 1814, in *Michigan Pioneer and Historical Collections*, (Lansing: Michigan Pioneer and Historical Society, 1886–1912) 15:581–584.

2. Lt. Colonel McDouall to Lt. General Drummond, 16 July 1814, in *Michigan Pioneer and Historical Collections*, 15:610–613.

3. Ibid.

4. Ibid.

5. Lt. Colonel McDouall to Lt. General Drummond, 16 July 1814, in *Michigan Pioneer and Historical Collections*, 15:610–613; "Seventy-two Years' Recollections of Wisconsin," in *Wisconsin Historical Collections*, vol. 3 (Madison: State Historical Society of Wisconsin, 1857), 271.

6. Lt. Colonel McDouall to Lt. General Drummond, 16 July 1814, in *Michigan Pioneer and Historical Collections*, 15:610–613.

7. Ibid.

8. Robert Dickson Orders, Michilimackinac, 28 June 1814, in *Wisconsin Historical Collections*, 11:303; "Seventy-two Years' Recollections of Wisconsin," in *Wisconsin Historical Collections*, 3:269–270.

9. Lt. Colonel McDouall to Lt. General Drummond, 16 July 1814, in *Michigan Pioneer and Historical Collections*, 15:610–613; "Personal Narrative of Captain Thomas G. Anderson," in *Wisconsin Historical Collections*, 11:194.

10. Lt. Colonel McDouall to Lt. General Drummond, 16 July 1814, in *Michigan Pioneer and Historical Collections*, 15:610–613; "Seventy-two Years' Recollections of Wisconsin," in *Wisconsin Historical Collections*, 3:271–272; Colonel McKay to Colonel McDouall, Prairie du Chien, 27 July 1814, in *Michigan Pioneer and Historical Collections*, 15:623–628.

11. "Personal Narrative of Captain Thomas G. Anderson," in *Wisconsin Historical Collections*, 9:295; "Seventy-two Years' Recollections of Wisconsin," in *Wisconsin Historical Collections*, 3:272.

12. "Seventy-two Years' Recollections of Wisconsin," in *Wisconsin Historical Collections*, 3:272–273;. Colonel McKay to Colonel McDouall, Prairie du Chien, 27 July 1814, in *Michigan Pioneer and Historical Collections*, 15:623–628.

13. "Seventy-two Years' Recollections of Wisconsin," in *Wisconsin Historical Collections*, 3:273.

14. Ibid.

15. "Personal Narrative of Captain Thomas G. Anderson," in *Wisconsin Historical Collections*, 9:195; Colonel McKay to Colonel McDouall, Prairie du Chien, 27 July 1814, in *Michigan Pioneer and Historical Collections*, 15:623–628.

16. Colonel Perkins to *Colonel McKay Michigan Pioneer and Historical Collections*, 15:619.

17. Colonel McKay to Colonel McDouall, Prairie du Chien, 27 July 1814, in *Michigan Pioneer and Historical Collections*, 15:623–628.

18. "Personal Narrative of Captain Thomas G. Anderson," in *Wisconsin Historical Collections*, 9: 195.

19. "Seventy-two Years' Recollections of Wisconsin," in *Wisconsin Historical Collections*, 3:274.

20. Colonel McKay to Colonel McDouall, 27 July 1814, in *Michigan Pioneer and Historical Collections*, 15:623–628; "Personal Narrative of Captain Thomas G. Anderson," in *Wisconsin Historical Collections*, 9:195.

21. "Seventy-two Years' Recollections of Wisconsin," in *Wisconsin Historical Collections*, 3:275–276.

22. Colonel McKay to Colonel McDouall, 27 July 1814, in *Michigan Pioneer and Historical Collections*, 15:623–628; "Personal Narrative of Captain Thomas G. Anderson," in *Wisconsin Historical Collections*, 9:195; "Seventy-two Years' Recollections of Wisconsin," in *Wisconsin Historical Collections*, 3:275–276.

23. Colonel McKay to Colonel McDouall, 27 July 1814, in *Michigan Pioneer and Historical Collections*, 15:623–628.

24. "Seventy-two Years' Recollections of Wisconsin," in *Wisconsin Historical Collections*, 3:276.

25. Colonel McKay to Colonel McDouall, 27 July 1814, in *Michigan Pioneer and Historical Collections*, 15:623–628.

26. Ibid.; "Seventy-two Years' Recollections of Wisconsin," in *Wisconsin Historical Collections*, 3:277.

27. Lt. Joseph Perkins, St. Louis, August 1814, transcript in Peter L. Scanlan Papers, Platteville Area Reseach Center, Platteville, Wisconsin.

28. Capt. Perkins to Lieut. Col. McKay, July 19, 1814, in *Michigan Pioneer and Historical Collections*, 15:620.

29. "Seventy-two Years' Recollections of Wisconsin," in *Wisconsin Historical Collections*, 3:277; Captain Perkins to Col. William McKay, 19 July 1814, and William McKay to Captain Joseph Perkins, 19 July 1814, in *Michigan Pioneer and Historical Collections*, 15:620.

30. Colonel McKay to Colonel McDouall, 27 July 1814, in *Michigan Pioneer and Historical Collections*, 15:623–628.

31. "Seventy-two Years' Recollections of Wisconsin," in *Wisconsin Historical Collections*, 3:277–278.

32. "Personal Narrative of Captain Thomas G. Anderson," in *Wisconsin Historical Collections*, 9:196; Colonel McKay to Colonel McDouall, 27 July 1814, in *Michigan Pioneer and Historical Collections*, 15:623–628; Lt. Joseph Perkins, St. Louis, August 1814, transcript, Scanlan Papers.

33. Colonel McKay to Colonel McDouall, 27 July 1814, in *Michigan Pioneer and Historical Collections*, 15:623–628.

34. Ibid.

35. Ibid.

### Chapter 10: American Attempts at Relief and British Successes

1. Donald Jackson, ed., *Black Hawk: An Autobiography* (Urbana: University of Illinois Press, 1990), 78.

2. Lt. John Campbell, St. Louis, 24 July 1814, transcript, Peter L. Scanlan Papers, Platteville Area Research Center, Platteville, WI; Jackson, *Black Hawk*, 78.

3. Ibid.

4. Lt. John Campbell, St. Louis, 24 July 1814, transcript, Scanlan Papers.

5. Jackson, *Black Hawk*, 78; Lt. Jonathan Riggs, Dardienne, 26 July 1814, transcript, in Scanlan Papers.

6. Jackson, *Black Hawk*, 79–80; Colonel McKay to Colonel McDouall, 27 July 1814, in *Michigan Pioneer and Historical Collections*, (Lansing: Michigan Pioneer and Historical Society, 1886–1912), 15:623–628.

7. Colonel McKay to Colonel McDouall, 27 July 1814, in *Michigan Pioneer and Historical Collections*, 15:623–628; Jackson, *Black Hawk*, 80.

8. "Events of the War," *Niles' Weekly Register* (Baltimore), 20 August 1814.

9. William McKay to Lt. Colonel McDouall, 1 August 1814, in *Michigan Pioneer and Historical Collections*, 15:630–631.

10. Colonel McKay to Colonel McDouall, 27 July 1814, in *Michigan Pioneer and Historical Collections*, 15:623–628.

11. Lt. Joseph Perkins, St. Louis, August 1814, transcript in Scanlan Papers.

12. Proceedings of a Court of Inquiry at Prairie du Chien, 3 January 1815, in *Michigan Pioneer and Historical Collections*, 15:2–32.

13. "Seventy-two Years' Recollections of Wisconsin," in *Wisconsin Historical Collections* (Madison: State Historical Society of Wisconsin, 1857), 3:278 Colonel McKay to Colonel McDouall, Prairie du Chien, 27 July 1814, in *Michigan Pioneer and Historical Collections*, 15:623–628.

14. William McKay to Lt. Colonel McDouall, 1 August 1814, in *Michigan Pioneer and Historical Collections*, 15:630–631; Lt. Joseph Perkins, St. Louis, August 1814, transcript, Scanlan Papers.

15. "Seventy-two Years' Recollections of Wisconsin," in *Wisconsin Historical Collections*, 3:279.

16. William McKay to Lt. Colonel McDouall, 1 August 1814, in *Michigan Pioneer and Historical Collections*, 15:630–631; "Personal Narrative of Captain Thomas G. Anderson," in *Wisconsin Historical Collections*, 9:196.

17. "Seventy-two Years' Recollections of Wisconsin," in *Wisconsin Historical Collections*, 3:279–780; "Personal Narrative of Captain Thomas G. Anderson," in *Wisconsin Historical Collections*, 9:194–196; Thomas G. Anderson to Lt. Colonel McDouall, 14 September 1814, in *Wisconsin Historical Collections*, 9:230–232.

18. "Personal Narrative of Captain Thomas G. Anderson," in *Wisconsin Historical Collections*, 9:196; "Journal of the Proceedings at Fort McKay . . . Prairie du Chien," in *Wisconsin Historical Collections*, 9:207–215.

19. "Journal of the Proceedings at Fort McKay . . . Prairie du Chien," in *Wisconsin Historical Collections*, 9:207–215.

20. Lt. Colonel McDouall to Lt. Grignon, 21 August 1813, in "Lawe and Grignon Papers," *Wisconsin Historical Collections*, 10:118–119.

21. "Journal of the Proceedings at Fort McKay . . . Prairie du Chien," in *Wisconsin Historical Collections*, 9:212–214.

22. "Personal Narrative of Captain Thomas G. Anderson," *Wisconsin Historical Collections*, 9:197–198.

23. "Journal of the Proceedings at Fort McKay . . . Prairie du Chien," *Wisconsin Historical Collections*, 9:211, 216, 221.

24. Thomas G. Anderson to Lt. Colonel McDouall, 29 August 1814, in *Wisconsin Historical Collections*, 9:220–221; "Journal of the Proceedings at Fort McKay . . . Prairie du Chien," in *Wisconsin Historical Collections*, 9:211, 216, 219.

25. Duncan Graham to Capt. Thomas G. Anderson, 3 September 1814, in *Wisconsin Historical Collections*, 9:224–225.

26. Benjamin Howard to Secretary of War, 1 August 1814, in *The Territorial Papers of the United States*, ed. Clarence Edwin Carter, 28 vols. (Washington, DC: Government Printing Office, 1934–1975), 17:3–4.

27. Benjamin Howard to Secretary of War, 17 August 1814, in Carter, *Territorial Papers*, 14:784.

28. "Skirmish at Rock River," *Niles' Weekly Register* 7 (Suppl.): 137–138.

29. Duncan Graham to Thomas G. Anderson, 3 September 1814 and 7 September 1814, in *Wisconsin Historical Collections*, 9:224–228.

30. "Skirmish at Rock River"; Duncan Graham to Thomas G. Anderson, 7 September 1814, in *Wisconsin Historical Collections*, 9:226–228.

31. Duncan Graham to Thomas G. Anderson, 7 September 1814, in *Wisconsin Historical Collections*, 9:226–228; Major Taylor to General Howard, 6 September 1814, quoted in "Skirmish at Rock River."

32. Duncan Graham to Thomas G. Anderson, 7 September 1814, in *Wisconsin Historical Collections*, 9:226–228.

33. Ibid.

34. Ibid.

35. Thomas G. Anderson to Lt. Colonel McDouall, 28 August 1814, in *Wisconsin Historical Collections*, 9:220–221.

36. George S. May, *War 1812: The United States and Great Britain at Mackinac, 1812–1815* (Mackinaw City, MI: Mackinac State Historic Parks, 2004).

37. Thomas Forsyth to Ninian Edwards, 12 September 1814, in *Wisconsin Historical Collections*, 11:330–331.

### Chapter 11: Tensions at Fort McKay

1. "Journal of the Proceedings at Fort McKay . . . Prairie du Chien," in *Wisconsin Historical Collections*, vol. 9 (Madison: Historical Society of Wisconsin, 1882), 9: 232–233.

2. Ibid., 235.

3. Ibid., 230–234.

4. Ibid., 235–243.

5. Invoices of I. Bleakley, in *Michigan Pioneer and Historical Collections* (Lansing: Michigan Pioneer and Historical Society, 1886–1912), 15: 644–649.

6. Instructions for the distribution of Indian presents by Maj. General R. H. Sheaffe, undated, in *Wisconsin Historical Collections* (Madison: Historical Society of Wisconsin, 1892), 12:118–120.

7. R. H. Sheaffe, Instructions for the distribution of Indian Presents, in *Michigan Pioneer and Historical Collections*, 15:649–651.

8. Report made by Capt. William McKay to His Excellency Sir George Prevost, 5 November 1814, in *Michigan Pioneer and Historical Collections*, 15:656–658.

9. Ibid.

10. Ibid.; Louis Grignon to Louis Crawford, 6 September 1814, in *Wisconsin Historical Collections*, 11:304.

11. Louis Grignon to Robert Dickson, 28 September 1814, and Louis Grignon to John Askin, 28 September 1814, in *Wisconsin Historical Collections*, 11:305–306.

12. Report made by Capt. William McKay to His Excellency Sir George Prevost, 5 November 1814, in *Michigan Pioneer and Historical Collections*, 15:656–658.

13. General Orders, Michilimackinac, 17 October 1814, in *Wisconsin Historical Collections*, 13:14–19; Andrew Bulger to M'Douall, Green Bay, 14 November 1814, in *Wisconsin Historical Collections*, 13:20–22.

14. Proceedings of a Court of Inquiry, Green Bay, 13 November 1814, in *Wisconsin Historical Collections*, 12:126–131; Andrew Bulger to M'Douall, Green Bay, 14 November 1814, in *Wisconsin Historical Collections*, 13:20–22.

15. Andrew Bulger to M'Douall, Green Bay, 14 November 1814, in *Wisconsin Historical Collections*, 13:20–22.

16. Andrew Bulger to M'Douall, 30 December 1814, in *Wisconsin Historical Collections*, 13:25–35.

17. Ibid.

18. Lt. Colonel McDouall to Captain Anderson, Michilimackinac, 21 August 1814, in *Wisconsin Historical Collections*, 9:228–230; Andrew Bulger to M'Douall, 30 December 1814, in *Wisconsin Historical Collections*, 13:25–35.

19. Andrew Bulger to M'Douall, 30 December 1814, in *Wisconsin Historical Collections*, 13:25–35; Lt. Colonel McDouall to Captain Anderson, 21 August 1814, in *Wisconsin Historical Collections*, 9:228–230.

20. A. Bulger to Joseph Rolette, 23 December 1814, Joseph Rolette to Capt. A. H. Bulger, 26 December 1814, and A. H. Bulger to Lt. Colonel M'Douall, 31 December 1814, in *Wisconsin Historical Collections*, 13:23-24, 36–37.

21. "Proceedings of a Garrison Court Martial held by order of Capt. Bulger," 2 January 1815, in *Wisconsin Historical Collections*, 13:41–42.

22. A. Bulger, Captain, to Lt. Colonel M'Douall, 15 January 1815, in *Wisconsin Historical Collections*, 13:54–60; Robert Dickson to John Lawe, 15 January 1815, in *Wisconsin Historical Collections*, 10:122–123; Robert Dickson to Captain Bulger, 31 December 1814, and Proclamation of A. Bulger, Captain, Prairie du Chien, 31 December 1814, in *Wisconsin Historical Collections*, 12:132.

23. Proceedings of Garrison Courts Martial and Garrison Orders, Fort McKay, 2 January 1815, in *Wisconsin Historical Collections*, 13:38–43; Robert Dickson to John Lawe, 15 January 1815, in *Wisconsin Historical Collections*, 10:122–123.

24. Robert Dickson to John Lawe, 15 January 1815, in *Wisconsin Historical Collections*, 10:122–123.

25. Robert Dickson to Captain Bulger, 3 January 1815, in *Michigan Pioneer and Historical Collections*, 16:3–4.

26. Court of Inquiry, 3 January 1815, in *Michigan Pioneer and Historical Collections*, 16:4–25.

27. Ibid., 16:25–31.

28. Documents of the Court of Inquiry held at Prairie du Chien on 5 January 1814, in *Michigan Pioneer and Historical Collections*, 16:31–32.

29. Ibid.; A. Bulger, Captain, to Lt. Colonel M'Douall, 15 January 1814, in *Wisconsin Historical Collections*, 13:54–60.

30. Proceedings of the Court, Prairie du Chien, 7 January 1814, and A. Bulger, Captain, to Lt. Colonel M'Douall, 7 January 1814, in *Wisconsin Historical Collections*, 13:48–52.

### Chapter 12: News of Peace

1. Francois Bouthellier, et al., to A. Bulger, Captain, 15 January 1815, and Captain A. Bulger, to Francois Bouthellier, et al., 15 January 1814, in *Wisconsin Historical Collections*, vol. 13 (Madison: State Historical Society of Wisconsin, 1895), 52–54.

2. A. Bulger, Captain, to Lt. Colonel M'Douall, 15 January 1814, and Interview between Bulger and Dickson, 26 January 1814, in *Wisconsin Historical Collections*, 13:54–62.

3. Robert S. Allen, *The British Indian Department and the Frontier in North America, 1755–1830*, (Ottawa: Department of Indian and Northern Affairs Canada, 1975), 81.

4. Correspondence between Robert Dickson and Andrew Bulger, 31 January 1815 through 9 February 1815, in *Wisconsin Historical Collections*, 13:63–72.

5. A. Bulger, Captain, to Robert Dickson, 9 February 1815, and R. Dickson to Captain Bulger, 10 February 1815, in *Wisconsin Historical Collections*, 13:70–74.

6. Lt. Colonel McDouall to Captain Bulger, 26 February 1815, in *Wisconsin Historical Collections*, 13:91–94.

7. Lt. Colonel McDouall to Captain Bulger, 16 February 1815, in *Wisconsin Historical Collections*, 13:74–78.

8. General Order from Adjutant Fort Michilimackinac, Michilimackinac, 23 February 1815, in *Wisconsin Historical Collections*, 13:85–91.

9. Lt. Colonel McDouall to Captain Bulger, 25 and 26 February 1815, in *Wisconsin Historical Collections*, 13:88–89, 91–94.

10. Robert Dickson to John Lawe, 15 January 1815, in *Wisconsin Historical Collections*, 10:122–123; Robert Dickson to John Lawe, 21 February 1815, in *Wisconsin Historical Collections*, 11:308–309.

11. William R. Manning, *Diplomatic Correspondence of the United States:*

*Canadian Relations, 1784–1860*, vol. 1 (Washington, DC: Carnegie Endowment for International Peace, 1940), 661, 662.

12. Ibid., 664–665.

13. Lt. Colonel McDouall to Captain Bulger, 26 February 1815, in *Wisconsin Historical Collections*, 13:94–97.

14. Lt. Colonel McDouall to Captain Bulger, 1 March 1815, in *Wisconsin Historical Collections*, 13:101–105.

15. Lt. Colonel McDouall to Lt. Grignon, 4 March 1815, and John Askin Jr. to John Lawe, 6 March 1815, in *Wisconsin Historical Collections*, 10:123–127.

16. Captain Bulger to Lt. Colonel McDouall, Green Bay, 10 March 1815, in *Wisconsin Historical Collections*, 13:110–115.

17. Duncan Graham to John Lawe, Prairie du Chien, 14 March 1815, in *Wisconsin Historical Collections*, 10:127–132.

18. Ibid.

19. Lt. Colonel McDouall to Captain Bulger, 19 March 1815, in *Wisconsin Historical Collections*, 13:118–122.

20. A. Bulger, Captain, to Jacques Porlier, 20 March 1815, A. Bulger, Captain, to Lt. Colonel McDouall, 22 March 1815, and Instructions to Interpreters from A. Bulger, Captain, Fort McKay, 8 April 1815, in *Wisconsin Historical Collections*, 13:123–126, 129–130.

21. A. Bulger, Captain, to R. Dickson, 8 April 1815, in *Wisconsin Historical Collections*, 13:127; R. Dickson to John Lawe, Prairie du Chien, 10 April 1815, in *Wisconsin Historical Collections*, 11:311–312.

22. A. Bulger to John Lawe, April 1815, in *Wisconsin Historical Collections*, 11:313–314.

23. Andrew Bulger, "Last Days of British at Prairie du Chien," in *Wisconsin Historical Collections*, 13:156.

24. Instructions to Mr. Guillroy, Fort McKay, 8 April 1815, and Instructions to Lieutenant Joseph Renville, Fort McKay, 8 April 1815, in *Wisconsin Historical Collections*, 13:127–130.

25. Andrew Bulger, "Last Days of British at Prairie du Chien," in *Wisconsin Historical Collections*, 13:154–156.

26. William Russell to the Secretary of War, 24 April 1815, in *The Territorial Papers of the United States*, ed. Clarence Edwin Carter, 28 vols. (Washington, DC: Government Printing Office, 1934–1975), 15:47–48.

27. William Clark to the British Officers on the Mississippi, 22 March 1815, Dispatch from W. Russell, 25 March 1815, and Taylor Berry to the Commanding Officer at Prairie du Chien, 10 April 1815, in *Wisconsin Historical Collections*, 13:126–127.

28. Secretary of War to the Indian Commissioners, War Department, 11 March 1815, Carter, *Territorial Papers*, 15:14–15.

29. Ibid.; William Russell to the Secretary of War, 24 April 1815, *Territorial Papers*, 15:47–48.
30. Transcript of an Indian Council held at Prairie du Chien, 18 April 1815, in *Wisconsin Historical Collections*, 13:127–129, 131–133.
31. Ibid.

### Chapter 13: Peace and Its Aftermath

1. Lt. Colonel McDouall to Captain Bulger, 25 April 1815, in *Wisconsin Historical Collections*, vol. 13 (Madison: State Historical Society of Wisconsin, 1895), 133–134.
2. Lt. Colonel McDouall to Captain Bulger, 1 May 1815, in *Wisconsin Historical Collections*, 13:135–140.
3. Ibid.
4. Ibid., 13:135–139.
5. Ibid., 13:135–140.
6. Robert McDouall to Andrew Bulger, 2 May 1815, in *Wisconsin Historical Collections*, 13:143–144.
7. A. Bulger, Captain, to R. Dickson, 28 April 1815, in *Wisconsin Historical Collections*, 13:135.
8. Report from Captain Anderson, 29 April 1815, in *Wisconsin Historical Collections*, 13:142.
9. A. Bulger, Captain, to Lt. Colonel McDouall, 1 May 1815, in *Wisconsin Historical Collections*, 13:140–141.
10. Lt. Colonel McDouall to Captain Bulger, 5 May 1815, in *Wisconsin Historical Collections*, 13:145–147.
11. Ibid., 13:146–147.
12. "British-American Diplomacy: Treaty of Ghent: 1814," The Avalon Project at Yale Law School, http://avalon.law.yale.edu/19th_century/ghent.asp. Source: *Treaties and Other International Acts of the United States of America*, ed. Hunter Miller, vol. 2, Documents 1–40: 1776–1818 (Washington, DC: Government Printing Office, 1931).
13. Lt. Colonel McDouall to Captain Bulger, Michilimackinac, 1 May 1815, in *Wisconsin Historical Collections*, 13:135–140; Andrew Bulger, "Last Days of the British at Prairie du Chien," in *Wisconsin Historical Collections*, 13:158–162.
14. Andrew Bulger, "Last Days of the British at Prairie du Chien," *Wisconsin Historical Collections*, 13:159.
15. Ibid., 160–161.
16. Ibid., 158–162.
17. A. Bulger, Captain, to Governor Clarke, 23 May 1815, in *Wisconsin Historical Collections*, 13:148–149.

18. A. Bulger, Captain, to Lt. Colonel McDouall, 19 June 1815, in *Wisconsin Historical Collections*, 13:149–151.
19. Lt. Colonel McDouall to Captain Bulger, 2 May 1815, in *Wisconsin Historical Collections*, 13:143–144.
20. Colonel Russell to the Officer Commanding . . . Prairie du Chien, 25 March 1815, in *Wisconsin Historical Collections*, 13:126–127; Secretary of War to the Indian Commissioners, War Department, 11 March 1815, in Carter, *Territorial Papers*, 15:14–15.
21. William Clark to Secretary of War, 17 April 1815, in Carter, *Territorial Papers*, 15:25–26.
22. P. Grignon to Louis Grignon, 17 June 1815, in *Wisconsin Historical Collections*, 19:375–376.
23. Thomas Forsyth to Commissioners, 30 May 1815, in *Wisconsin Historical Collections*, 11:338–341; *Missouri Gazette*, 17 June 1815; P. Grignon to Louis Grignon, 17 June 1815, in *Wisconsin Historical Collections*, 19:375–376.
24. *Missouri Gazette*, 15 July 1815.
25. Ibid.; Speech of La Moite, Michilimackinac, 28 June 1815, in *Michigan Pioneer and Historical Collections*, (Lansing: Michigan Pioneer and Historical Society, 1886–1912), 16:193–195.
26. Treaty of Portage des Sioux, 19 July 1815, in *Documents of United States Indian Policy*, ed. Francis Paul Prucha (Lincoln: University of Nebraska Press, 1990), 25; *Missouri Gazette*, 5 August 1815.
27. Lieut. Col. McDouall's Speech to the different Indian Nations, Michilimackinac, 28 July 1815, in *Michigan Pioneer and Historical Collections*, 16:192–193.
28. Ibid.; Speech of La Moite, Michilimackinac, 28 June 1815, in *Michigan Pioneer and Historical Collections*, 16:192–195.
29. Address of Black Hawk, Prairie du Chien, 3 August 1815, in *Michigan Pioneer and Historical Collections*, 16:195–196.
30. Anderson's response to Speech of La Moite, Michilimackinac, 3 August 1815, in *Michigan Pioneer and Historical Collections*, 16:195–196.
31. Address of Black Hawk, Prairie du Chien, 3 August 1815, in *Michigan Pioneer and Historical Collections*, 16:195–196.
32. Nicolas Boilvin to the Secretary of State, 24 July 1815, translation in Peter L. Scanlan Papers, Platteville Area Research Center, Platteville, WI.
33. Nicolas Boilvin to Secretary of War, 11 January 1815, translation in Scanlan Papers.
34. Nicolas Boilvin to Secretary of War, October 1815, translation in Scanlan Papers.
35. Robert Dickson to John Lawe, 15 January 1815, in *Wisconsin Historical Collections*, 10:122–123; Jeanne Kay, "John Lawe, Green Bay Trader,"

*Wisconsin Magazine of History* 64(1): 11; Colonel McKay to Lt. Colonel McDouall, 1 August 1814, *Michigan Pioneer and Historical Collections*, 15:630–631.

36. Rhoda Gilman, et al., *The Red River Trail: Oxcart Routes between St. Paul and the Selkirk Settlement* (St. Paul: Minnesota Historical Society Press, 1979), 2–5.

37. *Original Letters and other Documents relating to the Selkirk Settlement*, by Rev. Dr. George Bryce and Charles N. Bell, *MHS Transactions*, series 1, no. 33 (read 17 January 1889), The Manitoba Historical Society, http://www. mhs.mb.ca/docs/transactions/1/selkirkletters.shtml

38. Gilman, et al., *The Red River Trail*, 2–5; Robert Dickson to John Lawe, 19 June 1817, in *Wisconsin Historical Society*, 10:135–136; Robert S. Allen, "DICKSON, ROBERT," in *Dictionary of Canadian Biography*, vol. 6, University of Toronto/Université Laval, 2003–, http://www.biographi.ca/en/bio/ dickson_robert_6E.html.

39. "Personal Narrative of Captain Thomas G. Anderson," *Wisconsin Historical Collections*, 9:202–206.

40. Obituary of Joseph Renville written by Dr. Thomas Smith Williamson in 1846, Chippewa County Historical Society, Montevideo, MN.

41. Lewis Cass to A. J. Dallas, 20 June 1815, in *Wisconsin Historical Collections*, 19:376–379.

42. Ibid.

43. A. J. Dallas to President James Madison, 19 June 1815, in *Wisconsin Historical Collections*, 19:380–381.

44. Ninian Edwards to James Monroe, 3 March 1816, in *Wisconsin Historical Collections*, 19:401–404.

### Conclusion

1. William Woodbridge to Alexander J. Dallas, 10 May 1815, in *The Territorial Papers of the United States*, ed. Clarence E. Carter, 28 vols. (Washington, DC: Government Printing Office, 1934–1975), 10:536–537.

2. Lewis Cass to Alexander J. Dallas, 20 June 1815, in *Carter, Territorial Papers*, 10:573–575.

3. Alexander Dallas to James Madison, 19 June 1815, in "The Fur Trade In Wisconsin," *Wisconsin Historical Collections*, vol. 19 (Madison: State Historical Society of Wisconsin, 1910), 380–381.

4. Francis Paul Prucha, *Documents of United States Indian Policy* (Lincoln: University of Nebraska Press, 1990), 28–29.

5. W. H. Puthuff to L. Cass, Michilimackinac, 6 June 1816, and Pierre Rocheblave to Louis Grignon, Mackinac, 20 June 1816, in "The Fur-Trade in Wisconsin," *Wisconsin Historical Collections*, 19:415.

6. *American State Papers, Public Lands*, vol. 4, *Documents, Legislative and Executive of the Congress of the United States, from the First Session of the Fourteenth to the First Session of the Eighteenth Congress, Inclusive*, 34 vols. (Washington, DC: Gales and Seaton, 1834), 873–874.

7. John W. Johnson to Francis Bouthellier, Prairie du Chien, 23 June 1816, in "The Fur-Trade in Wisconsin," *Wisconsin Historical Collections*, 19:424–425.

8. *American State Papers: Public Lands*, 4:874.

9. John W. Johnson to Francis Bouthellier, Prairie du Chien, 23 June 1816, in "The Fur-Trade in Wisconsin," *Wisconsin Historical Collections*, 19:424–425.

10. James Lockwood, "Early Times and Events in Wisconsin," *Wisconsin Historical Collections*, 2:128; *American State Papers: Public Lands*, 4:874.

11. John O'Fallon to General Duncan McArthur, Green Bay, 24 September 1815, in "The Fur-Trade in Wisconsin," *Wisconsin Historical Collections*, 19:436–439.

12. William Puthuff to Governor Cass, Michilimackinac, 18 August 1815; John O'Fallon to General Duncan McArthur, Green Bay, 24 September 1815; and Jacques Porlier to Pierre Rocheblave, 1817, in "The Fur-Trade in Wisconsin," *Wisconsin Historical Collections*, 19:432–433, 436–439, 445–447.

13. Robert Dickson to John Lawe, eighteen miles from La Baye, 25 November 1815, in "Lawe and Grignon Papers," *Wisconsin Historical Collections*, 10:133–134.

14. James Lockwood, "Early Times and Events in Wisconsin," *Wisconsin Historical Collections*, 2:128–129.

15. Nicolas Boilvin to Secretary of War John C. Calhoun, 1 June 1818, online facsimile at www.stampauctionnetwork.com/f/f12114.cfm.

16. "To the Congress of the United States of America . . ." (manuscript petition by the residents of Prairie du Chien, Wisconsin, 1816); online facsimile at www.wisconsinhistory.org/turningpoints/search.asp?id=1755.

17. Land Claims in Michigan, in *American State Papers, Public Lands*, 4:851.

18. Ibid., 863.

19. Scanlan, "Nicolas Boilvin, Indian Agent," 160.

20. "Journal of the proceedings that took place, under a Commission to Genl Wm Clark & Govr L. Cass . . . at Prairie du Chien August 1825," online facsimile at http://digital.library.wisc.edu/1711.d/History.IT1825no139.

21. Ibid., 21–22.

22. Indian Speech at Drummond Island, 30 June 1828, in *Michigan Pioneer and Historical Collections*, 23:144–147.

23. Thomas Anderson to William McKay, 20 July 1828, in *Michigan Pioneer and Historical Collections*, 23:148–150.

# Acknowledgments

My research on the battle for Prairie du Chien began many years ago while I was curator at the Villa Louis Historic Site. The Dousman family home was built upon the same mound where Forts Shelby and McKay once stood. I found the earlier history of the site more captivating than the Victorian era and decided to learn more. My research report became the foundation for an event held each July at Villa Louis. After I left the site, I continued to research and investigate the July battle and the individuals who participated in and had a stake in the events of the summer of 1814. While involved in other research projects pertaining to the upper Mississippi Valley, I kept adding notes to my files. The more I learned, the more obvious it became that the battle of Prairie du Chien encompassed much more than three days in July 1814 two hundred years ago. The origins for the encounter at Prairie du Chien between American soldiers and British volunteers began in the years following the American Revolution and the outcome did not end with the conclusion of the War of 1812. Rather, the battle for Prairie du Chien was long in duration. When the two hundredth anniversary of the battle approached, I thought that I should do something with all the information I had accumulated.

There have been many people who have made my desire to share this story possible. Thank you very much to the Wisconsin Historical Society Press for their interest in my research and willingness to publish this book. Thank you to the individuals who read the manuscript in its various stages, and asked good questions and suggested directions that tightened the focus yet broadened the scope of my work. Thank you to the many people at the Press who worked on maps and illustrations to make my words become visual. A special thank you to Sara Phillips, my editor. Through all her readings, questions, suggestions, and edits to create continuity, and her patience with me, we accomplished a beautiful finished product.

# Index